Technology, Edu
The T

Series Editor: Marcia C. Linn
Advisory Board: Robert Bjork, Chris Dede,
Carol Lee, Jim Minstrell, Jonathan Osborne, Mitch Resnick

Leading Technology-Rich Schools

Award-Winning

Models for Success

Barbara B. Levin

Lynne Schrum

Foreword by Dennis Sparks

Teachers College, Columbia University
New York and London

Published by Teachers College Press, 1234 Amsterdam Avenue, New York, NY 10027

Library of Congress Cataloging-in-Publication Data

Leading technology-rich schools : award-winning models for success / Barbara B. Levin, Lynne Schrum ; foreword by Dennis Sparks.
    p. cm. – (Technology, education--connections)
    Includes bibliographical references and index.
    ISBN 978-0-8077-5334-7 (pbk. : alk. paper)
    ISBN 978-0-8077-5335-4 (hardcover : alk. paper)
        1. School management and organization–United States–Case studies. 2. School improvement programs–United States–Case studies. 3. Computer-assisted in-struction–United States–Case studies. I. Schrum, Lynne. II. Title.
    LB2805.L392   2012
    371.200973–dc23   2011049184

ISBN 978-0-8077-5334-7 (paperback)
ISBN 978-0-8077-5335-4 (hardcover)

Printed on acid-free paper
Manufactured in the United States of America

19   18   17   16   15   14   13   12   8   7   6   5   4   3   2   1

BBL: I would like to dedicate this book to all the school and district leaders, teachers, staff, parents, and community members who gave so graciously of their time so that we could learn from them and share their stories. Without them, this book would not be possible. I would also like to thank my husband, David Brown, for his continued support.

LS: I dedicate this book to educators everywhere who tirelessly work to encourage each learner and firmly believe that every child can learn; in particular, I thank the schools that welcomed us with joy, openness, and curiosity. I also thank my family for their support, love, and laughter.

Contents

3. Engaging in Systemic Planning: The Case of Rose Hill Junior High School, Lake Washington School District, Redmond, WA

Acknowledgments

We would like to thank our graduate students who willingly volunteered to help collect data in Virginia and North Carolina. They include Cheryl Ayers, Melissa Beeson, Jerad Crave, Jayme Linton, and Mandy Taylor from UNCG, plus Mary English and Lyndsie Galizio from GMU. Their interest and enthusiasm made data collection fun. We would also like to thank Brian Ellerbeck for encouraging us to do this work, and Dennis Sparks for writing the Foreword.

Foreword

As a young teacher I believed that principals made little difference in their schools and that good principals basically left teachers alone to do their jobs. Early in my career, however, I had the opportunity as a teacher leader to assume districtwide responsibilities which enabled me to closely observe a wide variety of schools whose leaders displayed varying degrees of effectiveness.

Thirty years later, one school in particular stands out in my mind. When I first knew this school it had a poor reputation for student learning and staff morale. Its long-standing principal was reassigned, and his role was assumed by a more able replacement. Over the next 3 years student achievement steadily improved, as did staff and community attitudes about the school. When that principal took a central office position her successor was, unfortunately, more like her predecessor. The school again spiraled downwards, to the dismay of everyone who had observed its rise. As a result of that experience, I became a close observer of what successful principals did and did not do, a habit that has remained with me to this day.

Barbara B. Levin and Lynne Schrum offer their readers the distinct advantage of compressing into a single volume what it took me decades to learn. They not only present the big ideas of effective school leadership, but bring them alive through case studies that illustrate how those ideas manifest themselves in leaders' day-to-day behaviors. It is because these ideas and practices are relevant to any major change initiative that readers can apply them in a variety of situations.

The case studies presented make it clear leaders that engage the school community in the effective use of technology to improve student learning:

- Possess clarity about the instructional and collaborative uses of technology and engage others in creating a shared understanding of the ideas and practices essential to those uses. Likewise, they are clear about the developmental appropriateness of various types of technology and the ways in which technology supports the school's purposes and the ways in which it does not.

- Appreciate the power of school culture to support or to thwart continuous improvement. They know that culture trumps innovation and so co-create, with the school community, cultures in which meaningful teamwork based on trust is the primary force of professional learning and continuous improvement.
- Understand that the most powerful forms of professional learning occur when teachers solve meaningful problems with their colleagues in professional communities. Such learning is meaningful, profound, and collaborative. These leaders initiate and encourage others to engage in the courageous conversations that are essential.
- Recognize that school leadership is too large a responsibility for any one individual. It must be shared with teachers and others in the school community who contribute their strengths and expertise to ensuring the success of improvement efforts. Together they distribute leadership by providing opportunities for others to assume meaningful leadership positions and by supporting them in the development of skills to ensure their success.

The case studies of secondary schools in this book reveal the essential role leaders must play in engaging the school community in the tasks of planning and implementing new forms of teaching based on technology-enabled instructional designs. The importance of that engagement was illustrated by the cognitive demands placed on educators by the vision held for New Tech High School in Napa, California, that, according to Levin and Schrum, "would prepare students for a technologically rich work environment that would require 21st-century skills including communication and collaboration skills, problem solving and critical thinking, and innovation and creativity. The curriculum for this public, non-charter, small high school was designed to be interdisciplinary, project based, and technology infused."

The only way in which any school can realize such a vision is when educators' professional lives closely resemble, for instance, the experiences of students attending New Tech High School: "a technologically rich work environment that would require 21st-century skills including communication and collaboration skills, problem solving and critical thinking, and innovation and creativity." In such settings, teachers and administrators would be absorbed in addressing the most pressing challenges of teaching and learning using sophisticated cognitive processes aided by technology and other relevant tools.

To stimulate educators' imaginations about the design of schools in which they believed everyone would flourish, I ask them to describe the attributes of such a school from the perspective of students, teachers, and administrators. I ask them to further imagine being assigned to one of those three roles and remain in that position.

Such an approach to school design requires that educators consider teaching and learning from a variety of perspectives, not just from the positions they currently occupy. The case studies provided in this book will help readers develop a more profound sense of the attributes of such schools. I encourage you to use the ideas and practices you find here to leverage technology to create schools in which all students and adults thrive.

–Dennis Sparks,
Emeritus Executive Director,
National Staff Development Council (now known as Learning Forward)

CHAPTER 1

An Introduction

Investigating Leadership, Technology, and School Improvement

No matter how much training teachers receive to prepare them for technology integration, most will not successfully employ that training without the leadership of the principal. (Dawson & Rakes, 2003, p. 30)

The leadership in a school largely determines the outcome of technology integration; however, administrators cannot fully or effectively support technology if they do not understand it. (Dawson & Rakes, 2003, p. 33)

This book includes case studies and a cross-case analysis to show how eight secondary schools and districts are using technology and making systemic changes to increase student engagement, improve achievement, and re-invigorate the teaching and learning process. Each case describes the ways exemplary school and district leaders are using technology in curricular, administrative, and analytical ways to meet the needs of the 21st-century learners, educators, and communities. This opening chapter includes our rationale for undertaking this research and the conceptual framework that guides our understanding of how technology, leadership, and systems thinking interact in school improvement initiatives. We also describe the methods we used to select and study our case study sites, and conclude with an explanation of how this book is organized.

School and district leaders have challenging and essential roles to play in supporting their schools through the process of changing and improving. This is especially true when a veteran staff has volunteered to pilot a 1:1 laptop initiative that will fundamentally change the way they usually teach. We know principals are essential to making things happen, but that sometimes it seems they have to be all things to all people! This was never more evident than when we conducted a focus group with several teachers at one of our school sites. During our conversation they described how their principal acted and interacted with them, and the variety of roles she played in their school. One teacher said that her principal "is very respectful of our time and builds in and supports collaboration." Another said, "I want a risk taker, who supports our odd electives, who recognizes that not everyone fits into a traditional class format so we need to let kids have a place to be comfortable." One veteran teacher reported, "I want someone to support the programs in lots of different ways, to be working as an ambassador with the district. You need an advocate to move through the bureaucracy." Other teachers described this school leader from the perspective of what they want and need in a leader. They said, "She is an instructional leader." She "challenges me to think about my teaching practice." "She is respectful of our time, builds in and supports collaboration." She has "principal power!" Based on the assistant principal's perspective, she said, "We are a team—she is really intentional so that I know what the thought process is and why we are doing it in a certain way. The staff sees we work together and give a consistent message." However, the principal told us,

> So I'm very systems oriented. Like, I look at something that isn't running well and I like to find something that makes it run better. And I'm really big on turning things to people; I don't make a lot of decisions. I bring a lot of problems to a table; sometimes I'll have ideas or proposals, but we make a lot of the decisions at the leadership team level. And whether it's my counselor, administrative team, or the building leadership team, or instructional leadership team, I like to turn that over to them and have them make that decision.

Rationale for This Book

Based on the assumption that integrating technology into the curriculum is a fundamentally important tool for transforming learning in 21st-century classrooms, and that leadership at the school and district level is key to doing this successfully, the purpose of this book is to provide case studies of exemplary, award-winning schools and districts that reveal how their leaders leverage technology to improve their schools. To fulfill this purpose, we studied eight secondary schools from across the United States in order to glean successful strategies that you can try or adapt in your situation based on what worked to transform the places we studied. However, the cases we provide demonstrate that just putting technology in schools may not change, reform, or improve anything. Rather, what we found as a result of our research are additional factors that have to be addressed (nearly) simultaneously if technology is to work as a tool for school improvement. Therefore, as you will read in these cases, school and district leaders also have to address the following: their vision, mission, and goals; planning, decision-making, and governance; school organization and structure; curriculum and instructional strategies; school culture, including student expectations, responsibilities, and policies; uses of data for assessment and evaluation; personnel and financial resources; professional development; partnerships with business, industry, and colleges and universities; and communication and relationships within the school community. Our hope is that by reading the cases in this book, leaders at both the building and district levels will learn strategies and models for successful reform that can be adapted for their own context.

We began our work on this book with the belief that many school leaders have a vision of what their school, district, or state's educational system might look like that includes ways that information and communication technology (ICT) might enhance learning, expand opportunities, and prepare students for their future. Many leaders hope that technology will increase student engagement, promote 21st-century skill development, raise student achievement, and develop a stronger culture of collaboration, shared leadership, and positive relationships with faculty, staff, families, and the surrounding community. This is the promise of technology; yet it has not always been realized. However, we know that in many places technology has been an effective catalyst for change, while in other places it has not. So, we asked: What happens in places where school and district leaders successfully leverage technology to improve their schools?

Unfortunately, it has been said that our students "power down" to come to the classroom, and when they do this, "students also power down in the way they access information and think" (Frey, Fisher, & Gonzalez, 2010, p. 110). Most of today's students (and many of their teachers) are always connected digitally and use multiple technologies outside of school; Web 2.0 tools have become almost commonplace (Alexander, 2008). Clearly, technology has had a positive impact on our youth, even if it has not yet resulted in wholesale educational transformation. Possibly this is because there are other unaddressed mediating issues. For example, disparities in educational outcomes still exist, the digital divide remains large, too many of our youth still drop out of school and do not reach their potential, teachers are not always comfortable with using new technologies in their classrooms, and students are disengaged from learning in many schools today.

We know that everyone in the field of education is eager to improve achievement, engagement, and other outcomes for their students. We are all aware that this is an enormous task that is complicated by many factors that are frequently outside the control of most educators: Our students today are not the ones for whom our schools were created, our society has become more diverse and complex, funding has been cut and resources are limited, and metrics for evaluating school progress have narrowed significantly while the pressure to meet them has increased. Nevertheless, in our research for this book we saw strong leadership, exciting curriculum, and innovative teachers who used technology to encourage students to explore, develop, create, and question. Therefore, it is our contention that we haven't yet fully embraced or shared some of the tools that we can employ to prepare our students to learn and thrive in the 21st century. This book provides examples of how successful school and district leaders do just that, and how their leadership makes exciting things happen.

Those who study education know that leadership matters, and agree with Drago-Severson that "The principal is key to building a better school. A strong and supportive principal can enable a faculty to succeed in the most challenging conditions" (Drago-Severson, 2004, p. xvii). Darling-Hammond, Meyerson, LaPointe, and Orr (2010) concur when saying, "The critical role of principals in developing successful schools has been well established" (p. 179). Given this premise, we wanted to understand how exemplary leaders at both the school and district level handle the enormous tasks that confront them daily when they employ technology to improve their schools and districts. Specifically, we wanted to know how they prepare students for the realities of the 21st century by developing, creating, or supporting an educational environment that reflects the increasingly pervasive role of technology in our society.

In a previous book (Schrum & Levin, 2009), we wrote about what school leaders need to know about using technology to move their schools into the 21st century. We think of that book as the 30,000-foot view of the knowledge, opportunities, and challenges that leaders need to consider when using technology to lead 21st-century schools. That book talks about what leaders need to know and understand; for this book we wanted to learn more about what exemplary schools, districts, and their leaders are doing with technology, and how they are doing it. How do they communicate and implement changes and expectations? What are they doing to support 21st-century learning, and what types of ICT are they rolling out? We also wanted to learn what teachers do with technology and how they are affected when their leadership includes technology as a key factor in school improvement plans. Therefore, in this book we provide detailed case studies about what the schools and districts we studied accomplished by using technology as a lever for school improvement. We do this so we can offer lessons learned by the schools and districts in this book that may be useful to other educators. Of course, we realize that we have not studied every exemplary school or district out there. Many other school and district leaders are also doing wonderful things with technology and seeing improvement because of their efforts. Their stories need to be shared as well, but these are the eight we have to share for now.

Framework for Understanding Technology and Leadership

We began our research with an assumption that technology is a critical component of a 21st-century education for a variety of reasons. Evidence exists that using technology in student-centered ways can positively affect student performance (Abramovich, 2006; Brown, 2007; Lei & Zhao, 2007). Being literate in the 21st century requires more than knowing how to read, write, and compute. The Partnership for 21st Century Skills initiative (http://www.21stcenturyskills.org) helps us see the necessity of infusing information literacy, critical media literacy, and information and communication technology literacy into every subject taught in our schools. Without these skills and others (visual literacy, multimedia literacy, and cultural literacy) our students will not be able to adapt to changes coming their way.

This book is also grounded in the knowledge that leadership matters for promoting teachers' uses of technology (Anderson & Dexter, 2005), and that school administrators need to be increasingly involved in the technology projects in their schools to model and support its use (Dawson & Rakes, 2003; Stuart, Mills, & Remus, 2009; Williams, 2008). Many suggest that school leaders also need to effectively and quickly make shifts in their knowledge, skills, and practices (McLeod & Richardson, 2011; Schrum, Galizio, & Ledesma, 2011).

Despite what we think we know about leadership and technology, at a recent meeting of educational technology specialists we were discussing the past 20 years and wondering why we are still asking the same question: "With all the energy, effort, and spending on educational technology, why don't we see the potential truly realized in the teaching and learning process?" For a long time we discussed barriers that affect full implementation and obstacles that serve as constraints to successful integration of technology: teachers unwilling to change their practice, inadequate funding, students unfamiliar with the educational technology, or administrators not fully cognizant of what they need to be doing. We then looked at the situation again and determined that in reality a school or a district is a system, or just one part of a system, that is made up of interacting, interrelated, and interdependent components. Further, these components must work together when making changes if they are to be sustained and embraced by all (Kopcha, 2010). Changing just one part of the system is not enough to make a difference. All parts of the system have to be addressed in concert, and adding one component (like technology) to the system affects other parts of the system. Furthermore, an educational system can also be seen as a community situated within a specific type of environment, and the context and environment influence the educational system, and vice versa.

Based on the premise that systems thinking also needs to be considered when discussing leadership and technology, another goal of this book was to examine the actions and interaction among school and district leaders, the context of the schools and districts, and the roles and practices of a myriad of other individuals in the system. We believe that taking a systems approach helps us to better understand how exemplary school and district leaders are able to leverage technology to organize, implement, and promote student engagement and achievement, increase school success, and reinvigorate teachers. However, in order to proceed, a theory of leadership was essential to our framework, and we determined that distributed leadership provided the appropriate and logical lens through which to analyze and interpret our data.

Spillane, Halverson, and Diamond (2001) suggested that to understand leadership, it is important to look beyond what one person can do, or knows how to do, and look instead at what each person brings to the task, build on strengths, and collaboratively tackle the issue. They suggest, "Consequently, to understand the knowledge needed for leadership practice in these situations, one has to move beyond an analysis of individual knowledge and consider what these leaders know and do together" (p. 25). Their central premise is that school leadership is "understood as a distributed practice, stretched over the school's social and situational contexts" (p. 23). They go on to describe four functions of distributed leadership: "leadership tasks and functions, task enactment, social distribution of task enactment, and situational distribution of task enactment" (p. 23). Moving forward, Spillane, Diamond, and Jita (2003) concluded,

> We define school leadership as the identification, acquisition, allocation, coordination, and use of the social, material and cultural resources necessary to establish the conditions for the possibility of innovation in teaching and learning. The distributed leadership framework incorporates the practice of those multiple individuals in a school who work at mobilizing and guiding school staff in the instructional innovation process. (p. 535)

While Spillane and his colleagues (2001, 2003) provided the notion of a distributed leadership style, others have contributed to our understanding of the complexity of the idea. For example, Gronn (2002) suggests that leadership is a dynamic concept, and Mayrowetz (2008) agrees that leadership is best when distributed or "stretched over" multiple people and that examining and understanding the tools they use would be helpful to understand the practice of leadership in schools. This research suggests that

> As distributed leadership initiatives in schools and empirical research continue to flourish, the field will benefit from scholarship that clearly articulates what is meant by *distributed leadership* in studies that are both responsive to central problems of practice and anchored in relevant theory. (p. 433)

Essentially, what we noted while observing many examples of distributed leadership in the schools and districts we visited is that it assumes "a set of direction-setting and influence practices potentially enacted by people at all levels rather than a set of personal characteristics and attributes located in people at the top" (Leithwood, Jantzi, & McElheron-Hopkins, 2006, p. 20). Early on Hallinger and Heck (1998) also noted that most accounts of school leadership pay little attention to the practice of leadership; rather, they concentrate upon the people, structures, routines, and systems. More recently, Murphy, Smylieb, Mayrowetz, and Louis (2009) suggest that administrators distribute leadership with a goal of building strong relationships with teachers, rethinking conceptions of power, and fashioning organizational structures. Therefore, in analyzing and presenting our data we looked for examples to share about how distributed leadership practices were enacted around technology initiatives in the schools and districts we visited.

However, we also found in our analysis that distributed leadership was only one aspect of the complex system we call education as it occurs in schools today. In the context of school reform researchers argue, and we agree, that the purpose of educational leadership is to improve student learning and to foster equity in educational outcomes (Firestone & Riehl, 2005). Principals and other school leaders also are responsible for organizing the action, or practice, of leading. Spillane, Camburn, and Pareja (2007) suggest that what happens is constantly "emerging from *interactions* among school leaders and followers, mediated by the situation in which the work occurs. In our view, practice is more about interaction than action" (p. 70). Therefore, examining the practice of leadership is important because "Putting practice center stage allows us to focus where the "rubber" of school leadership and management meets the "road" of instructional improvement" (p. 70).

Other aspects of our educational system are also pertinent to how we interpreted data from the sites we studied for this book. For example, Moos and Johansson (2009) suggested that "Schools are looking for support from parents; they are forming partnerships with social and cultural institutions that can support them in addressing challenges that cannot adequately be met within" (p. 778). Most schools are now acknowledging more than previously that students learn not only in their schools but also well beyond the traditional boundaries. For example, today influence comes "in their relations with peers, their attitudes towards (and influence by) the mass media, and their facility with information technology and the internet" (p. 778). They also found that these successful principals are "effective communicators—they listen readily and intently, and they openly share their thoughts and visions" (pp. 776–777). In general, they follow guidelines to develop teachers, create leadership teams or "webs," and challenge teachers to build capacity.

Also of importance is the work of Ertmer and Ottenbreit-Leftwich (2010) who identified key variables associated with teacher change and technology integration that include knowledge, pedagogical beliefs, and school culture. In fact, teacher knowledge about technology and their content area, teacher beliefs about pedagogy, and school culture all play a part in whether or not teachers actually integrate technology into instructional practices. Furthermore, there appear to be reciprocal relationships among these variables in that changes in school culture may positively influence teachers to embrace technology initiatives, but a school's culture can also be against technology integration. Given the influence on the culture of schools and school districts that leaders have, teacher knowledge, their pedagogical beliefs, and school culture are additional aspects of the educational system we have to consider when looking at leadership, technology, and systems.

Relatedly, Harris (2006) suggested that distributed leadership has a descriptive dimension, stating that "it describes the forms of practice implicit in the workings of professional learning communities or communities of practice" (p. 41). This is reminiscent of Wenger's (1998) perspective of communities of practice in which he promulgates the notion that all ideas and tasks are distributed by their form and individuals' skills and functions. Harris (2006) said, "In short, principals are responsible for setting the internal structural and cultural conditions within which distributed patterns of leadership can flourish" (p. 42). Katz and Kahn (1978) maintain that the focus on leadership moves from one group upward to the entire organization. They defined leadership as "the exercise of influence on organizationally relevant matters by any member of the organization," and suggested that the organization was more effective when the leadership was shared (p. 571).

In another informative study, Camburn, Rowan, and Taylor (2003) identified 100 elementary schools in which distributed leadership was one way the leadership team attempted to improve student achievement and school functioning. They surveyed formally designated leaders in each school to examine the distribution of responsibility for leadership functions, including principals, assistant principals, program coordinators or facilitators, subject area coordinators or facilitators, mentors, master teachers, or teacher consultants. In particular, they found that the common perception of one "heroic" leader was not the way these schools were functioning. They concluded that there had

> emerged a new vision of effective leadership, one in which multiple school members are seen as exercising powerful instructional leadership, sometimes in redundant fashion, in order to effect programmatic change and instructional improvement. Clearly, this is *not* a model of a single, "heroic" leader standing atop a hierarchy, bending the school community to his or her purposes. (p. 348)

Case Studies of Effective Leadership

Case studies of how effective leadership proceeds in K–12 schools also informed our research, given that our goal was to develop case studies about the schools and districts we visited. Case study research on school leadership provided examples of what others have found, but not all of these studies focused on secondary schools, which is our focus in this book. For example, Park and Datnow (2009) conducted a qualitative study of four urban school systems and found that leaders at all levels co-constructed the vision and implementation of data-driven decision-making, distributed decision-making authority to empower staff members to use expertise, and "directed their resources on building human and social capacity mainly by focusing on modeling and knowledge brokering amongst their staff" (p. 477).

Crum, Sherman, and Myran (2009) conducted interviews with successful elementary school principals; they found these successful principals engaged in activities that were designed to develop others' leadership, delegate responsibilities, empower others in their team, and to communicate and develop rapport. They concluded, "This study identified vital practices of successful elementary leaders that enabled them to facilitate high levels of student achievement and to dispel any notions that success is not possible in a high stakes environment" (p. 48). In a case study of one school instituting a distributed leadership model, Murphy et al. (2009) found that a strong participatory style of management that was "predominantly informal" resulted in an understanding and helped "explain the success of the distributed leadership initiative" (p. 203). Timperley (2005) studied the leadership processes in elementary schools involved in a school improvement initiative over a 4-year time span, and included observations, interviews, and the analysis of student achievement data for each year. She found interesting changes over time; however, she also cautioned that quality of leadership activities is an important aspect of distributed leadership to focus on, but concluded with a caution that "Distributing leadership over more people is a risky business and may result in the greater distribution of incompetence" (p. 417).

Dimmock (1999) conducted a case study investigation into one school to examine how a principal solved difficult problems while restructuring a school. He concluded that "It seems a common experience for principals in school systems to face the ambiguity caused by being part of a system while at the same time developing school-based management. Dilemmas seem to be generated by this ambiguity" (p. 111). A study by Mulford, Edmunds, Kendall, Kendall, and Bishop (2008) found similar results and concluded that successful principals "adapt and adopt their leadership practice to meet the changing needs of circumstances in which they find themselves" (p. 67). Crum and Sherman (2008) found in their study of 12 principals that they were not only using data for decision-making, but were also dedicating themselves to using longitudinal data to accomplish their goals. They suggested that "Relationship building was often seen by the principals as a part of a community building process. They spoke to their ultimate goals of creating a cohesive community with a foundation of positive, trusting relationships" (p. 56).

In all, we found that the case studies of principals, schools, teachers, and students have shown remarkable similarity in the actions of successful leaders and the challenges all schools face. Yet few of the case studies we reviewed were about secondary schools or focused on technology as one of the levers to move forward in improving student achievement, solving problems, and promoting shared governance. Thus, with these studies and others in our mind, we began our efforts to select appropriate sites for case studies for this research.

Identifying Our Cases

We spent considerable time identifying the eight cases upon which the book is built. The goal of the selection process was to identify exemplar cases, or what Yin (2008) calls *intrinsic* cases, so we could learn how school and district leaders use technology as part of their plans for school improvement. From the outset we established parameters for the types of schools we would include or exclude; for example, we did not want to include private schools, schools that limit their student population by academic achievement or parent participation, or public schools within non-diverse communities. Rather, our goal was to find schools with ethnically, linguistically, and socio-economically diverse students in diverse communities, including those facing the types of challenges that many schools in the country face: changing demographics, limited resources, expectations from parents for safe schools, mandates from the government for meeting adequate yearly progress (AYP), and requirements from business and industry for workers prepared for the 21st century. Ultimately we contacted over 24 possible schools and/or districts, and felt very pleased to have so many exemplary locations as possible sites in which to conduct our research.

Working from this pool of nominated and/or recommended sites, we selected eight cases through purposeful sampling (Patton, 1990) based on their having received state or national awards as exemplary technology-using schools (e.g., state or regional awards, or from the International Society for Technology in Education [ISTE]), or because they have received more than one technology grant (e.g., from foundations like the Gates Foundation; or from the state, such as IMPACT grants in North Carolina; or PT3 grants from the federal government), or through a snowball system of nominations based on the school or leader's reputation at the state or national level. One criterion we did not compromise was the need for settings as diverse as possible; therefore, our final selection of sites for case studies was based on additional criteria that included geographic region, school level (middle or high school), and accessibility, including their willingness to allow us to do interviews and observations, and also to collect documents. Ultimately we identified eight schools representing all parts of the country, urban and rural settings, and large and small school districts.

Among the eight cases represented in this book, five are traditional public schools, one is a public charter school, and two are magnet schools. The school sizes range from about 400 students to more than 2,000, and the districts range in size from 1,700 students to more than 103,000. The percentages of free and reduced lunch range from 33% to as high as 90%, and all sites are diverse in numerous ways. The schools are located in the following states: California, Colorado, Maryland, Michigan, Minnesota, North Carolina, Virginia, and Washington.

Considering Appropriate Methods

In determining the appropriate methods for studying these schools and districts, their leadership, and interactions within the system, we again turned to the literature for guidance. Once we identified schools and leaders, it became important to use our theoretical framework and the case study literature to refine our methods (Merriam, 1998; Yin, 2008). Each of our case study sites is a bounded system, which is a set of interacting parts that fit within a functioning whole. Additionally, the bounded systems are social, and have recognizable edges between the inside and outside, with different functions occurring in different spaces (Creswell, 1998; Stake, 1995). For most of the cases a single school is the bounded system, but in some of the smaller districts we visited, the schools within it are so interconnected that together they and the district are the bounded system.

As much as interviews were essential and significant in establishing our understanding of how leaders and others in each of these sites acted and interacted, observations were also desirable. Berends, Bodilly, and Kirby (2002) argue that a rich set of indicators are needed to understand school processes, and Timperley (2005) explained the need for observations in addition to interviews as follows:

> However, if quality of activity and its consequences are of interest, it is difficult to develop an adequate understanding of that activity without observing it directly in order to understand the situation as it unfolds from the perspective of theories-in-use. (p. 417)

Timperley (2005) also suggested that "on-the-ground observations are essential to developing these important concepts further" (p. 398). Additionally, we gathered documentation from each school and district in order to understand the ways in which the leadership documented and communicated its activities (Spillane et al., 2003).

In sum, our data sources included multiple formal and informal interviews using separate research protocols for key informants (principal and other administrators at both the school and district level, teachers, support staff, and occasionally parents in leadership roles and school board members) during a 3-to-5-day visit at each school, plus the collection of documents (e.g., school improvement plans, agendas and minutes of meetings, internal and external publicity documents, student achievement data, school leader blogs, etc.). Focus groups were used to supplement interviews whenever practical in order to respect the busy schedules of people in the schools and districts we visited. Also, we used protocols that yielded detailed field notes while observing in as many classrooms as possible during our on-site visits. In all, we recorded over 150 interviews or focus group participants, logged more than 300 hours of observations, and collected hundreds of documents. Of course, each school district granted formal approval, and each researcher's institution granted Institutional Review Board approval. We also collected consent forms from all participants.

Data analysis was based on transcriptions of interviews and detailed content analysis of observations and documents to identify the practices used by the leadership in these schools that appeared from both the insider's (emic) perspective and the outsider's (etic) perspective to contribute to improving their schools in ways that led them to be considered exemplary, award-winning schools. We used the constant comparative analysis method (Lincoln & Guba, 1985) to analyze the interview and observation data both within each case and across the cases. We wrote descriptive case studies and shared them with key informants at each school through member checking (Merriam, 1998; Patton, 1990) to verify that our analysis and interpretation was valid before we undertook the cross-case analysis of the lessons learned from all eight cases.

Summary and Organization of the Book

The initial goal of doing the research was to learn from exemplary, award-winning schools and school leaders about the role technology and a myriad of other factors played in their efforts at school improvement. As a result, this book includes eight descriptive case studies based on multiple interviews and observations of exemplary secondary schools (both middle schools and high schools) from various regions of the United States. Each of the schools and districts we visited has been recognized for effectively using technology as an integral part of transforming their schools. While the eight case studies share some characteristics, they also represent diverse communities, challenges, and other considerations that make them unique because of their contexts. Nevertheless, each case elucidates how technology was leveraged for school improvement with a focus on the many ways each school's leadership team transformed their context such that it became an exemplary, award-winning school. Further, these cases reveal a myriad of other important factors addressed by the leadership of these schools and districts that go well beyond what they did with technology. The other factors we observed included changes in school culture, curriculum and teaching, and uses of assessment data, in addition to how the schools and districts addressed financial considerations, technology infrastructure and support, and involvement with the community. While one of our goals was to identify similarities across cases based on lessons that can be learned from each case, each situation is remarkably different, and we believe our obligation is to represent what we found in each case with fidelity.

Each of the next eight chapters in this book is the story of one of our case study sites. Each case includes similar information to situate it, including relevant demographics, history, and culture of the school. For each case we also describe the context of the focus school as well as the district; we look at the leadership from multiple perspectives; and we provide details about the curriculum, teaching, and learning, technology infrastructure and use, and aspects of professional development within each context. Each chapter ends with challenges and specific "lessons learned" that we feel are worth others' consideration based on what we learned from that case study.

However, it is worth noting once again that the context of each case is unique. Therefore, in some cases the focus is clearly on one school with most of the data coming directly from that location. In other situations the district is more of a focus (usually because of its small size) and one or two schools are highlighted. A brief description of each case and the kinds of technology we found at each site appears at the beginning of each case to help the reader get oriented.

We could have ordered the presentation of the eight case studies in many different ways. However, after much consideration we chose to begin with the sites we visited that have the least experience with technology as a tool for school reform and to conclude with the cases that have the most years of experience, and arguably the most success, with using technology as an integral part of forming and reforming these schools. In organizing the cases this way we leave it to our readers to select cases that best fit their own context based on size or level of experience with technology; however, we strongly believe that the story of each school and district offers much to share with others, whether it is a case study of a school or district that is small or large, urban, rural, or suburban, more or less financially poor or wealthy, more or less ethnically or linguistically diverse, or more or less experienced with using technology as a lever for school reform and school improvement.

We conclude this book with a chapter that looks across all eight case studies to summarize the lessons learned from these cases. Our goal in this final chapter was to capture the many ways that the leadership of these schools and districts address the challenges all schools face while trying to improve, reform, or transform, namely, limited resources, changing student populations, continuous efforts to hire and keep the best teachers, and the national and state initiatives for student achievement measured by tests. However, the final chapter is not a typical cross-case analysis that reduces the lessons learned to a few general patterns and themes that may lose their impact because the details are lost. Rather, we offer a synthesis based on numerous examples of the many valuable lessons learned from the exemplary, award-winning schools and districts we visited to highlight the main findings from our research. Overall, as a result of our research we found that employing technology as a tool for school reform, or just believing in or even acting on the principles of distributed leadership is not nearly enough. What we found is that school reform/improvement is very complex and dynamic, which we believe is what we capture in each of the case studies in this book.

CHAPTER 2

What Visionary Leaders Do
The Case of Walton Middle School, Albemarle County Public Schools, VA

"Raise the bar and push kids up."

This is a case of a small, rural middle school with a long history of piloting new technology. It is also the case of the very beginning of a 1:1 laptop program for 6th-graders. This case is set in a Virginia school division recognized by the governor and Board of Education for using assessment data to make progress toward the state's comprehensive plan for strengthening public education. The efforts of both the principal and the superintendent to use technology as a way to leverage opportunities for all students are highlighted.

At the time of this study, this middle school of about 400 students had three and a half computer labs with PCs in them, plus two laptop carts, two iPod Touch carts, and several sets of clickers available for checkout to use with the interactive whiteboards and projection systems in all 7th- and 8th-grade classrooms. In addition they have new laptops for every 6th-grader, and all teachers have laptops and iPads. The school is wireless and teachers are regularly using a variety of free Web 2.0 tools ranging from Moodle to Wordle, as well as programs like Discovery Learning (an educational service that offers digital content, interactive lessons, real-time assessment, and virtual experiences to schools), and Rosetta Stone (language learning software)–purchased by the school.

When we returned to the school at 6:00 PM for Expo Night, the upper parking lot was already full, so we parked in the lower lot and walked up the steps. As we entered the building there was a buzz of excitement in the air. Families both large and small were making their way to the cafeteria where barbecue was on the menu. Along the way students were pointing out various projects they had completed and posted on the walls. Donating canned goods for a local food pantry got you a free meal, but otherwise the Parent Teacher Organization was only charging $3 a plate. As we took our food and spread out to sit at different tables we wondered if this enthusiastic turnout for Expo Night at Walton Middle School (WMS) was larger than the first one last year, or not? Each of us talked with kids and adults at our tables, and told them what we were doing. Universally, the parents told us that they were very happy with WMS and that they were excited to see what their children were learning. The well-regarded WMS band was playing while we talked and we didn't have permission to tape-record conversations with students anyway, but we did want to gauge the pulse of the community at this event. Later we listened and watched in various classrooms, as well as in the hallways as the students showed their parents and siblings what they had been learning so far this year. The 6th-graders were especially anxious to show off their laptops and the work they had completed using them because they were not yet allowed to take the laptops home. That would come a little later in the year. The 7th-graders wanted their parents to play some of the computer games that had been set up in their math and science classes, and the 8th-graders, while a little more subdued, showed their family members what they had been learning as well. One father told us that he had recently moved to Albemarle County from another part of the country and how thrilled he was with how well WMS was run, how easily his children had settled into their new school, and how impressed he was with the teachers and their efforts to both teach and care for his children. Later, the principal told us that the turnout for Expo Night was even bigger than the previous year.

Context

Walton Middle School is a small middle school (grades 6–8) in a rural part of Albemarle County, Virginia. WMS serves about 400 students with a staff of 37 teachers, including core and specialists, along with another 20 support staff. The student population is 80% White, 13% African American, 4% Hispanic, and 3% Asian/Pacific Islander. The principal, Betsy Agee, was in her fourth year at Walton at the time of this study, and the assistant principal, Jim

Asher, was in his second year, having moved to WMS from a nearby high school because of his longtime desire to work in a middle school. Prior to the arrival of the current principal the school's administration had been "a revolving door," according to several teachers.

WMS is one of five middle schools in Albemarle County Public Schools (ACPS), which is located near Charlottesville, Virginia, and serves about 13,000 students. There are 16 elementary schools, five middle schools and a middle charter school, four comprehensive high schools and a Math, Engineering, & Science Academy, plus four other schools with alternative programs in this district. Although school districts are called divisions in Virginia, we will use the more common term—district.

District leadership in ACPS is described by both outsiders and insiders as innovative and quite stable. The superintendent of ACPS, Dr. Pam Moran, was originally a science and staff development coordinator in this district with a long history of successful collaboration with the University of Virginia. The director for professional development, media services, and instructional technology, Becky Fisher started teaching in the division as a high school physics teacher. Both these leaders have held district-level positions for over 15 years. Dr. Moran's service as superintendent was preceded by many years as a principal and a teacher and Ms. Fisher's as an administrator and teacher, respectively. From interviewing both of these district leaders, it is clear they see the value and need for technology integration in support of learning, and they have been strong advocates and leaders in this area for many years. Their relationship with the principal of WMS, Betsy Agee, is highly supportive. Both administrators were clearly knowledgeable about the many technology initiatives at WMS, including the 6th-grade 1:1 laptop initiative that was originally suggested by the teachers, as well as the use of interactive whiteboards (IWBs) and iPod Touches in several classrooms, plus a new project to try out digital fabrication in an 8th-grade classroom that was studying the intersection of math and architecture. As the assistant principal at WMS told us, the district is aware of the initiatives with technology at WMS, and has been working on getting more technology for many years—hardware and software. He said, "I think the county recognizes that we are trying to move forward. . . . We have always been ones to present when the county has tech days . . . we're kind of out here in the forefront."

Walton Middle School was selected for this study for two main reasons: First, WMS has a long history of trying innovative things with technology, often sparked by participation in a 19-year partnership with the University of Virginia and successful applications for internal and external grants. For example, over the past few years teachers at WMS have piloted the use of Palm Pilots and other PDAs, Texas Instrument (TITM) calculators, document cameras, iPod Touches, and most recently the 1:1 laptop initiative in

6th grade. Previous leadership at WMS purchased several interactive white-boards and LCD projectors, though not for every classroom, and last year every staff member received an iPod Touch to try out in addition to the laptops that teachers have had for a number of years. Additionally, there are three computer labs located at the school and several laptop carts in use. As one 6th-grade teacher said, we have been "ahead of the curve for a long time . . . [and] we get excited about it." Second, Albemarle County Public Schools (ACPS) recently won an award from the state of Virginia for using technology to help close the achievement gap. ACPS was among only 15 school systems in Virginia to receive the Board of Education's Excellence Award for making progress toward educational goals advocated by the governor and by the Board of Education as part of its comprehensive plan for strengthening public education across the state.

At WMS the goals for the 1:1 laptop initiative include not just to expose students to new technology tools for learning, but also to "raise the bar" and "help push kids up." That is the principal's mission, "to create an optimal environment for kids to learn and feel supported." If that means resources, activities, or whatever, she wants to do whatever it takes to help the students achieve, have new experiences, and be ready for the 21st century. Additionally, projects like the 6th-grade 1:1 laptop initiative at WMS, along with a history of other technology-based pilot projects over the years, positioned WMS as a good place to assess how this initiative would work and compare to other pilot projects in other schools in the district.

Students and Opportunities

The students at WMS come from economically diverse families that range from very needy to very privileged, and there is an achievement gap between these two groups. Although WMS did not make AYP during the last 2 years due to lack of success in the economically disadvantaged sub-group on state-mandated tests, it had made AYP in previous years. In past years WMS also struggled with chronic discipline problems. However, together with the staff, the current principal made discipline a priority, created a new system called FOCUS (Focus on Curriculum and Using Support), and the current statistics on referrals bear out success in this area. Now the focus of this administration is on building "Rigor, Relevance, and Relationships," which are the cornerstones of their school-improvement plan, along with closing the achievement gap. As a part of these goals, school climate is a priority, by which the principal said she means "kids, community, and teachers." In fact the assistant principal, Jim Asher, told us that building teamwork, collaborating, and trying to create both common purposes and a positive culture are key:

> You have to build the team and collaborative environment where
> people are working together . . . you have to have a culture where
> people are working together with a common goal. It can't just be that
> we are in the same place, but we have to have a common goal and we
> have to communicate about it—the communication becomes a strategy.
> . . . We have to also pay attention to the morale of the teachers. . . . We
> are building a culture with the teacher leaders we have here. . . .

Raising the bar and increasing opportunities for students are priorities
at WMS, and we observed many examples of this goal. For example, engagement in the arts has increased and WMS is one of only two middle
schools in the district with a drama program as well as a very successful band
program. As part of the World Languages program at WMS every student
has access to a copy of Rosetta Stone, as does any teacher interested. The
principal initiated the Rosetta Stone project after returning from a College
Board–sponsored trip to visit schools in China and realizing during that trip
that Walton students would be at a disadvantage without exposure to the
global community. Starting with languages made sense to her—and the staff.
There have been several opportunities for students to learn about world cultures through travel and student and teacher exchanges, and there is a strong
Advancement Via Individual Determination (AVID) program—including a
special world cultures class for the AVID students—as well as a new Safe &
Healthy Schools grant that provides additional counseling services. WMS is
also adding higher-level math courses for everyone with the goal of giving all
WMS students access to the algebra curriculum before entering high school,
and there is the 1:1 laptop initiative for all 6th-graders that began in the fall
of 2010. The purpose of the 6th-grade laptop initiative was to raise the bar
and raise achievement for 6th-graders in all core subject areas, according to
the assistant principal. Additionally, the purpose was to expose students to a
tool they will use in their future work life.

WMS is known in the community for what they do to support all students
and for trying new things to benefit the students, including the many technology innovations over the years. Families in the community, both those who
have lived in the area for many generations and newer residents, are very loyal
to the school. Families come to school events like Expo Night where dinner
was provided by the Parent Teacher Organization and student work was displayed throughout the school, as described at the start of this chapter.

Leadership Practices

With regard to new initiatives at WMS, we learned that some of them come
from the administration and some come from the teachers. For example, the

principal told us that they take a consensus vote on many things at WMS, but that discipline was her decision because she had to get it under control when she first arrived. However, the idea of a short-term timeout room came from the teachers, and the laptop initiative came from the 6th-grade teachers as a result of discussing what it would take to be a successful 6th-grader and brainstorming ways this could be achieved.

Structurally WMS has several groups that form their leadership team and both the principal and assistant principal believe in shared leadership. For example, lead teachers from each content area (two representing Language Arts, and one each representing math, science, and social studies) meet monthly with the administration to discuss the curriculum, assessment data, and common assessments. Team leaders representing each grade level, Health/PE, and other specialists also meet monthly with the administration to discuss organizational issues, schoolwide events, and scheduling. Together these groups constitute the school's leadership team, which also includes representation from the Library/Media and Guidance departments. Additionally, the administration, members of the Guidance Department, and people from various community agencies meet weekly as a Positive Pupil Support (PPS) team.

In addition, some of the hallmarks of the leadership at WMS include their valuing and striving for open communication with the faculty and staff as both a goal and a means to achieve success. Everyone was very transparent about how things were going with technology use while we were there, and people we interviewed shared both successes and areas for improvement. Assessment of how the technology initiatives were progressing at this school included surveys sent to teachers to gather their feedback, discussions at staff meetings, and communications sent to parents and families in a variety of ways—including Twitter, which is used extensively throughout this district for communication purposes. Furthermore, teacher leadership was cultivated, highly valued, and recognized publicly, which not only goes to open communication but also to sustaining the positive school climate for innovation at this school. Of course, this means that the school leaders had to know their faculty well, know their strengths and interests, and then offer opportunities for them to take on various leadership roles—both formally and informally.

The superintendent's style is one of distributed leadership. Ideas for moving the students forward and giving them better learning opportunities are encouraged from faculty and administrators alike, although she has a clear vision for the future that includes a focus on lifelong-learning standards that are articulated in the district's document called a *Framework for Quality Learning*. This document articulates how teachers can and should make use of 21st-century pedagogy. The superintendent also told us that she believes in job-embedded professional development through Professional Leaning Communities (PLCs) supported by instructional coaches and school administrators. She also believes in technology as another lever for school improvement:

> And then the third piece, I think, is the focus on trying to roll out what I would call research and development innovation work in technology. And the focus of that being, "How do we make technology more about learning technologies versus the technologies that are strictly focused on, for example, test prep, data management, administrative applications for either teachers or principals?"

When ideas come from the superintendent, they typically are discussed at the building level where they can be customized to suit each school. Both the superintendent and the principal at WMS understand the value of buy-in, but the superintendent is not interested in having cookie-cutter schools or classrooms. As she told us, she is interested in systematic change and building capacity:

> So if we give teachers permission to innovate, what we end up with are people who really are building different ways of approaching how kids do inquiry, how kids do project-based learning, how spaces really accommodate the needs of kids in a particular school that's not random and is not about people, you know, sort of, some people saying, "Well, I don't want to learn this new technology because I've only got three years before I retire and so I'm not going to do it at all," but really saying, "Everybody here has potential to be part of the innovation team." Everybody's using these technologies, but they're going to use them in different ways. . . . I've learned deep change does not happen overnight. It can't be mandated. . . . That it's easy to get the pioneers and the scouts on board. It's not as hard to get the next wave of people who will follow the scouts and pioneers that were just waiting for them to cut the path. . . . So I guess that would be what I would say, is that systemic change takes a lot of time. That systemic change means you have to build the capacity of the organization to sustain it and to move it beyond just the early adopters . . . systemic change takes an up and down the organization vertically and horizontally level of distributed leadership support, that it can't be about any one person. At its best it looks like an ecosystem where you have nodes and hubs of leadership, including kids being part of a leadership group, so that those connected nodes and hubs of leadership are able to support each other when the times get tough, when you hit those resistors. So that's what I think is probably the really critical thing that I try to do is to continue focusing on systemic change, building capacity, distributed leadership, making sure that we're building

that ownership vertically and horizontally across the organization, and that we're not throwing too many things at people so that if we—because when we do that we just overpower our capacity to make the changes that we need to make. And we lose ground.

In sum, decision-making and governance are distributed across a variety of school leaders at the building and the district level in Albemarle County, and at WMS we saw many teachers and staff members without official roles being recognized for their leadership in various ways. For example, during our visit to WMS several teachers were mentioned by name as "leaders, but not on a team" and several other teachers were acknowledged by the administrators at a monthly faculty meeting we observed for helping with a variety of tasks: cleaning up defunct websites, creating an exemplary website over the summer, overseeing the planning for Expo Night, and organizing and chaperoning the next school dance. As the assistant principal at WMS told us,

> You have to build the team and collaborative environment where people are working together . . . you have to have a culture where people are working together with a common goal. It can't just be that we are in the same place, but we have to have a common goal and we have to communicate about it—the communication becomes a strategy. We have to also pay attention to the morale of the teachers. . . . We are building a culture with the teacher leaders we have here. . . .

And as the principal realistically described her staff,

> We are making progress; we have rock stars and others who are still progressing. I think it is our united vision that guides us. Are there still a few people in the life raft, not in the boat, and we are having to drag them along? You bet. . . . We are not all the same but most days we are moving in a common direction.

And what this principal sees that gratifies her regarding their common focus on helping students also relates to the laptop initiative:

> The laptop initiative actually came from our 6th-grade teachers, spilled out of our talking about what would a 6th-grader—What does it look like to be a successful 6th-grader at Walton? What if they could participate in discussions outside the class? What if they all had computers? So it came from the grade-level teachers. They are doing some cool stuff, with TodaysMeet, Edmodo, and one of our 6th-graders who is not strong has generated enormous materials on what they are

reading, on their work, and especially on Shakespeare of all things. I bet that child generated more content about this than he did all last year. I have jaw-dropping moments at this school.

Professional Learning Communities (PLCs) are also in place at WMS, and teachers spend their weekly meeting time looking at assessment data and talking about two primary questions: What now and what next? As with all schools today, raising student achievement is a priority, and the ultimate goal for everything undertaken at the school, but building relationships with students in order to determine the best ways to support them is also a priority at WMS. District-provided instructional coaches also meet with PLCs and individual teachers to both assist and push teachers to the next level. The instructional coaches work with teachers in a variety of ways—depending upon a teacher's request—whether it be helping with classroom management strategies, assisting with technology, curriculum support, etc. Also, they try to observe the teachers, and then have reflective, strategic conversations, for example, about how to use technology to purposefully develop critical thinking. Their job is to support teachers to be successful by helping them with whatever they need or want. Also, all the instructional coaches meet together weekly so that good ideas from one school can be cross-pollinated at other schools.

As mentioned earlier, both the principal and assistant principal at WMS are focused on creating opportunities for students that will raise the bar, push the kids, and close the achievement gap at the same time. Principal Betsy Agee told us her goal is "to create the optimal environment for kids to learn and feel supported," which means providing resources, activities, or whatever else it takes. She and assistant principal Jim Asher are focused on Rigor, Relevance, and Relationships, and they even use these goals to organize the agenda for faculty meetings. For example, we observed one faculty meeting that included a quick online poll of the staff about Thomas Guskey's (1995) work on what effective teachers attend to first (beliefs and attitudes of teachers, teachers' behaviors, or student learning), followed by a brief video showing African American girls talking about their learning needs, a discussion of the principles of culturally responsive teaching. Following this, the principal asked each teacher to commit to focusing on at least one tenet of culturally responsive teaching in order to improve relationships with students, to increase rigor, and to improve relevance in their instructional practices.

Professional Development

The culture at WMS is one of collaboration and sharing, and both the teachers and the administration make an ongoing effort to share and model new

ideas for using technology and to help one another learn. In fact, during focus groups with teachers at each grade level, they told us that they see WMS
as a community, and they have a long history of co-teaching with EC and
ESL teachers whom they call Collaborative Teachers.

There is some in-house professional development offered during faculty meetings, as well as opportunities through the school district's resource
center (through the ARC, Albemarle Resource Center), and through professional development days called "Making Connections" where teachers from
across the district present and share their successes. Teachers can also attend
various conferences (e.g., the Lausanne Laptop Institute) on request. However, while there are some planned opportunities for professional development
around the use of new technologies at WMS, many teachers expressed to us
that they wish there were even more professional development opportunities, more sharing, and more time to figure out how to make best use of new
tools like the iPod Touches, the laptops, and new software. While some teachers are happy to experiment and to teach themselves, others say they feel
slowed in their implementation and level of use because they are not finding
or making the time to learn on their own. For example, some of the 6th-grade
teachers were shocked when the students' laptops came with OpenOffice instead of Microsoft Word and felt this slowed their use of the laptops because
they weren't feeling competent with the new word-processing program. Not
feeling the same need for professional development himself, the assistant
principal said, "Some people ask when are we going to have professional
development, but was there professional development for Facebook? For
shopping online? You don't have to wait." He believes in just plunging in and
doesn't expect that every attempt will be a success. Nevertheless, there is lots
of support and modeling provided by the principal and assistant principal, as
well as many of the teachers who are taking on leadership roles in this area.
But while some teachers do just figure it out and are willing to experiment
with new programs on their own time, including during the summer, others need more formal training opportunities, either one-on-one or in small
groups. This issue of ongoing professional development was a concern at
every school we visited for this study, and some handled it in better ways
than others.

Technology and Technology Infrastructure

In the Albemarle County Public Schools (ACPS) every school is provided
with computers based on a funding distribution model that provides a set
number of desktop computers for labs, plus more computers based on enrollment, as well as one laptop cart per school, with additional laptop carts based
on enrollment. Computers are required to support online testing required

by Virginia during a 3-week period in the spring, so additional laptops are available from the central office and are moved around as needed. At WMS this means there were three computer labs with class-size numbers of PCs in them, plus two laptop carts and two iPod Touch carts, interactive whiteboards and projection systems in the 7th- and 8th-grade classrooms, in addition to every 6th-grader having a laptop.

Adding to these budgeted funds, competitive innovation grants called SEED projects are funded annually from cost savings from other projects in order to move forward on the district's goal of creating more student-centered classrooms where teachers differentiate instruction. Increasing students' level of engagement and achievement is the intended outcome of funded SEED projects. While WMS has a history of receiving funds for various technology projects from SEED funds, and also from its partnership with UVA over the years, teachers have written other grants to get funds for technology-based projects. However, Walton's most recent 1:1 laptop initiative for all 6th-graders was funded from instructional funds because of a recent policy change that made these funds available not just for textbooks but for all learning resources. Such policy changes are becoming more and more common as a way of funding technology; they were also the case in the other districts we studied.

Besides the instructional coaches there is technical support staff provided by the district and housed at WMS, although both coaches and tech support personnel have to attend to multiple schools. The instructional coaches work with classroom teachers to help them improve instruction and the technical support staff tries to keep all the systems working. While both instructional coaches and technical support staff are assigned to or housed at Walton, they are also responsible for other schools, so they do not always as feel as much a part of Walton as they would like. The technical staff also wants teachers to be successful in using technology, and they are often found troubleshooting if they are in the building. However, they told us they would also like to be more involved in planning and implementation in addition to providing technical support.

Changes in Teaching and Learning

Changes in teaching and learning as a result of ubiquitous computing in the 6th grade were just beginning to happen when we were observing WMS. However, we saw many teachers using the laptops in interesting ways at this grade level, and we saw many other exemplary uses of technology in other grade levels as well. For example, in one 6th-grade Language Arts class we saw a teacher use four different tools rather seamlessly to review work they had been doing for several weeks on the students' identities as readers and writers, a big idea in the 6th-grade language arts curriculum. In this lesson a Web 2.0 tool called Edmodo was used to review how students were defining identity as they answered this question: How does individuality affect how you understand what you read and what you write? Then another program called TodaysMeet (a Web 2.0 tool for synchronous discussions) was used by the students to generate a list of vocabulary to describe their own personal identity, and the teacher set goals to encourage them to use multi-syllable or rare vocabulary words that are positive rather than negative. Because they used their laptops, the composite list of words was available for both the teacher and everyone in the class to see, and the teacher was able to monitor and encourage students individually as well. Next, students were asked to use the word-processing program in OpenOffice to list at least ten words or phrases to describe their personal identity, following the same guidelines for the previous activity. The teacher then showed an example of how last year's students used another Web 2.0 tool, Wordle, to generate a collage of words describing her as their teacher. Finally, the students were given directions for making their own personal collage on Wordle by cutting and pasting the words they had generated in the previous activity. Parameters for using Wordle were written on the whiteboard for students to follow, and once they printed their personal word collages students were able to fill them in with colored pencils and put them up in the hallway to be viewed during Expo Night. Every student was engaged and successful in completing these activities on their laptops, and did so with minimal problems—most of which were related to low batteries. While parts of this lesson could have been completed without laptops, the lesson would have become more teacher-directed and less student-centered without the use of laptops. Furthermore, the Wordle collage could not have been completed very easily without laptops.

In other classrooms we also saw student response systems, fondly called clickers, being used with the SMART Board so that the teacher could poll the students and check for understanding during discussions in an 8th-grade class. In both math and science classes at all grade levels we observed interactive, reusable learning objects called widgets being used to model or demonstrate a process, along with online games being used in some classes. iPod Touches were being used in a 7th-grade science class, and the laptop carts were being used in several classes so the students could search for information on the Internet, write reflections, or post responses to questions as blog posts. In a 7th-grade Language Arts class the teacher used the iPod Touches to have students answer and then discuss questions about their relations with their siblings today by using Poll Everywhere. The purpose was to make a personal connection to their upcoming reading selection from Mark Twain's *Tom Sawyer*, which they then read on their iPods before getting together to rewrite the rather arcane language in more modern language. Following this, the teacher took these students to the computer lab across the hall so they could use a Web 2.0 comic-book-generating tool to create their own version of the scene they read in *Tom Sawyer*. We also saw TodaysMeet used in several grade levels for students to post responses to questions asked by the teacher, and Edmodo was another popular Web 2.0 tool being used in many classrooms at WMS. In math classes we saw students using drill and practice programs to review skills that were related to an upcoming benchmark test, and we also observed several different uses of interactive whiteboards, such as projecting results from graphing calculators, showing students' work samples, and displaying and discussing parts of a lesson. In world languages classes, Rosetta Stone is used on a routine basis, and video clips were shown regularly, especially in social studies and science classes because teachers have access to Discovery Learning.

Another lesson we observed involved an 8th-grade teacher with a small group of exceptional students trying to understand the meaning of several amendments to the Constitution. To help them understand the right of eminent domain and just compensation as described in the Fifth Amendment to the U.S. Constitution, the teacher pulled up Google Earth and displayed it on his whiteboard. By doing so the students could observe the distance that houses in their neighborhood stood from both improved and unimproved sections of the highway that ran through their county, and on which they traveled to and from school every day. It was clear from real-time Google Earth images that the newly constructed four-lane highway had taken away the front yards of many homes, making them now very close to the highway, compared to those houses where the highway was still only two lanes and there was plenty of land between the road and the homes. This graphic illustration made the students sit up and take notice because it helped them see how the Fifth Amendment to the U.S. Constitution relates to their lives today.

The school also has Scholastic's READ 180 program and Math Navigator, both intervention/remediation programs with a computer component that are used to support students with special learning needs, in addition to other similar programs. In fact, the special educators at the school are very pleased that so much technology is being used by all students because now they feel that their students don't seem any different from any other student in their classes. In observing one of the special education teachers, who also is viewed as one of the technology leaders in this school, he used a variety of computer-based exercises with his students in his Language Arts class. For example, he had them access Wikispaces for a word-study activity, and then asked each student do a different activity with vocabulary words using their laptops. During the writing portion of the lesson the students used OpenOffice to write about what they like to eat, drink, and do for fun; what their favorite classes were;

which TV shows they liked; and what other activities they liked, which they then pasted into Wordle and printed. The teacher provided the students with direction cards he made about how to use Wikispaces and Edmodo, and he also had directions on cards about how to post, Google sites, and how to solve a WebQuest so the students could be independent once they were introduced to these tools.

Noteworthy Outcomes

Overall, the teaching practices we observed at WMS indicated to us that the vast majority of teachers are working very hard to incorporate technology into their lessons on a regular and routine basis. Most were doing this in ways that engaged the students and seemed to fit logically into their lessons. Furthermore, they were teaching with technology in ways that seemed to shift the focus away from the teacher as the sole source of information, the prover-bial "sage on the stage," in favor of more student-centered lessons where the students were more actively engaged. In addition, or perhaps as an outcome, the culture of this school has become a safe, student-centered, community-oriented environment where teachers and staff collaborate in many ways to improve the learning opportunities for students.

Engagement appears to be a positive outcome based on our observations, but the academic results of the 1:1 laptop initiative in 6th grade won't be known for quite a while, as we were visiting WMS at the beginning of the initiative. Nevertheless, we heard about some more transformative attempts to use the technology to do joint Language Arts projects collaboratively with students in other states that would increase the potential to accomplish the leadership's goals of providing opportunities for students they wouldn't oth-erwise have without using the technology to change the way the curriculum is delivered, to expand their horizons, and to push them up.

Challenges

While the laptop initiative at WMS was just getting started, there was already talk about how to sustain this initiative, and we found sustainability to be a concern in the other schools and districts we visited. Also, many questions were still unresolved regarding this pilot project: Would the 6th-graders keep their laptops as they moved on to 7th grade? Would the 7th-grade teachers get professional development on the tools the students have been using in 6th grade, or would the students be way ahead of them? Would the district be able to fund laptops for both 6th- and 7th-graders the following year? Could the entire school become a laptop school, or would this experiment stop with 6th grade and they would recycle the laptops to incoming 6th-graders each year? Would the district ever be able to afford 1:1 computing devices, whether laptops, netbooks, iPads, iPods, or something new, for every student starting in 6th grade? What are other models of starting up an innovation that could be used? These and many other questions have to be resolved by this school and district, just as they will in all other schools and districts that start pilot projects in certain school or grades but not in all schools and grades.

Sustainability is always an issue with 1:1 initiatives for a number of reasons, not the least of which is cost. For example, while every high school physics student uses a netbook to access an online physics curriculum, we were told that the netbooks have not held up well over time, so maintenance and replacement costs are a consideration when selecting equipment. At WMS, limited battery life of the laptops that had been selected for purchase, and lack of suitable power outlets in classrooms were also concerns. The administration had to buy power strips for classrooms, but with plugs snaking all over the room, we wondered what the fire marshal would say upon inspection.

And, given that the Apple Classroom of Tomorrow (ACOT) studies (Sandholtz, Ringstaff, & Dwyer, 1997) showed that it takes teachers 3–5 years to change their practice to be more student-centered than teacher-directed, even with ubiquitous computing and tech support, we wondered if the leadership would be patient, or if they would expect some kind of payoff sooner than that. Would there be an implementation dip or an implementation bubble in the test scores of 6th-grade students? What other expectations or markers of success would be acceptable to warrant the continuation of 1:1 computing? The superintendent expressed understanding that systemic change takes time, but would the parents, teachers, and other administrators, much less school board and community members, be as understanding? And how will the teachers handle learning about and incorporating new hardware and software that comes along almost daily in a fast-changing technology-centered world? So, at WMS they are watching the data closely to see if pushing the students to achieve higher standards, especially in math, will work as they hope it will. They are "making progress, [but] want to make more."

Lessons Learned: Key Factors for Success

Although WMS was just starting its 1:1 laptop initiative for 6th-graders when our research team (consisting of the two authors of this book and four doctoral students) visited to collect data for this case study, we feel that this school's history with piloting many technology initiatives offers lessons that other school and districts can learn. This case may be especially useful for leaders of schools or districts with financial challenges because the school serves students with disparate levels of family income, and because the leaders have strong community ties and a deep commitment to improvement. At WMS the leadership wanted more and better opportunities for all students, and capitalized on their teachers' desire to use different kinds of technologies in various ways to promote achieving that for their students. Many other schools and districts have these same goals for their students; therefore, we think others will benefit from reading about this school's experiences with technology integration for the purpose of school improvement. Further, the district leaders in ACPS are all about finding ways to create 21st-century schools without getting hung up on every school having to do everything the same way. Everyone sees putting technology in the hands of students as a value-added proposition, and believes that increased engagement is a necessary first step, and perhaps a catalyst, for improving student learning. Therefore, based on our interviews (N=18), focus groups (N=3), and observations (N=20), these are some lessons learned that we think are valuable for others.

- Leaders have to have a clear vision about what they want to accomplish, and in this case the leadership at both the school and district level knew that changes in current teaching practices were needed in order to better prepare their students to live and work in the 21st century. At WMS this vision was articulated in three words—*Rigor, Relevance,* and *Relationships*—which became the mantra for guiding every decision and action they took to help "Raise the bar and push kids up."

- Having leaders at the school and district level who believe in, understand, and operate from the principles of distributed leadership was evident in this case. For example, at WMS, the principal was intentional about identifying strengths in various teachers that they may not have recognized in themselves; then she encouraged them to become leaders and both supported and publicly recognized their efforts.

- Further, district leaders were open and transparent about how things were progressing with new initiatives and communicated this at the school level. Open communication among the leadership, faculty, staff, and community was an explicit goal, which included publicly acknowledging everyone's contributions to the school's goals. In addition, both district and school leaders constantly modeled new ways to use technology for their faculty and staff, which was another way they demonstrated leadership.

- Planning at the district and in the school was guided by an understanding that systemic change takes time and requires buy-in at all levels. At the district level, the superintendent recognized that sharing within and across schools serves to cross-pollinate good ideas, but at the same time the superintendent encouraged schools to customize district goals to meet their own needs. She did not want cookie-cutter schools.

- Changing the district's textbook policies to include funding technology as a learning resource was an important step in planning for technology integration in this district, as was creating mini-grant opportunities for teachers who wanted to try new innovations with technology. At the school, the leadership described their planning as providing students with resources, activities, or whatever it takes for them to be successful. While this school had a long history of co-teaching, the leadership worked hard to make time for joint planning time so that co-teachers could collaborate with each other.

- Two technology support staff were provided by the district and housed at WMS, but they felt spread too thin by having to serve five other schools, which was the norm in this district. As a consequence, the tech support staff didn't always know what was going on or feel as connected as they wanted to feel to this school.

- As a form of professional development, the district provided instructional coaches to work with teachers in whatever ways the teachers requested, including how to better use the technology they had available for instruction. These instructional coaches were also the agents for the cross-pollination of ideas throughout the district. However, the teachers at WMS wished for more formal opportunities for professional development, and were not satisfied with being told to just try things on their own.

- Working on a positive school culture that includes a safe and orderly environment was very important in this case, as was the fact that the culture at WMS was clearly student-centered. Having photos of student activities displayed around the school and shown during lunchtime in the cafeteria was just one manifestation of this. The student-centered focus at WMS was also evident in the school leadership's concern about educating the "whole child," not just the academic side—an explicit focus on building relationships with students in order to determine the best ways to support them—and the use of small mentor groups of 12–15 students assigned to one teacher or staff member so that all students had adults who knew them well.

- The leadership in this school also believed strongly in raising the bar for students, doing whatever was needed to push them up. They also understood that engaging students is a first step to increasing their achievement. Integrating technology, and in particular starting a 1:1 initiative, was one way to accomplish these things, as were many other things that could expand opportunities for students.

- Co-teaching had been a common practice at this school for many years, and it was clear that the school valued collaboration on multiple levels. This kind of collaborative culture easily morphed into a culture of sharing ideas about how to use new technology, new software, or Web 2.0 tools among the staff. This collaborative culture also was bolstered by publicly acknowledging everyone's contributions to the school's technology goals, and was further manifested in using their Professional Learning Communities to look closely at student data, which was both a school and district goal.

- One other aspect of this school's culture was an expectation that everyone would plunge in and try new things with technology, which included allowing teachers to experiment at their own pace with regard to integrating technology into their curriculum. Thus, a culture of experimentation without specific mandates about how often technology had to be used was established.

- Changes in curriculum and instruction at WMS were tied to the leadership's goals of providing students with resources, activities, or whatever it took to be successful, wanting to expose students to tools they could use in their future work lives while finding opportunities to expand global awareness. Besides rearranging the schedule to make time for tutoring as well as for enrichment, various types of technology and software were sought out to support different kinds of learners. For example, to meet the special needs and interests of individual students, the school provided an advanced world language class online for one student, online tutorials and remediation for other students, and numerous Web 2.0 tools for still others.

- Virginia uses technology for online testing, and the district has been acknowledged for using data to help eliminate the achievement gap. In addition, this school worked to create common assessments across disciplines and grade levels to help assess student progress, while also focusing on including the tenets of culturally responsive teaching in their curriculum. And while creating responsible, digital citizens became an explicit part of the curriculum, the leadership at WMS was also looking for creativity and higher-order thinking in lessons—especially those that included a technology component—all the while believing that every lesson did not have to include technology.

- Although there was not a lot of industry nearby WMS, the school and the district understood the value of partnerships, and the school had a long-term relationship with a nearby university that provided reciprocal advantages for both institutions.
- Finally, involving and educating parents at the front end before the laptops were rolled out to the 6th-graders was critical, as was being transparent about how things were progressing with this new initiative.

Postscript

In the spring, 20 students from the 6th grade facilitated a school board work session on the 1:1 initiative in which they had participated during the school year and shared why they believe that 1:1 computing helps students be more successful in school. Teachers in the spring also met and discussed the possibility of becoming the first school in the county to go fully 1:1 and the commitments they would need to make to realize that goal. They created a Google Doc to record questions and concerns as well as respond to one another. In the early spring, they decided as a whole to take the initiative to 7th and 8th grades with funding support from the district. They met with central staff to confirm that they had close to 100% buy-in in late May. During the summer, they worked in professional development to extend and expand their own competencies. In the first 9 weeks of the 2011–2012 school year, every student will receive a new laptop and the school will scale to 1:1.

CHAPTER 3

Engaging in Systemic Planning

The Case of Rose Hill Junior High School, Lake Washington School District, Redmond, WA

> Every Student Future-Ready Prepared for college • Prepared for the global workplace • Prepared for personal success (Lake Washington School District)

> Our Rose Hill Junior High community cares for each other, embraces learning, and prepares students for a successful life.

This is a case of how the leadership in one of the least affluent junior high schools located in a wealthy school district in Washington is successfully juggling several new initiatives: changing into a middle school, building a new school, and piloting a 1:1 laptop program. This school was selected for us by the superintendent, who has received several awards for outstanding leadership, is known for using technology to further the district's educational goals, and has committed significant funds to advancing educational uses of technology in its schools.

At the time of this study, this junior high school of about 440 students had 171 desktop PCs available in four labs and classrooms, a cart of netbooks available for checkout, and 180 netbooks for the 7th-grade 1:1 initiative. In addition, there is a well-equipped digital media classroom and one of their electives is a Robots and Roller Coasters class. Teachers all have desktops or netbooks connected to their interactive whiteboards, and the use of a variety of software programs as well as more and more Web 2.0 tools. United Streaming is available, and although it was a challenge, this 40-year-old building is now wireless.

Well before 7:00 AM on a Wednesday morning, with the fog slowly lifting above the school, we arrived to attend a Continuous Improvement Plan (CIP) meeting at Rose Hill Junior High School. Students were already populating the halls and the energy in the school was quite evident. Students seemed happy to be there, and there was clear evidence that their netbooks were being used as students sat or stood together in clusters looking at someone's screen. While some students moved down the hall to the band and orchestra room, others headed for the library, and still others gathered in the lunch area to work together on assignments and activities. In the conference room the Continuous Improvement Plan committee began its work by discussing ways to reach each child, support each teacher, and meet the goals it had helped to set for the school. The people on this committee included the grade-level chairs and several administrators, about ten people in all. Large posters on the walls around the room were covered with brainstorming notes, lists, schedules, and calendars indicating the ongoing work of the leadership teams at this school. One of the posters listed three major changes that were happening simultaneously at Rose Hill: planning for the construction of a new building, transitioning from a junior high school to a middle school model, and expanding their 1:1 laptop initiative. A lot was happening at this school and we were anxious to learn more about how things worked at Rose Hill.

District Context

Lake Washington School District (LWSD) sits in an area southeast of Seattle between Lake Washington and the Cascade Mountains. Covering 76 square miles, LWSD is the public school district for the cities of Kirkland and Redmond as well as for about half of Sammamish. On the north end of the district, some Bothell and Woodinville residents also attend LWSD schools. The district is also near several major technology companies—in particular, Microsoft is very close. Approximately 25,000 students are part of LWSD, spread across 31 elementary schools, 12 junior high schools, and eight high schools; LWSD employs 2,600 staff members and of those 1,600 are teachers. It is the sixth largest school district in the state of Washington. The demographics of this rather affluent district are such that 72% are White, 15% Asian, 7% Hispanic, 2% African American, 0.5% Native American, 0.3% Pacific Islander, and 2% Multiracial. Only 13.9% of students in the district receive free or reduced-price meals (compared to the state average of 38%), 12.3% of students receive special education services (the state average is 13%), and there is bilingual support for 5% of the students (the state average is 8%). The on-time graduation rate is 90.2% and the dropout rate is 2.6%.

This district is exceptionally successful in many ways. Dr. Chip Kimball, superintendent of the Lake Washington School District since 2007, was named in 2010 as one of the top ten superintendents who best demonstrate outstanding leadership in using technology to further educational goals by *e-school News*. He also was nominated for and received Superintendent of the Year from the Washington Library Media Association in 2010 for supporting libraries and technology in schools. Prior to becoming superintendent, Dr. Kimball was the assistant superintendent, chief information officer, and responsible for all the information-technology functions in LWSD for many years. Additionally, *Bloomberg Businessweek* ranked Redmond as the top place in Washington to raise a family and gave credit to its excellent schools. *Forbes Magazine* determined that this area is one of the best bargains for housing, and also cited its excellent schools. The district also supports its teachers in their efforts toward National Board Certification (141 have now achieved this recognition), and LWSD has a well-entrenched system of New Teacher Support to provide coaching to all new teachers.

Lake Washington School District has also committed significant funding over the past few years to advancing educational uses of technology in its schools. Beginning in 2008–2009 the district created an "ActivClassroom" plan to install a package of an interactive whiteboard, projectors, document cameras, and FrontRow speakers and amplification in every classroom. In addition, the district began in 2009–2010 exploring the use of 1:1 computing by field-testing netbooks in five elementary schools and two high schools, and tied these tools to teaching the curriculum (specifically to math and Language Arts/social studies). During the 2010–2011 school year this 1:1 pilot was expanded, and every 7th-grade student at Rose Hill Junior High School received a netbook to be used at school and at home.

Funding for all this technology was explained to us during interviews with LWSD superintendent Kimball and the chief information officer (CIO) (now the assistant superintendent), Dr. John Vaille. Realizing a few years before that they needed a major influx of funds to allow this district to be able to meet its goal of having every student ready with the 21st-century skills they would need in their future careers and lives, they proposed a $42.8 million bond issue that was passed in 2010. These funds have allowed LWSD to update and move forward toward achieving its goals, and they plan another such bond issue in 2014. Furthermore, the availability of these funds allows LWSD to consistently secure better prices for equipment than they expected, so they are able to stretch their funds even further than they initially planned. In distributing these funds we were told that approximately 33% are allocated for technology for students and teachers, about 5% for infrastructure, about

7% for administrative staff, approximately 18.5% for instructional and enterprise software, and fully 50% for professional development, which works out to be more than $23 million available for PD over a 4-year period.

School Context

Rose Hill is a school described by its principal, Dr. Laurynn Evans, as "experiencing a demographic shift. . . . You're going to see a growing number of minority population, especially Hispanic oriented, in our attendance zone." In general it replicates the district's statistics (69% White, 13% Hispanic, 3% African American), but it does have a higher percentage of students receiving free and reduced meals (35%) than the district as a whole, and a growing population of English learners—almost enough to warrant a full-time ESL teacher. In addition, Rose Hill has a reputation for volunteering to take on challenges, no matter how risky or exploratory they might be. For example, it was one of three junior high schools that agreed to become part of a Microsoft Math Partnership grant, a project to support coaching for math teachers, and as such, teachers welcome a colleague/coach (at Rose Hill it is the chair of the mathematics department) into their classroom to jointly explore ways to improve the teaching of mathematics.

It was no surprise to the district's superintendent and CIO that Rose Hill and its principal were willing and eager to be the pilot school for 1:1 netbooks for the 2010–2011 school year even though this was added to two other major initiatives, all of which were tackled simultaneously. In asking these two district leaders why they recommended Rose Hill for participation in the 1:1 laptop initiative and as the site for our research, they responded that they had confidence in the leadership at Rose Hill, the school's ability to think about student learning outcomes, and the relationships necessary to make sure everyone was on board with the 1:1 project. Dr. Kimball stated, "The crux of the issue is effective teaching. The 1:1 is simply a tool to enact the vision and mission."

Leadership Practices

Dr. Laurynn Evans is in her second year as a leader at Rose Hill, having previous experience as an assistant principal, dean, and teacher in other districts, and yet it is obvious that she has had an impact already. In our first interview Dr. Evans described the three significant changes the entire school community was experiencing simultaneously. First, a new school building was in the process of being constructed over the following 2 years. She said, "So 2013, we'll move into the new facility. The new facility is completely different from this one. So pods, multi-level, big culture shift in terms of how the community and the staff work and collaborate." The second initiative is a total reconfiguration from the current "junior high school" model of serving 7th- through 9th-grade students to a true middle school serving 6th- through 8th-grade students. As a result of this change, Dr. Evans explained that the entire curriculum will have to be reconsidered, staff positions will need to be reviewed, and there will be some uncertainty about how that all this will work. She said, "We're going to be shifting down to a six through eight. Again, a huge culture shift." And finally, the school eagerly volunteered to be a pilot location for a 7th-grade 1:1 laptop initiative that began this year and looked forward to it being expanded to the entire school the following year.

Dr. Evans explained her philosophy of leadership as being systems oriented, rather than manipulative.

> So I'm very systems oriented. Like, I look at something that isn't running well and I like to find something that makes it run better. And I'm really big on turning things to people; I don't make a lot of decisions. I bring a lot of problems to a table; sometimes I'll have ideas or proposals, but we make a lot of the decisions at the leadership team level. And whether it's my counselor, administrative team, or the building leadership team, or instructional leadership team, I like to turn that over to them and have them make that decision.

As an example of her penchant for considering the entire system when making decisions, becoming a middle school has some staff members concerned about their positions, and what they will be teaching. In response, Dr. Evans has told them that there will be a place for everyone who wants to stay, but that the specific place is going to be determined by her, and that there will be a blank slate to begin figuring out who's going to teach what. She suggested that "The only way to be fair to everyone is to be fair to nobody. A commitment to stay at Rose Hill Middle School is a commitment to teach anything in your endorsement area, at any of the grade levels that will be at Rose Hill Middle School." Her guiding principle is "based on what's best for kids and I say that a lot, too, what's best for kids. That's the North Star, that's what we orient ourselves to."

The principal and assistant principal at Rose Hill also model ways they collaborate when working together. Mrs. Bowser, the assistant principal, stated, "We are a team—she is really intentional so that I know what the thought process is and why we are doing it in a certain way. The staff sees we work together and gives a consistent message." She also reports that she sees Dr. Evans as "an instructional leader in every sense." They often do joint observations of teachers, and more than anything, they work hard to "show that it has to be collaborative."

Dr. Evans discussed some other ways her leadership has made an impact during these 2 years. She explained that the school has done "a lot of intentional focused work about welcoming, and the Rose Hill way, and having to sometimes change and going through that." Her arrival resulted in developing a well-defined decision-making plan, and also an examination of the vision for Rose Hill. "Okay, we're going to do vision and mission, it's really important to know. If you don't know where you're going and your road's going to get you there, we need to know what is our road." She also explained that one of her guiding principles is to support her staff. "I'm not one of those people who go and win awards and do that kind of stuff. But I try to push other people up, so maybe they will." She also works to build relationships within the community. "I get good parent feedback, which I think is important, and the PTSA relationship is really good. I am giving them kind of an inside path to the principal's office," she explained.

History of Technology Integration at Rose Hill

It is important to recognize that while the new 1:1 netbooks, fully rolled out at the start of this year as a 7th-grade pilot with students taking the computers home and using them daily, is a significant part of this school's story, it is not the only use of technology that is worth discussing at Rose Hill. As evidence of the school's innovative approach to curriculum, many impressive, exciting, and pioneering activities have been taking place in this school for many years; following are just two of these:

Robots and Roller Coasters. A science teacher created and teaches an elective class entitled "Robots and Roller Coasters," where the students learn to build and conduct hands-on activities using computers, Legos, and programming. He explained,

> This started as an after-school Lego club, and then became an elective, and now I get to play with these things one period a day. I wrote a grant to the Lake Washington Schools' Foundation but also to others and we were able to get materials and equipment.

He described the course content; in the first part of the semester students learn programming with machines, with the incorporation of math into the designs, and then they develop their skills so they can make the robots accomplish more sophisticated things, such as moving in the shape of a polygon. He works hard to help them understand the fundamentals, such as what kind of angle the robot must turn, or what really is a polygon. He reports, "They don't necessarily realize all they are learning. For example, if we are determining the average speed of one of the robots, there is some time/distance graphing and of course that is learning about velocity." Interestingly, the school does not have room in its schedule for an advanced Robots and Roller Coasters elective, but some students sign up as "teaching assistants" and complete advanced activities in science, engineering, and mathematics.

Digital Media 1 and 2. A veteran teacher who has been at Rose Hill for 25 years designed and teaches an elective called Digital Media, a course that makes him very proud. He explained, "I started about five years ago and developed this digital media program from scratch." He found funding at the district level and got support from the faculty and administration. He said, "I really feel that kids can learn that and have fun with it, and it is important." He went on to describe how Rose Hill has an auditorium and a fund grew from the public that was paying to rent that auditorium. The district allowed him to use that fund to buy 30 copies of Adobe Premiere, Premiere elements, some external drives, and other materials. He described how he solved the problem of printing student projects:

> I figured out a way to use the district system for printing in color, so we use the drop box; the students can print through the district printing offices, and they turn it around in about a day, and the students have copies of whatever they need—newsletters, for example.

Rollout of 1:1 Initiative

Rose Hill might not have been the logical place to start the pilot of 1:1 netbooks, given two other major changes that were going on at the same time in the school; yet it was not a surprise to the staff or to Dr. Evans that they would take on one more major initiative. In fact, when she asked the faculty if they wanted to lead the way, and set the standard for using netbooks, or instead be told how it is going to happen after others have set the standard, they wanted to jump right into it. We heard many times that Rose Hill has a strong tradition of being early adopters. One teacher said, "We raise our hand—and even though the core group has changed in 25 years—but we stay that way because we want to meet the needs of learners on many things, but more so on the technology side." The library media specialist said, "We have lots of technology leaders on the staff; we ask what can we pilot, like online grading. Our model is the man who has been teaching 30 years and still just wants to explore and learn new things!" However, as she went on to explain, as others had, the current school building was a major challenge structurally for a true wireless 1:1 rollout. She said, "They may have wanted to show how we can do it when it is a challenge. Test of worst-case scenario!"

In order to prepare for the laptops, several specific items were put into place. As Dr. Evans told us,

> What I did do was insist that we had carts out at the end of last year, to kind of warm up to using them in the classroom. And John [the CIO] and the team were very good about not putting any pressure on the staff about it.

Additionally, Dr. Evans contacted a colleague from another district that had rolled out a 1:1 project to find out what that principal had done up front, what he wished he had done, and what he would do differently. This information helped Dr. Evans and her leadership team put some procedures in place that turned out to be very useful.

The assistant principal clarified some of the systems put into place before the netbooks were distributed. She said, "Laurynn met with the parents the spring before and let them know about the computers, and then on our prep day (before school starts), we talked to them about their netbooks." She explained that the first month of school students did not have a netbook assigned to them, but they used them in all their classes. They became comfortable with them, and then had to have permission and acceptable use agreements signed before they could get them checked out.

Dr. Evans also explained, "I'm a systems person. So, like, the whole thing of, like, setting up a checkout, getting it into kids, pre-selling to parents. Like, I came up with most of that and then they made it happen." In fact, the school staff seemed very proud that they managed to check out the netbooks (almost 180 of them) in less than 45 minutes. Dr. Evans explained the way things have worked so far.

> So we're the only school doing full checkout, one-to-one kids have their netbooks, are taking them home, and bringing them back. My staff are the guinea pigs. And we asked for it. We talked about it last spring and had a lot of conversation. It's gone really well. We've been very well supported with that, which I think leads to a lot of the reason why they're game to go full school next year.

We asked everyone why Rose Hill was chosen as the junior high to start with the netbooks, and Dr. Evans's pride in her school and staff was quite evident. She reported,

> We were selected for this because of the comfort level of my staff with the computers. But the other thing is, it's like "New York, New York" by Frank Sinatra. If it can work here, it can work anywhere, because of the physical structure. I mean, we've got, you know, concrete

and brick walls. Beaming Wi-Fi is not exactly what we'd call easy, portable areas, so all of that.

One teacher explained Rose Hill's reputation:

> What we have is a very strong cadre of teachers who are very tech savvy. I would say we have a core pocket of about eight who are really tech savvy. I would say that goes to about fifteen to sixteen who are very, very competent, including our librarian, which is really helpful.

Technology Support

While no technology specialist was assigned to the school, there is a district-level technical person who spends some time at the school and who is readily available to them. The library media specialist remarked, "We just let them know if we have a problem with an online form submitted to the district and we get service almost immediately."

Other district and school efforts support the implementation of technology at the classroom level. There is a district technology instructional specialist who is helpful in pulling together what individuals and schools are doing and identifying the challenges faced. The library media specialist explained,

> She is primarily charged with consolidating ideas, putting them out there. They have the teachers in the pilot meet every month for field test meetings and they talk about, how are you using them? What's been working? What isn't? What's a natural way of integrating?

Another districtwide effort that is having an impact on Rose Hill is district's IT2 initiative. The CIO, Dr. Vaille, explained this system: Each year the district identifies a specific technology to focus upon. A school-based individual volunteers to become the "expert" on that technology, software, skill, or system. Then, for each teacher who documents that she or he has mastered this new technology, a bonus of $1,200 is available to claim; this is repeated each year. The CIO explained that every teacher is encouraged to participate in this effort, and as a result many teachers at Rose Hill have become experts with specific technologies and then taught others how to use them.

Using Technology for Assessment

Technology used to support assessment has been a boon to the teachers and building leaders in LWSD. For example, the district has a system-wide gradebook program, and Rose Hill has a 2-week update agreement that Dr. Evans says she takes advantage of regularly. She said,

> It's great. I really love it, because I can go in and see—I have a group of kids I'm following, who have not been doing well. And so I can just yank their grades up anytime and kind of hold their feet to the fire.

In addition, Rose Hill's counselor, who has been at Rose Hill for 29 years, is considered to be the school's "data guru." He explained that the school began looking at data seriously about 7 or 8 years ago. It started with concerns about their 9th-grade students "who were leaving our school credit deficient." With new technology systems, and the way teachers are able to enter their grades quickly and easily, he described to us what is happening almost daily:

> Now we're looking at teacher performance and we're providing data for teachers so that they can see what percentage of grades am I giving? You know, how are kids doing in my class? How do I compare with other teachers? Am I offering instruction in a different style, different way that is beneficial to students?

And, while he acknowledged that this may be a bit of a concern to some teachers, it is something they are all eager to do. He said the attitude at Rose Hill is, "Let's look at teacher performance, let's look at student performance." He further suggested that access to these data has developed into ways to begin collaboration and conversations, "And now we're at the point where that is freely shared with teachers that may meet as departments and start to look at it, and then we can break it down and actually give them the names of all."

So now, teachers are using technology to systematically monitor their students' learning and identify what is going on. As just one example, a science teacher explained his routine use of the (Promethean) Active Votes system connected to his interactive whiteboard:

> I have been creating content for the ActivBoards, and am becoming more sophisticated in how I use it, and develop content, and it is becoming part of the classroom. It gives me a chance to know if what I am teaching is being received and I know what I need to reteach. I do look at my data each week and know what the students know. If there is going to be technology in my classroom I want them to use it as a tool.

Changes in Teaching and Learning

Although our visit to Rose Hill was only 6 months into the 1:1 initiative, we observed a wide variety of uses for the netbooks but never felt the teachers were using them just because they were there. Further, teachers at Rose Hill told us they were not throwing out their curriculum or previous plans and starting over, but were using the netbooks as they made sense in their lessons. For example, one English teacher had planned for students to look up words they were studying in an organized way; students used their netbooks to check an online dictionary and share the meanings with a neighbor. Students clearly were comfortable and confident in using the netbooks and also in lowering the lids when asked to show their readiness to proceed. The library/media specialist summarized what she had observed over the course of about 6 months regarding how teachers were using the netbooks. She said,

> They are focused to look at what the computer can do for the student. I had one class with netbooks who were able to do in two days what learners without netbooks took three days to do. I have also seen the teachers being able to add more differentiation to document students' learning and assessment. And third, I see more spontaneity in their teaching. If something comes up regarding evolution, you can jump to information on the Scopes Trial.

She added that, "Overall, the positives for the students far outweigh the challenges of a few broken or problematic ones." This sentiment was shared by many teachers.

One 7th-grade social studies teacher described her focus on cooperative learning and how she uses artifacts, the Internet, and other activities to "hook" the children into a new unit. During our observations in her classroom it was clear that the students understood the purpose of the different types of activities they were doing, and each group seamlessly used their netbooks only insofar as it was necessary to accomplish their goals. This teacher also reported that she uses WebQuests as a bridge from one chapter or unit to the next to help her learners in "sewing those pieces together." She stated that she

> taught the faculty this week on the way that students think about their lives, and used a map of Facebook as a way to consider what is in their minds: instant gratification but with the friends, autonomy, multitasking, blogging, and social network concepts to help them learn.

She also described her delight when one of her students surprised her by asking, "Can I create a video game to explain the causes of World War I? Can that be my assessment? I asked if he knew how to do that, and he said yes, so I said, 'Knock yourself out.'"

The math coach also reported some specifics about what she observed regarding the technology that was being used for individualizing instruction, teaching a math lesson, or supporting their video club, the latter in which teachers volunteer to have their lessons taped, viewed, and discussed by other teachers participating in the grant. And some of the science teachers also explained ways in which they integrated the netbooks into their teaching. For example, at the time we were on-site, the 2011 Japanese earthquake had recently occurred. Students conducted a lab in which they created and monitored a virtual earthquake and were able to record, evaluate, and estimate the repercussions from it. Another science teacher said,

> If you're going to be having kids do graphing, because they use some Probeware and measure the velocity of a car that they made as it releases from a rubber band, you already are recording it on Probeware. So instead of having them hand-graph it, why not plug it into a netbook and use Excel, right? I mean, that's the way of the future.

Still another teacher commented on the buy-in with the technology by the students. She said, "We have to be flexible, and so on; teachable moments that may have been lost previously, now I can do it on the fly." And another 7th-grade Language Arts teacher spoke eloquently about the impact of the netbooks, but first explained that she loves technology so for her, this transition has been easy. She described her reasoning:

> In the past, the ninth-grade classes most frequently used the computer labs, and every month when the schedule came out, the teachers of seventh and eighth grade were lined up at the door to try to schedule the lab. Now we can plan for full class use for any activity or assignment, rather than for the entire period once in a while. And now I can rely on the fact that the learners have reliable technology at home, so I know what they have available.

This teacher also explained that the most challenging aspect to learn was how to manage 30 netbooks at once while making sure everyone was on task. But she and her colleagues are sharing good strategies for this, and the students have come a long way since they started the school year with their netbooks.

Teachers' Views of Leadership

Several of the words we heard to describe the leadership at Rose Hill include *organized, hard working, good communicator, decisive, open, honest, trustworthy, confidential, thoughtful,* and *forward looking.* In describing what they both need and want in order to accomplish their individual and schoolwide goals, several teachers shared specifics about their principal. For example, one teacher said, "I need autonomy, too! Don't give me busy tasks, but if there is something I need to do that is important, I will absolutely do it. Laurynn is very respectful of our time and builds in and supports collaboration." Another said, "I want a risk taker, who supports our odd electives, who recognizes that not everyone fits into a traditional class format so we need to let kids have a place to be comfortable." One veteran teacher reported, "I want someone to support the programs in lots of different ways, to be working as an ambassador with the district. You need an advocate to move through the bureaucracy." And, as an example, he described the digital media class that requires each student to have a large amount of space on the district servers, which was a bit of a problem at first, until the principal helped negotiate by explaining why it was important and reasonable. He said,

> I call that "principal power!" which made my work much easier. Or, in my advanced digital media elective class I only have fifteen students and a principal could easily say we need to cancel it because the standard here is thirty. Those are the important things to me.

Another teacher explained his view as follows: "We need time to collaborate; find the best ways to these tools." Yet another agreed that time is the largest challenge, "Not just time to plan but time to really collaborate, which we are good at doing!" In fact, Dr. Evans appeared to recognize the importance of inspiring her teachers to try new things. She said,

> I've tried to encourage teachers, at least once per unit, to have a really heavy, netbook-intensive lesson, that's really creative and just kind of go[es] outside the box. And if we just keep doing that, over time we will get this really solid repertoire of good lessons, and so far, that's been building in nicely.

Professional Development

As described earlier, the district's model for professional development (PD) is a train-the-trainers model that offers monetary incentives to teachers who are willing to learn new technologies and then go back to their schools to teach other teachers. However, significant energy is required to support teachers in learning how to use their netbooks effectively, so time for professional development is an important consideration in any school with a 1:1 initiative. The principal's strategy at Rose Hill was not to push but to support the teachers in their uses, which is a pattern we saw in many other schools we studied. Dr. Evans said her model has been to tell teachers to look for opportunities that make sense, perhaps to turn a PowerPoint into an interactive flip chart, or use a document camera for student presentations. She said she tells them, "Look for those opportunities. It's the low pressure approach. I'd say that's probably why we're doing so well with teacher support on this."

When asked how professional development takes place at Rose Hill, we were not surprised to hear this response: "The PD for this has been peer-to-peer, almost exclusively. I've given them time to do that. The district has paid them to do that." And, we observed that the culture of the school appears to support peer-to-peer assistance. One teacher reported, "We are always sending each other things we find, or ideas that will be useful, or answer a question that person had." Another teacher explained that they are comfortable working and sharing together and that it is a characteristic of their school. She said, "We work in departments and also in team teaching across the departments, like the honors block, when the students stay together for social studies and Language Arts, and we co-plan for many units and self-directed projects."

Noteworthy Outcomes

While it is too early to know how or if the introduction of netbooks will end up having an impact on student achievement or learning outcomes at Rose Hill, or if they will see increases in student engagement or teacher collaboration, it does seem clear that a variety of benefits have already emerged. Several teachers reported that because they are always discussing the netbooks, "I think the teachers are more collaborative based on the need to keep on top of what they are doing and how they are doing it." Others told us that the students are working harder. The assistant principal said, "I did not know this group of students before the netbooks, of course, but they seem to be very enthusiastic, fearless, and willing to be taught the one way to turn in assignments, and such."

Further, anticipated challenges around the netbook rollout—especially concerns about how junior high school students would take care of them—turned out to be much less than the staff worried about. As an example, the assistant principal said, "I anticipated that I would come in each day and have students lined up outside my office. But so far we only have had one major incident and very few minor issues." She continued, "Surprisingly, what has not been hard is student misuse, abuse, discipline-oriented stuff. That's been pretty easy and surprisingly, we haven't had parents be opposed to it." We inquired about the issue of insurance for the netbooks, given that 7th-graders are not necessarily known for being responsible, but Dr. Evans said,

> The joy of the netbook, they're so cheap, right . . . the insurance is rolled into the component of the netbook. So the district holds the policy and it doesn't cost very much, because I think per unit, these are five hundred bucks or less. So unlike a traditional laptop one-to-one.

Looking ahead, Dr. Evans indicated that she is ready for the next stage. Before they knew that the netbooks would be extended to the entire school in 2011–2012, she was already prepared.

> I'm going to be doing some structured sharing. I anticipate having 7th grade teachers do some PD for their peers about, here's how I'm integrating it, here's what it looks like. We'll meet in some people's classrooms, we'll have a cart, and the teachers can be the students. And just kind of go through, here's how you would use Synchronize, or here's how you would have kids present, or here's what I did when I had a dead battery. Anything from instructional to managerial!

Challenges

Of course, there are challenges with any innovation. The literature is filled with reports of those issues, and this school was no exception. However, by the time we arrived the glitches with going wireless in a very old building had been ironed out, and the learning curve with a new gradebook program was over. However, this school was still working on three monumental changes at once—reconfiguring the school to a middle school, managing the many tasks of moving to a new building, along with working through the necessary change in pedagogy that a 1:1 initiative required. With the entire school going 1:1 the following year, Dr. Evans explained that a few faculty members are not yet prepared to move to a 1:1 system, and that may not be good for the school or the students. She considered that she may need to have a "conversation with them, you either need to or it may be time for you to think about moving on to greener pastures, because we've got to do this." She went on to remark, "I mean, we are doing a disservice to our kids if we don't teach them how to be capable and competent on a technology platform."

Teachers also reported that it would be good to have the students all get a bit more preparation on the basics of using their netbooks. One remarked, "We need to have some ideas for how to do the usual things on a netbook, add a printer, find the drop box, etcetera, so that it does not take class time." He went on to suggest that perhaps someone could make tutorial videos with Camtasia or have the students in Digital Media 2 create them. He also discussed how he tries to assuage any concerns the students may have by saying, "My mantra is something is going to go wrong today with the technology so the kiddos don't freak out."

Other things the teachers "wish for" include "Time is what I need, money, and also more collaboration for getting the creative ball rolling, help people be a bit more willing to take that leap." Others wanted more teachers so the class size could be lowered, or more interaction with parents; over-all, though, most teachers and administrative staff seem exceedingly pleased with the 1:1 rollout, the upcoming change to middle school, and the adventure of a being in a brand-new building.

Lessons Learned: Key Factors for Success

Most of the lessons learned from this case have to do with the role that leadership, planning, and school culture play in transforming a school. Many of these lessons are valuable for other schools, although we have to acknowledge that the financial strength of the Lake Washington School District is probably not typical in most parts of the country today. However, because many schools have multiple initiatives going on simultaneously, Rose Hill's story should be familiar to many school leaders who are trying to balance multiple projects. Therefore, even if your school or district is not well supported financially there are several lessons that can be learned regarding how to establish a collaborative school culture so that technology integration and other innovations are not as challenging to lead as you might imagine. Based on our interviews with administrators and teachers at Rose Hill (N=11), attending various leadership and grade-level meetings (N=4), and our classroom observations (N=18), these are the lessons we think are most valuable to share:

- The leaders in this school and in the district know that you have to create a vision so that you know where you are headed. They also know that you have to be forward thinking and willing to try new things. Just one example is the superintendent's willingness to redirect funds creatively—in this case, using rental fees for the school's auditorium to fund software needed for the Digital Media classes at Rose Hill.
- The superintendent of this district, who is an award-winning leader himself, directed us to this school knowing that the young principal would have a lot to teach us about distributed leadership in practice because she builds relationships with teachers, staff, parents, and students; advocates for teachers and students to the district and the community; and believes in creating a culture of positive support for teachers and students.
- Regarding distributed leadership, the principal talked explicitly about the importance of empowering others to be leaders in the school and the value of listening, asking questions, and gathering information from others, as well as watching, reading, thinking, and planning before making any

decisions. She told us that her style is to suggest possibilities and offer choices to her leadership teams and to lead without micromanaging, which she does by turning problems over to the people involved to help make decisions. She also likes to enable teachers with good ideas for innovative courses, grants, projects, and so on; further, she likes to support early adopters as they lead the way.

- Regarding systems thinking, this school leader told us that she is able to see the big picture and take a systems approach to making changes. She is also adept at managing multiple projects and changes at the same time, and always plans for several possible contingencies. She likes creating clear models and rolling out systems for decision-making, procedures, systems, etcetera, so that everyone understands the process as well as the outcome.
- This school leader believes in planning, planning, and more planning, having no hidden agenda, and being intentional and transparent with every decision that is made. One example of systems thinking and good planning in this case was the rollout of available technology on carts for teachers to try out during the year prior to the 1:1 rollout for students, a demonstration that every teacher appreciated. The actual deployment of the student laptops was also quick and efficient because of careful planning, thinking through all possible contingencies, and involving parents and families up front.
- Planning should be data-driven, and this school's leadership team uses data to make decisions about both student and teacher performance. They have found technology to be invaluable for this purpose, and very useful for scheduling as well. For example, the leadership team reorganized the schedule so they could provide tutoring for students Monday through Thursday, saving time for assemblies or other schoolwide events on Fridays only.
- Improving school culture and school climate was a priority for the leadership in this case, and the principal worked tirelessly to create a culture of positive support for teachers and students by building relationships with teachers, staff, parents, and students.
- A part of this school's culture related to technology is their use of peer-to-peer sharing as major form of professional development for technology integration, and establishing times for teachers to collaborate with others and share their uses of the technology. In fact, as part of a grant

from Microsoft, the math teachers in this school conduct peer observations of each other by using videos of their classes with the goal of supporting teacher learning and collaboration. The district also supports a trainer-of-trainer model for technology professional development, and offers generous financial incentives for teachers who take part in district-sponsored professional development and then pass it on to their peers at their school.

- In addition to establishing a positive school climate, this leadership team values using data to make decisions about student performance, recognizes that different students need different niches to be successful, and tries to accommodate their differing needs. This positive school culture is also manifested in taking time in grade-level and subject area team meetings to discuss the needs of individual students so that no student falls through the cracks. Furthermore, with the learning management system they have, data are available to students so they can track their own progress.

- With regard to changes in the curriculum, the faculty at this school is moving toward models of interdisciplinary teaching, but the leadership lessens the pressure by expecting just one new netbook lesson per unit of instruction, and continues to enable teachers who have good ideas for innovative courses, grants, projects, etc.

- Relatedly, the leadership encourages teachers to take advantage of grant opportunities that are available locally, such as Microsoft's Math Partnership Grant, and the Lake Washington Foundation grant to support programs like the Robots and Roller Coasters course, among other innovative ideas.

- In addition to partnering with business and industry, the leadership in this school believes in opening the school to parents who want to be involved and encourages their assistance, which fits in with the principal's goal of building relationships with teachers, staff, parents, and students.

CHAPTER 4

Working Towards a Cutting-Edge Vision

The Case of Godfrey-Lee Public Schools, Wyoming, MI

Vision: Godfrey-Lee Public Schools will provide the comprehensive, innovative, and creative instructional programs that prepare each learner to succeed in a global society.

Mission: Prepare each student for college and career in a 21st-century global community.

Motto for Technology Integration: Anytime, Anywhere, Any Device

This is the case of a very small school district (1 square mile) in Michigan that is ethnically diverse, where 86% of its students receive free or reduced-priced meals, and is under mandated school improvement due to chronic low performance. This district is also juggling several initiatives designed to increase student engagement and achievement, including a 1:1 netbook program for 6th-graders, and an open access network and cloud computing so that high school students can use their own electronic devices at school. This district was nominated through snowball sampling because the superintendent is seen by other superintendents as someone who "walks the talk" and thinks outside the box in order to get technology into the hands of students.

At the time of this study, the entire student population in this district was about 1,800, with about 350 students attending the high school, which provides wireless access through a secure school portal, and where every student in grades 6–12 has an email address to use with personal and school mobile devices. In addition to the BYOD (bring your own device) plan at the high school, the 6th grade began with a 1:1 netbook initiative in fall 2010 and 7th-grade teachers had access to carts of netbooks to prepare their students for a 1:1 rollout in fall 2011. To save money and paper, students and teachers use free tools like Google Docs to complete assignments for their teachers. The district also purchased Scholastic's READ 180 and System 44 programs with federal school-improvement grants for low-performing schools.

The superintendent related the following story to us that seems representative of his leadership style as well as his passion for this district and for each child. Mr. Britten is a runner and very proud of his students' running group; he started this long ago and always has a following of students who run with him. He said,

A couple of days a week we will meet after school, or in the summer we meet at the park over here a couple of nights a week and run. If they run with me and they stick with it, I give them all a free t-shirt at the end, Runnin' Rebels (school mascot) t-shirt. They love that. Last year I was trying out the barefoot running. So I'd go down at two o'clock in the spring and get on the track before all the kids got down there. One day all the Kindergartners are out on the track and they're walking, jogging, and the teachers are walking with them. It's kind of their little fitness thing. Most of them recognize me and they're jogging along when they ask me, "Where's your shoes?" I said, "I love running barefoot; it feels so cool." All of a sudden I see the teachers waving, "Stop, stop!" The students had all taken their shoes off, they're everywhere, scattered everywhere and they're all running barefoot with me on the track. The teacher says, "We're never going to find their shoes again!"

Context

This very small school district, almost surrounded by the metropolis of Grand Rapids, Michigan, has survived several efforts to consolidate it, has had major demographic changes, and yet is still moving in strong and forward-looking ways. The district serves grades pre-K–12 for a total of about 1,800 students in five schools: one high school, one middle school (these two schools share a building), an elementary school with grades 3–5, an early childhood center serving pre-K–2 students, and East Lee Campus (formerly Vision Quest), an alternative school that serves 10th- to 12th-graders and adult English-language learners. In all, the school population is 61% Hispanic, 20% White, 17% African American, and less than 1% either Native American or Asian/Pacific Islander. The district provides free or reduced meals to 86% of its students. In addition, of the 61% Hispanic students, 40% are designated as having limited English proficiency (LEP), which is the highest percentage of LEP students in the state. The entire district is 1 mile square so there is limited bus service, and it is provided to the youngest elementary students only; the remaining students either walk or get a ride to school. A few high school students drive. The makeup of the community has changed dramatically over the past several decades. The secondary principal, Peter Foote, explained, "At one time, perhaps 1960, the district had a predominantly White population and the curriculum was of two tracks, college-bound and preparation for workers in industry." The population has changed to the broad demographics described above. Now approximately 89% graduate and 30% go to some sort of post-secondary institution.

Godfrey-Lee Early Childhood Center (ECC) and Godfrey Elementary both continued to meet adequate yearly progress (AYP) under the federal No Child Left Behind (NCLB) Act. Michigan's Education YES! school report cards gave the ECC an overall grade of "A" while the elementary school continued to earn a solid grade of "B." Lee High School has made progress and achieved AYP, but its staff is aware that they must work harder to try to remove the state designation as a "persistently low-achieving" school in reading and mathematics. In fact, because of persistently weak ACT scores, Lee High School fell into the bottom 5% of schools in Michigan and was therefore eligible to apply for a very competitive federal School Improvement Grant (SIG), which the district did receive.

Given this context, we should explain that we included this very small school district in our study of award-winning, exemplary districts that have used technology as a lever for school reform based on the results of snowball sampling. That is, while studying other schools and districts, we asked superintendents and other school leaders about other districts they knew were using technology as a key to their improvement and that had strong leadership. David Britten and Godfrey-Lee were nominated based on these two criteria. We were also interested because of this district's forward-thinking plans to encourage students to bring their own personal computing devices to school, including smartphones, iPads, laptops of any kind, iPods, netbooks of any kind, etcetera, and to provide a robust, wireless network that would allow students access no matter what personal electronic device they had available to them. The district's motto of "Anywhere, Anytime, Any Device" seemed to warrant study.

Given this, it is also important to understand the dichotomy of "place" in this district. On one hand, many of the teachers and administrators have strong ties to the community and the school system. Mr. Foote, the secondary principal overseeing the middle and high school, as well as the alternative school, explained, "I was a student at Lee and ultimately kept coming back to teaching after other career choices." His family has stayed here and a family member is a teacher in the high school. Mr. Britten, the superintendent, while not graduating from Lee, grew up in the area, has a family history with the district and a close family member is teaching there currently. His passion for the place is clear, indicated as follows:

> A lot of the board members grew up here with me, and at about the same time period. And so there's a lot of connection to the past, which is a very different past than the kids in the families that are going here now have. I'll retire here or be carried out on a stretcher.

He also talked about changes in the community and the large amount of mobility in the students.

> I am always out in the schools and there are a lot of kids there that I don't know; that bothers me. A lot of it is because they haven't come through our system. We have a lot of transiency, so we get kids at a lot of age levels.

To put this in context, the assistant principal explained that every year they give a "Rebel for Life" award to anyone who started Kindergarten in the district and stayed through their K–12 education. (It is worth noting that the mascot was chosen to help students see they can rebel against stereotypes; Mr. Britten explained, "If a student believes he can go to Harvard, then he should be able to go to Harvard!"). He said, "Each year out of sixty or seventy who graduate only ten or so earn that award." From a teacher perspective, we suggested to a group of 7th-grade teachers that their incoming students would be very savvy with computers since they would have had them in the 6th grade, and one responded, "It is not unusual to have twenty-five to thirty percent totally new students in one year, so that is not really an expectation we can make." The reality of the changing population is important in the planning and implementation of new initiatives.

Leadership Practices

A hallmark of this district's leadership is the way in which it employs a distributed leadership model, encouraging and supporting department chairs, teacher leaders, and others. During our visit, teachers and other administrators in the district described Superintendent Britten's leadership using the following terms: *forward thinking, trustworthy, allows us to be involved in decision-making, shares responsibility, energetic, encouraging, shared leadership, follows Stephen Covey's ideas about having an abundance mentality and sharpening the saw, focused, learns from others, good communicator, shares new ideas with us all the time, has a practical agenda,* and so forth. Yet many individuals point to the superintendent as the one having the vision, being relentlessly and passionately involved, and encouraging everyone to be the same. As mentioned above, Superintendent Britten has lived in the area for a long time, grew up in the district, and actually attended district schools for "a couple of years"; but he also has a history through family members who graduated from the district. He explained how he became superintendent:

> I got a call from a friend of mine saying they were looking for a middle school principal and he talked me into coming up here. And then two years later, I took on the high school as well and then of course a few years ago was asked to move up to superintendent.

Mr. Britten describes himself as a hands-on superintendent who often conducts Skype sessions with children in the district, and said, "Yesterday, I spent most of the late morning over with the Kindergartners," and then said,

> The day-to-day management things, that's not me. I'm an in-the-classroom type of person. But I have had to spend far too much time lately on budgets and everything else because of the [financial] disaster going on.

The core plan is that everyone must stay focused on two or three key things at a time, and Mr. Britten explains that he is always asking more from his teachers: "What does this have to do with student achievement, or student engagement? And the teacher leadership has been fantastic in supporting our goals." Also, because the secondary principal is being forced to retire due to state regulations, Mr. Britten will take on that role for the coming school year, and there will be a leadership team in place to manage everything. However, this was a purposeful decision, as he explained, "It's really a disguised effort to say, okay, I've got second-level administrators and teacher/leaders and I'm not going to be there every day; they're going to have to really step up and be leaders and this'll be a good thing."

Mr. Britten knows how to deal with and encourage the changes he wants to see. He knows there may be some reluctance on the part of any group of people to accept change. It is normal behavior not to want to change. He said, "You go head-on you're going to hit the defense, and you might find yourself in a minefield, but you can go up to it and push a little bit." He acknowledges that sometimes you have to step back, and give them "a chance to rebound a little bit, but they won't come all the way back. And maybe then you can go and push a little more."

When asked why they thought this district was selected for this book, almost everyone gave the same answer: "Our superintendent's habits for communication, making this a one-to-one school, and encouraging progress." Given this, we were particularly interested in knowing what the educators and administrators feel are the strengths of Mr. Britten's leadership style. Overall, we heard almost everyone say that he lives and models what he wants others to do, and that "he walks the walk as well as talks the talk." It appears he also routinely "leads by example, uses Facebook, Twitter, goes all in with it," said one teacher. Another commented, "I trust him without question." The consensus is that an important part of leadership is to be organized and to provide a vision. One said, "He knows where we are going and how to get there, but also how the students and we will benefit from it." One visual image of a "good leader" seemed to be clearly talking about Mr. Britten. As one teacher commented,

> You can have a leader who sits in the office and comes up with all these ideas but if they are not connected, out and about here, don't know how many ELLs are in your classroom, what challenges you face, then they are not really leading.

Similarly, the current assistant principal suggested that the leadership must be shared and let others make some decisions and show ways they can lead. The SIG manager suggested that in Godfrey-Lee they use the model of "if one person shines, we all shine" and that we are all better when someone has a good idea. She said, "We build each other up, what do you think about this, how about that? Our superintendent is 'relentless' as a learner and energizer; he keeps sending us information about new things and how they may support our goals." The assistant principal laughed and said, "We might get two or three suggestions, ideas, links, from him just over the weekend or in a single day."

Principal Foote has a shared leadership style as well. He told us that he believes in "cross-training for faculty and students; if I'm not here, someone needs to be able to take on the tasks for collaborative work." He also believes that technology now is like a "pencil, it's a tool; it doesn't take the place of the craft of teaching and it doesn't take the place of genius or humanity, but it is a tool and as such, we need to exploit it one hundred and twenty-five percent."

As mentioned earlier, due to forced retirement by the state system, Mr. Foote will be leaving the district; many are clearly not happy to see him forced to retire, because his work as the principal has allowed him to support many of the initiatives of the district. He has helped institutionalize the SIG grant and make sure it was successful. He also said,

> I don't believe in just giving every student an iPad because it's a short-term fix if you don't have a plan for it, to embed it, or you don't know how to provide for its continuation; it is all about people.

In summary, Superintendent Britten and Principal Foote share the qualities of putting the students first and caring about the teachers as people. In fact, Mr. Britten said he told the SIG manager, "You need to hammer me over the head if I'm doing something that's getting in the way of their success."

Implementation Process: Three Different Initiatives

Initiative One: School Improvement Grant (SIG). The school district and thus this chapter must be framed by three significant initiatives. It is important to understand this small district with regard to the impact and influence of these initiatives. First, the district was the recipient of a federal grant award administered by the state, designated as the School Improvement Grant (SIG). Due to its history of academic challenges, during the 2009–2010 school year Lee High School was placed on the list of the 5% lowest-performing Michigan schools. While that was a disappointment to the entire staff, they used it as an opportunity to seek funding from the state to improve their educational system by applying for this very competitive grant. Ninety-seven schools in Michigan applied for this grant and 26 were selected to receive the funding; Godfrey-Lee was one of those. It received $2.3 million for a 3-year period to focus on improvements at the high school, and it was clear to us that the SIG grant was important in our understanding of what was happening in Godfrey-Lee. Mr. Britten explained, "This is our opportunity to bring many things together," and Mr. Foote stated, "The grant got things moving in the district. In one year our ACT scores went up nine points."

The implementation of the SIG grant brought about many changes. First, a former colleague of the superintendent's was asked to come to Godfrey-Lee to serve as the grant manager. She has the role of being all things (evaluator, data collector, organizer, and so on) for the grant. She works closely with the administrators and teachers in the high school. Second, they instituted Scholastic's READ 180, which is a supplemental reading program that required English classes to use almost all available computers in the school for those who needed this program. One of the English teachers who teaches READ 180 and is also the program coordinator explained,

> The program requires an hour with three specific segments (computers, reading, small group with teachers) and there is strong buy-in from the teachers. Before the grant was written, teachers had input and this is what they wanted. Now we are able to bring in things that other school districts have but we just don't have the money to do. Our plan is to shift READ 180 to middle and elementary as we have fewer and fewer in high school, so that they will be ready when they get to the high school.

In addition to the inclusion of READ 180 plus the complementary program for those who are significantly lower, System 44, the district also partnered with Central Michigan University's Center for Excellence in Education. The grant requires that all recipients base their plans on a strong research base, so three individuals connected with this center each provide 120 days of consulting during each of the 3 years. They bring to the district their expertise in mathematics, literacy, and leadership and are able to provide both professional development and feedback to the high school and middle school teachers, assisting them to improve student engagement and boosting their ability to use a model of continuous assessment. In talking with these three consultants, they clearly believe that the district has made progress in improving school culture, in creating an orderly and safe environment, and in expanding teaching strategies and models employed.

Even though the first year of the grant has been focused more on reading, a strong effort has been made to improve mathematics instruction. At the time of our visit, the district had asked the state for an additional half a million dollars to implement a focus on mathematics instruction, similar to what had been done for literacy. They want to bump up what they are doing by including more technology, more coaching and teaching strategies, and to work on ways for students to excel in math. The math consultant said, "We are seeing more efforts at collaborative teaching and making their practice public. We know next year there will be more emphasis on math but the reading won't go away." Following our visit, we learned the district did in fact receive an additional $250,000 to start up a rigorous math intervention using a blended learning approach provided by Carnegie Learning. All Algebra I classes will now incorporate Carnegie's online Cognitive Tutor system for differentiating instruction based on the needs of each student.

The SIG grant manager said, "We hope to retool our ability to decipher assessments, how to use assessment more effectively, and focus on the data from assessment." She also explained that at first they had not realized how much effort was needed to refocus the culture and climate of the school, but that it quickly became apparent. She reported that now

> there is a Culture and Climate Committee and we strive to recognize the students for what they have done, and what they can do. We want to support them "owning the future" for themselves; this is harder to measure but equally essential.

After only 9 months of the program, the school staff members have seen changes in students' attitudes and reading abilities. They now celebrate students making strong or exemplary progress through a plaque in the main hall; for example, two of the students made the ACT honor roll and their names are on this plaque. In addition, Lee High School was cited by the local newspaper for achieving the highest gains on the annual ACT test this past spring in comparison to all other area high schools. Also, they celebrate when students move up from one level to another level in READ 180, or make significant progress in the Lexile scores (Lexile scores are measures of either an individual's reading ability or the difficulty of a text). The SIG grant manager said,

> We have had students jump one year or two years in their Lexile scores already and they are proud of it, thrilled with themselves about it. The students have come to learn what this means, how to check their work in the READ 180 system, and so on.

Everyone in the district has seen advances in the students' ACT scores, and now students don't need to wait for the teachers to tell them they are doing better. So far, teachers appear to be taking the strategies they learned from the consultants and their own informal sharing. Furthermore, they are using these new strategies, looking at assessments, and eager to make sure they know how to do their best.

Initiative Two: Technology Integration Anytime, Anywhere, Any Device. The Godfrey-Lee district has made a significant commitment to using technology for teaching and learning as another major focus. This commitment is evident in talking with their technology team, which includes one technology integration specialist, a network administrator, a library/media specialist, and a technical support person in addition to a director of technology, who had been at Godfrey-Lee for 6 years. One example of the commitment is the director's work to make sure that the role of the technology integration specialist remains flexible and available. The administrator said, "At first, they wanted to give her a computer lab and have her teach spreadsheets or word-processing classes! That is so not what we are about."

Instead, the district made a decision that they needed to use any and all means to reach their educational goals, so Macs, PCs, and Linux, "Anytime, Anywhere, Any Device" is their motto. One member of the tech team explained, "Somehow we were saying, but wouldn't it be cool if it could be anything, Mac, PC, smartphones, whatever it is that someone has!" The network administrator said, "The 'any device' is the most difficult to manage, but whatever it is, whatever users can get their hands on, we want to support." He explained that a lot of schools ask students to turn off their electronic devices when they come to school, but "we want them to bring the devices and then also be able to reach the network and do what they need to do."

Some time ago the district used mostly outsourced technology support, but about 5 years ago an entire new technology department was created. The network administrator explained that with contracted services there was "no innovation, no vision, and no purposeful or intentional direction." The goal was to keep financial considerations in mind while also enabling a faster response to help teachers and others. One member of the tech team explained,

> Then the picture grew of what could be; we had a sort of synergistic happenstance; as the technology department began to grow, the media center became more involved, then technology integration grew, and at the same time Britten came on as superintendent, and he had the vision.

Now the entire team works together to support that vision. Today, all classrooms have data projectors, a few have interactive whiteboards, and teachers are experimenting at all levels. The network administrator explained the transition as follows:

> Any device—it really is an organic process as it seemed to evolve through the entire administration. We found a product called Stoneware that allows you to provide a web-based portal and only requires a browser. So we determined that if this was really going to

work, we needed to focus only on things that can be accessed through a browser.

Their web portal, called "RebelNet," was mostly created during the past school year. Mr. Britten told us how they "opened" the network:

> Mid-year the network administrator called me and said he was about to flip the switch to let the students get onto the network with their devices. I asked what has to happen for the students to actually log on. Then I saw a student with an iPod Touch, and he says, "I got on the network, I'm in the system." We didn't even have to make any formal announcements before the kids were on it!

The elementary-level classes typically had software applications that had to be installed on a desktop, so, according to Mr. Britten, "We started searching for web-based alternatives to whatever they were using." They began to encourage the teachers to "take ownership of that process and we told them that everything we deliver is going to be through the web." Now Google applications are used for all aspects of the district's work, and all students can have email accounts. When we asked how they go about helping teachers with all the new applications and materials with which they need to become comfortable, the technology integration specialist said,

> It is hard to keep up but I try to do some of everything—come to them, they come to me. I'm big into Twitter so I find a lot of things that way, and when I find something I know a particular teacher would like, I send that to her. I created a social bookmarking site where I have everything organized and it is available to all the teachers in the district. The only thing we really had some difficulty finding was a video editor, but we have found things for that, too.

There have been a lot of successes with this bold initiative. The technology team explained that everyone in the school system is using the web portal now, and people can do it from home, or wherever and whenever they want. The network administrator said,

> Teachers sort of learned that they could do things and suddenly they were totally available. Last year we also did total wireless public access and everyone figured it out and was using it instantly. Of course, our policy for its use came after turning it on, which is our usual style! My goal is to let them know more about what they can do and make it really seamless to actually bring any device, to really help with access.

The technology team at Godfrey-Lee is still working on developing this system and getting it to more seamlessly include parents; they can access the portal now and can see what their students are doing, communicate with the teachers and, so on; however, not too many are doing that yet. One technology team member said, "It would be neat if there were a way for parents to be able to collaborate more." As the system expands, they hope eventually to have every student bringing his or her device without having the district have to invest the funds to buy hardware, and we learned from the 6th-grade teachers that, at least in their grade level, 90% of the students have a computer at home, even though 80% are receiving free or reduced meals. As the network administrator said:

> [If we] give the Internet access, storage, email, and then it really would be ubiquitous. But have them available for those who don't have it to let them use a device in the school and still go home and use any device they have at home. It would be interesting to gather more data about what devices the students really have at home or access to.

Clearly their goal has been to build infrastructure in support of what they wanted to do "instead of in reaction to what was being done." The director of technology said,

> We have a highway in place. Now they see it, and we already have it ready to go. I really want to do this, as part of a unit; sort of like we built this nice smooth highway and you can pick what kind of car you want to drive on it. You want a Prius, great, but if you want a Suburban, they have open highway and ability to do it. I am very proud of my staff and they were chosen for their skills, fit for the district, and our goals.

The network administrator also explained that when someone wants to do something, the first measure is, "How does it fit our measure, Anytime, Anywhere, Any Device? If it fits, then we go to the next step of curriculum justification, How does this fit my curriculum plan, and third, how much money does it cost?" But they also continuously try to find free materials that replace expensive ones. If a teacher wants a class set of the TI-83 calculators, "Well, these are free online so do we need to buy physical ones if we don't need them?" Further, Superintendent Britten explained the push is to move things forward quickly, when he noted, "My emphasis is on the one-to-one. We're not going to make teachers experts; we're going to make them comfortable. They're going to learn right along with the kids."

Sometimes new technology is part of a collaborative effort—for example, the local parks and recreation department received a grant that resulted in buying Adobe Premiere and other high-end software and installed it on the district's computer lab machines. Thus, "During the day we can use it but then they offer after-school classes; a sort of win-win collaboration," said the director of technology.

Funding for technology is a consistent challenge for all districts and is particularly relevant in this difficult time; but, as the director of technology explained,

> I have never had issues with my budget. It was given to me when I came here and then we passed one bond for the new 6th-grade campus and the one-to-one, so it is all now part of the general budget to sustain the initiative; fluctuating is the PD [professional development] for the technology staff, which costs more each year.

We wondered about the metrics for success of these districtwide technology initiatives. She responded, "It is not my job to measure student success, it is my job to support teachers in promoting student success." However, she explained that in determining which netbook to buy, they selected a sturdy one, and made sure that their technicians could do a lot of the repairs themselves. They also wanted to make sure they could afford to buy enough extra netbooks to supplement and ensure there were enough.

Initiative Three: One-to-One Laptops and 6th-Grade Campus.
When Mr. Britten became the superintendent, he took a bold step in creating a new space for collaboration, technology, and student success. His predecessor had gone to the community for a $1.2 million school bond issue to build a 6th-grade "campus" located immediately outside the middle school/high school building, but Superintendent Britten helped to shape how this space would look. The 6th-grade campus is the location where the 1:1 laptop initiative was started this year; each 6th-grade student has her or his own netbook. A teacher explained, "Mr. Britten thought sixth was the best grade because it is the transition grade." Britten said, "Originally we were going to put fifth and sixth grade in there, and there were going to be ten classrooms." He said the plan was for 200 5th- and 6th-graders overseen by ten teachers, and a "bowling alley hallway and just boxes along the hallway. It would have been a disaster." Instead the building is more of a group of rooms surrounding a variety of collaborative spaces and everything is on wheels; one of the rooms is double size and has a sliding wall so that two classes can meet at one time for projects. Another key component is lots of glass windows, both interior and exterior, allowing everyone to see what's going on in any of the learning spaces.

The 6th-grade teachers explained that the development of this new building was done within "an environment of openness. We were invited to planning meetings and picked out furniture, but it has been the [design of the] building that really was needed to create this." They explained that they now have a common planning period in addition to a personal prep time, so "every day we do common planning." Unfortunately, it is worth noting that due to significant budget challenges that common planning may be lost in the coming year.

We asked how 6th-grade teachers prepared for the 1:1 laptops. One teacher explained, "We started with a single cart last year, but this year it was scary. We were told, 'Here is your netbook and here you go.'" The students did not know the basics of how to use it for learning, saving files, finding things, and so on; so the management of the netbooks had to be addressed in about 2 weeks of purposeful lessons at the beginning of the year. They learned from this. As one teacher put it, "Fifth grade now has one cart but some of the teachers are getting excited about the carts and netbooks so we think next year and on[ward] the students will be coming in with more skills."

To assist in building their professional skills, all the teachers in Godfrey-Lee have early release Fridays every other Friday for almost 3 hours for professional development. At first these sessions included time for learning about the technology, software, and teaching ideas, but the teachers reported that lately they have "sessions to support the school-improvement grant projects." One explained, "It would be good to do both. We need more training." However, they still note many changes in their teaching, including more hands-on and interactive activities completed online. As one teacher explained about the technology,

> This helps me individualize my lessons, especially reading, audio books, and text to speech. I use it on a daily basis; the tech team has built a social bookmarking system so that all we have to do is to go look for a topic. She has resources and has vetted them so they are good and safe.

One decision made early on is that the students do not take their laptops home. "If they went home who knows what they will do, maybe they won't come back the next day when we need it, and what will happen at home. We just cannot imagine," explained a teacher. For homework they use a mix of paper and pencil and computer assignments, and those students who don't have access to a computer at home typically find ways to work with friends who do have such access, or they go to the library. The teachers have found that the students are much more independent and proactive regarding finding answers for themselves, and they can troubleshoot if they lose their connection. Their early efforts to teach the students have clearly paid off rather quickly. The 6th-grade team, for example, explained that 6 months ago, "We did not know what Google Docs was and now we use it all the time; we give tests using Google forms, the students know how to use Edmodo and you only have to say, go to Edmodo and look for sixth-grade math for today." Another teacher added, "It is really nice that it is all web-based, so we can work from home and get that test set up or whatever." The teachers have noticed that some parents are starting to check online to make sure their students are returning homework and completing assignments, or asking for duplicates of assignments they are missing. Teachers did report that unfortunately this is not true for all students.

Professional Development

Professional development has always been a focus for the district but with the addition of a 1:1 initiative it clearly had to be expanded and deepened. However, it was clear that the plan was not to just teach how to use the technology. The goal was always to improve teaching and learning, support innovative integration of the technology, and improve student outcomes. Furthermore, part of the SIG grant was to identify consultants to assist teachers, move the district forward, and implement growth in literacy, math, and leadership. The SIG manager explained that Mr. Britten created a process to find the appropriate consultants: "To his credit, he picked the ones from Central Michigan University because they work in the classrooms not just in large groups. That has turned out to be one of the best things to support our transformation." The consultants' willingness to go into the classroom, provide demonstration lessons, and model their suggestions in the larger group sessions makes their impact substantial. She continued, "It is something where we all can learn from each other."

End-of-summer PD sessions on technology were mentioned by almost every teacher we interviewed. Since the district mascot is a rebel, they named their session Rebel U; it was apparently unusual for its practical aspects. Teachers were able to choose some of the sessions, and also had shared sessions on using tools. This year the plan is to expand the number of "choice" sessions instead of the traditional "sit and get" sessions, but in all instances this kind of PD was a hit with the teachers in Godfrey-Lee.

The technology integration specialist tries to keep consistent opportunities open for teachers to ask questions and learn. She created a Bits and Bytes newsletter, a "12 Days of Ed Tech" cheer around the holidays, and developed a robust social bookmarking system that was mentioned previously. A system of identifying teacher leaders for technology has also been created, and ongoing professional development sessions are available. Prior to the initiation of the laptops the tech team created a "boot camp" for the 6th-grade teachers; this will be repeated for the 7th-grade teachers in the coming summer and 6th- and 8th-grade teachers can also attend. The district's goal for every teacher seems to align with this technology specialist's statement: "If we make the teachers comfortable, that is a big part of our job. If they feel supported, know we are here to help them, it will be a big change, [we will go] from a [long] lag time to [being very] responsive." They intend to try to simplify the technology for the teachers, break down the barriers, and to help them "see it as a tool rather than an annoyance."

One complication of the professional development plan is the current financial crisis. As such, teachers and the tech team are not sure who will be teaching what next year, so the 7th-grade teachers cannot get their laptops before the summer. The teachers desire more professional development in the area of technology, would love to visit other schools to see what they are doing, and would also like to have technology coaches who could help them throughout the year, but they do seem to recognize the limitations of funding, time, and the requirements for the SIG grant, which does provide coaches for math and literacy. One group mentioned they would like more feedback as an outcome of formal and informal observations; however, they are also well aware of the reality of limited time and administrators' multiple obligations.

Changes in Teaching and Learning

We asked all teachers and administrators to tell us examples of the ways teaching practices and outcomes have changed as a result of integrating technology. We were told that many teachers still feel they must do double planning; one teacher explained, "I have this for the technology if it works, and oh maybe if it does not work, I better have some alternative planning in reserve." Other teachers talked about now being able to offer students more choices for how to complete assignments. For example, during a class session we observed, one teacher remarked, "Here are three activities to practice graphing in Edmodo and you can pick which one you want to do."

The district's portal, RebelNet, is apparently used every day and multiple times a day, as teachers access Google applications, the calendar, Infinite Campus student data manager, or search for online resources to use with their students. We were told that quite a few teachers are looking at more project-based learning approaches, and are becoming more open and comfortable asking for help. And, as a result of the professional development they have received through the SIG grant, they are using many more cooperative learning and active, student-centered strategies. Thus, both teachers and administrators reported that the culture of the district is changing. One example demonstrates this shift. Superintendent Britten relayed the following story.

A seventh-grade teacher wanted to do a project with the computers on the cart but she did not know how to do it. The students said, "Yeah, we'll show you how to do it." I was walking by and she says, "Come here. You should see what these kids taught me how to do, and look at what they're doing; I was scared to death at first, but this is great."

Other changes have been noticed. One teacher said, "There was leadership from the district to make this happen. That was a clear vision when Mr. Britten became superintendent, and it became the district vision." One of the things the SIG manager noticed is that "Those teachers involved in the READ 180 are taking that model and using it in their traditional classes; that is, they are dividing up the time for small group, independent work, and computer reinforcement." She was very pleased that they were following this structure, so the student owns the learning and is responsible, and giving the students three different ways to learn content.

Grade levels without netbooks are being supported with tech carts so teachers can still do lessons that call for using computers with all the students, and the school's wireless network allows them unlimited access to websites and use of many online tools. One teacher explained, "We did get more labs, and they were used a lot, then came the netbooks, and those are all being used especially in Language Arts and science." The 7th-grade teachers were clearly planning for their 1:1 netbooks next year. One teacher explained, "We are doing some projects and then a collaborative project across courses, we have done Prezi, and I let them use their iPods." Another teacher said, "I use interactive math labs and we have a good site that prompts them if they are not graphing linear equations correctly." And yet another reported, "I use an algebra planet blaster–they can blow up their planet if they solve the algebra problem correctly. Kids loved it and knew right away that they got it correct or not." Other teachers told us about their use of Dashboards (a type of presentation program), flip cameras, Google Docs for peer editing, and many other tools. One told us how her practice has changed:

> I have an overwhelming urge to print everything out and scribble all over the paper. Last year the kids did their final papers, they did it by email. So I have a "papers to grade" folder; I attach the rubric, and send it back.

And another teacher managed to find a program and Wiimotes (Wii remotes) to turn the regular whiteboard in her room into an interactive whiteboard for about $80; another said, "I have tech envy for that, and need to try to figure it out." We heard about the teacher responsible for this in two other interviews, so clearly it was becoming a topic of conversation.

Noteworthy Outcomes

It is important to think of this case as more than encompassing only one school. This is partly because Godfrey-Lee is a very small district and its three main initiatives are focused beyond just one school, but also because of the way the superintendent and others have overseen changes, and the way they are articulated throughout the entire district. The people we interviewed are very proud of many accomplishments related to culture, climate, student attendance, and achievement. Mr. Britten said, "We are starting to attract kids here. We've grown two hundred–over two hundred in the last five years. For an eighteen hundred student district, that's quite a lot."

As an example, due to funding from the SIG grant, a new project called "Rebel Prize" will begin to extend the school year 10 additional days for remediation, credit recovery, and enrichment classes in core content areas. Students signed up for it and teachers planned to teach these classes. The additional days will include new and exciting classes (e.g., Paranormal Science, Film as Art, and local history), and those who need remediation will get some of that, too. There will be guest speakers, the days will start at 9:30 rather than 7:50, and the 2 weeks will end with a schoolwide barbecue and a "gallery walk of learning" to showcase products from the classes.

As of now, everyone has a data projector, the 6th-grade students and teachers have laptops, teachers who currently have desktop machines are seeing those replaced with laptops as they wear out; the 7th-grade team has laptop carts and every 7th-grader will have a netbook at the start of the 2011–2012 school year. The 8th-grade students and teachers will receive them in the summer of 2012, but for the next year several laptop carts will be moved into 8th grade so the teachers can start using them. Plans also include leasing a full cart of Google Chromebooks for a pilot in the 8th-grade Language Arts classroom. The director of technology explained that there are a lot of exciting teaching activities with technology going on. She notes that she stays busy: "I wish I could have had the time to celebrate the really excellent things going on in the classrooms, but there is a time issue. When I watch the classrooms, it is hit or miss, but some great things are going on." The 7th-grade teachers said, "We hear sixth-grade students are awesome in what they know. We honestly think they will be teaching us; they know so much more than we do. They are excited about being inventive, creative, and knowing more than me!"

Another area of pride is seen in changes at the alternative high school, which is now known as East Lee Academy. Students are there for a variety of reasons, and up until this year many problems were evident, including fights, truancy, and lack of academic progress. The new assistant principal at this alternative site has worked collaboratively with staff and made a significant number of modifications to change direction. As a result, the numbers for fights and dropouts are much lower, the hours have been changed to fit a more traditional school model with some flexibility through evening classes, technology has been added throughout the many different programs at this school, and graduation rates, attendance, and ACT scores are up. The assistant principal said, "If a student shows up she should get the best we can offer. If a teacher shows up, she should feel safe and be able to teach. Now we are trying to refocus and they [the teachers] are using technology to do that." They have added an online GED program, hardware (laptops and interactive whiteboards), and more project-based learning and service learning. They also provide English-language support and job services for adults who are mainly ELL students. Superintendent Britten said, "Actually, we're trying to gear up our alternative education to be more STEM focused and to provide a cyber component where we can attract kids from around the state back into school." Planning is also underway to offer a cyber component that will be intended to encourage dropouts from any part of the state (or country) to return to school, and to take online courses taught by the resident faculty at East Lee Campus.

Challenges

The changes in Godfrey-Lee over the past few years are significant; this district is not without both successes and continuing challenges. Financial setbacks may change the time for joint planning, the numbers of students in each class, and other items, but it is a positive that the high school's SIG grant still has 2 more years of funding. Additionally, the district has had some difficulty in building better communication with families partly due to the language barrier. The SIG grant manager suggested, "Another area where we really were not successful yet, but will devote more energy to, is the parents and wider community piece." She went on to say, "We are not where we need to be in that arena. We really need to build this into next year, making it more of a partnership and stress how we need to work together."

Superintendent Britten seconded that goal and also said he wants to make the wireless network more available in the general outside area of the schools. He also has plans to seek funding for an addition using the currently open courtyard within the Lee Middle and High School building, explaining, "We envision a glass roof dome on that and that becomes the community center for technology and media."

Lessons Learned: Key Factors for Success

There are several lessons that can be learned about vision and leadership from tiny Godfrey-Lee School District that are valuable for other schools and districts, large or small. These lessons exemplify what can be done with very limited resources in a very poor and very diverse school and/or district when the leadership is willing to think outside the box, even when there are several initiatives underway and the school or district has been mandated for school improvement. Based on our interviews in Godfrey-Lee (N=13), focus groups (N=3), and observations (N=13), these are the lessons learned that we think are valuable.

- The importance of having a strong vision and then leading by example, with passion, and focus was a clear lesson in this case. The superintendent of this district realized that students have changed and need something different to stay engaged in their schooling. This led to a vision for creating new kinds of collaborative learning environments for 21st-century students, and believing that teachers and staff wanted to change for the better as well. This vision also included being willing to try things—in this case, encouraging students to bring and use their own wireless devices to school when it was clear that the cost of a 1:1 initiative would defer the vision of a 21st-century education for students.

- This superintendent's vision also included technology being used for instruction as opposed to test preparation and administrative purposes. He also believed in supporting and trusting new policies and initiatives to help stretch the limits of what is possible. However, the superintendent also believed in knowing your own talents and strengths as a district, school, or teacher leader.

- Believing that distributed leadership can help accomplish your vision, this leader said it is all about the people—your students, their families, and your teachers and other staff. Further, he allowed people to find their niche and lead based on their varying strengths. Another example of distributed leadership in operation in this district was building successful teams and hiring good staff members who are dynamic and passionate about their subject, even beyond school hours. In this case, one example of building a successful team was creating a technology team that consisted of the library/media specialist, a network administrator, one tech/media support staff, a technology integration specialist, and the district technology director who made the BYOD (bring your own device) initiative a reality, while also supporting a 1:1 netbook program for 6th-graders that would expand annually.

- In order to enact one's vision, the leader of this district said he was thinking and planning for several years down the road, not just for the next year or two. Furthermore, he connected and communicated with other school leaders who are passionate about technology and who also think outside the box. Also, to enact his vision, this superintendent believed in being an integral member of the community, acting as more than just a building or district leader.

- The culture in the schools we observed in this district included acknowledging even small successes, building on each success, and celebrating successes publicly. The culture was also one of trusting students to be responsible with technology when the policy was changed to allow students to bring their own computing devices to school.

- Further, the leadership in this district did not believe that all younger teachers already knew how to use technology in their teaching, or assume that all the experienced teachers were going to be reluctant to change or learn to use new technologies. Instead, the district provided ongoing and consistent PD in a wide variety of ways, which included manipulating the schedule to make time for collaboration and joint planning, and budgeting for unstructured time for the teachers to spend together with their materials and with technology guidance.

- In order to achieve their vision for using technology to engage students and improve instruction, the leadership in this district had to find ways to do so with very limited funding. One way to do this is to move toward using more web-based applications and ceasing the purchase of software licenses, which they did. Another way is to limit textbook purchases and move toward 100% use of online learning materials. The superintendent also told us that he was also willing to "blow up" and rebuild programs that were no longer working, and devote enough resources to the technology team because in the long run this would save money, speed up response time, and support the plans to achieve the vision. He was also willing to seek bond issues and grants, even when he was unsure of the probable success of doing this.

- When the district did receive a school-improvement grant, a lot of planning and professional development ensued. Using technology for instruction more than for testing and administration was already an important goal, and the district planned effectively by placing laptop carts at grade levels prior to moving toward 1:1 for that grade in the following year. Further, the leadership leveraged the benefits of this grant to improve every aspect of the school rather than one targeted content area.

- Curriculum changes were also planned, including the implementation of new research-based programs that promised to increase student achievement. Broadening the traditional Senior Capstone Project to include technology components, online learning, or internships related to technology education was also a change; and continuing to fund the district's full-day Kindergarten program in a location where full-day programs are not required remained a priority.

- Collaboration with nearby colleges and universities brought consultants into the district to provide professional development related to the goals of the school-improvement grant. However, because of their focus on active teaching strategies, time was limited for desired technology professional development according to the teachers we interviewed, which is indicative of the challenges in balancing competing needs that leaders always have to consider.

Epilogue

On August 27, 2011, the Michigan Department of Education released the revision to the "Top to Bottom" school rankings, along with an update on the 5% Persistent Low Achieving (PLA) list. Lee High School improved dramatically, reaching the 33rd percentile in the state's ranking, and was removed from the PLA list. While the high school will continue for at least 2 more years to be under the watchful eye of the state reform officer to ensure the transformation continues, the success achieved by the high school staff, students, and parents will no doubt serve as a foundation for continuing student achievement growth in future years to come.

CHAPTER 5

When Funds Are Limited

The Case of Simley High School, Inver Grove Heights Community School District, Inver Grove, MN

Learning environments for high student achievement so all learners are academically and socially prepared for lifelong learning.

This is the case of a small and relatively poor but academically successful district that strives to provide a 21st-century education for its students rather than rest on its laurels. This is also the case of a superintendent and her Technology Leadership Team trying every way possible to get technology into the hands of students in a context where the resources for doing so are limited. This district received a Technology Leadership Award in 2010 from Minnesota TIES for its efforts, which is one reason why it was selected for this book.

At the time of this study, this district of about 3,660 students had 70 interactive whiteboards (IWBs) across the district's five schools (about half of the classrooms), including IWBs in all Advanced Placement classrooms at the high school. In addition there are two PC labs at the high school, 64 older Macs in common areas in the new middle school, plus ten class-size and three smaller labs at the middle and high school, all with dual-boot Macs. All middle school and high school teachers have Macs with dual-boot capabilities, and all other teachers have laptops or desktops. There is video conferencing equipment at all the district's schools, and the administrators all have iPads.

One of the classes we observed was the Alternative Learning Program (ALP) at Simley High School. This class of juniors and seniors who are at risk for dropping out of school was housed in a very large classroom that allowed several different workspaces for 23 students and the two teachers who were co-teaching this group. Prior to this year students who needed to recover credits and who were not succeeding in their regular six- or seven-period-per-day classes came to the ALP whenever they liked, completed packets of worksheets while they were there, and took tests to earn credits. According to the superintendent, both the attendance and the success rate of students in this program were atrocious and something needed to change. As a result of the administration's determination to try something new, two young teachers without much experience, but with a lot of enthusiasm, were asked to create a new program that would include laptops for every student and a flexible but full-day schedule that used problem-based and challenge-based learning as primary methods for organizing all the required curriculum that students had to complete successfully so they could get back on track to graduate.

What we observed in this room were students working independently and together, engaging with their peers in groups but also participating in direct instruction from one of the teachers, and using their laptops for research, writing, and posting assignments. They appeared to be engaged in their learning because the teachers made a concerted effort to learn each student's strengths and weaknesses and care deeply about each student's success. Further, these teachers expressed their willingness to do whatever it takes to teach the curriculum in ways that make it relevant for these formerly disengaged students. The classroom culture, which was purposefully and carefully established at the start of the school year, has developed into one of trust and respect among the students and their teachers. As a result, learning is occurring and students are motivated to work more than they ever were in regular classroom settings.

We asked to observe this ALP because we heard the high school students were collaborating with 4th-graders at another school in the district on a Going Green challenge-based learning project. The teachers had all attended the same professional development sessions about challenge-based learning and discussed working together on a project. The plan for the day we observed was to use the video conferencing equipment so that high school students could talk with their elementary school partners and brainstorm ideas for recycling projects they could do in their schools. Even though the video was not working, the students could still hear one another. It was amazing to see once disaffected high school students encouraging and guiding their 4th-grade buddies toward realistic plans for completing a Going Green project that they would eventually do together. As we watched, the high school students listened and offered suggestions, and the 4th-graders also listened and offered suggestions. When one of the older students talked about biodegradable products, she found herself in the position of teaching younger students what that term meant. You could see the pride on her face when her much younger partners understood this term, and you could hear the enthusiasm in everyone's voices as they brainstormed ideas for projects such as having a recycling fair for their community, arranging for recycling areas at their schools, going outside to pick up litter, and having a campaign to promote the use of biodegradable products. The level of collaboration going on would not have been feasible without the technology that both classrooms had available.

Of course, the ALP students had to learn the science behind recycling and were studying other important issues in environmental science, applying their math skills to interpreting and creating graphs, and also using their reading and writing skills to meet required high school science and English competencies, but they were doing this in a way that was engaging and relevant to them. From our perspective, and that of their teachers, it was clear that this new version of the ALP at Simley High School was much more challenging for both teachers and students than completing packets of worksheets, and it was clearly an improvement in everyone's eyes because these students were getting back on track to graduate.

Context

Inver Grove Heights is a very small school district in Minnesota located a little south of St. Paul, but close enough so that most people living in the town commute to jobs in the Twin Cities. Inver Grove Heights has a population of about 34,000, an estimated median household income in 2009 of about $64,650, and a median house or condo value in 2009 of about $224,700. The Inver Grove Heights Community School district is comprised of three elementary schools plus a middle school and high school located on the same property as the school district office. In fact, you can remain completely indoors and move easily between these three buildings, which must be especially nice in the winter. It also means that the superintendent, other central office staff, and the administrators in the middle school and at Simley High School have easy access to one another. The students in all five schools are taught by 244 teachers and the district has a total staff of 462. The ethnic breakdown of the district's population of 3,663 students is 72% White, 14% Hispanic, 8% African American, 5% Asian, and 1% Native American. About 12% of these students are English learners, 18% receive special education services, and 31% are eligible to receive free or reduced-price meals. Since 2002 the district has offered a magnet program called Atheneum for highly gifted students in grades 2 through 5, which is followed by honors and Advanced Placement courses in middle school and high school, respectively.

By all measures educators in Inver Grove Heights Community Schools (IGHCS) provide a good education for students because they meet or exceed the state average on all measures. For example, the graduation rate is 97% (79% for the entire state average) and the passing rate on Minnesota's required tests are: 92% for Writing (91% for the entire state average), 78% for Reading (78% for the state), and 60% for Math (58% for the state). Furthermore, the Inver Grove community is very involved in their schools, and there is an active volunteer program to put adults in schools, as well as a rich tradition of both tangible and intangible support over the years. Students who benefit from the community's support, kindness, and generosity also give back to their community in many ways. However, the district struggles to finance all its needs due to a low property tax rate for schools ($806 for a $200,000 home) and an aging population in the community who do not have children in the schools. In fact, IGHCS spends about $400 less per pupil each year than the state average. That is, the district spends $8,763 per pupil compared to the Minnesota state average of $9,116 per pupil. To help remedy this situation, IGHCS is currently seeking an annual increase in the tax levy to fund capital project costs, which will include funding for critical health and safety upgrades and for computer and technology infrastructure repairs and replacements. And a unique way they are trying to involve and educate all voters in the community is to offer a Saturday morning Technology Fair, which both the chair of the school board and the superintendent told us will involve students as teachers. As the superintendent told us,

> We're going out for referendum this fall, and I'm also going to propose a technology referendum. I think there's about a fifty-fifty chance, which is good, it's good to have a fifty-fifty chance at anything. I think that people understand more and more that the students need to have access to it [technology]. There's still a good portion of persons who believe that technology is sort of extra and we don't really need it. Those same people are going to doctors . . . where doctors are now carrying iPads, you know, when they go to the doctor. We have a community of many elderly citizens. I came up with this little

brainchild, and I don't know if you heard about that or not, but we're going to have a half-day event where the students actually are going to be providing like a sectional, kind of breakout sections, where you can go and learn how to do whatever on an iPad or an iPod. And the students are actually going to teach that. I thought, "Well, if this community's going to see a benefit to it, it's going to come from them being able to see the students do things." I think we have support from the parents who have students in the schools. I don't know that we have a lot of support from the rest of the community and only about 17% of our taxpayers have students in schools here.

Despite the fact that funding technology purchases continues to be a struggle in this small district, as it is in so many other schools and districts for a variety of reasons, we selected Inver Grove Heights and Simley High School as a site for our research for several reasons. First, the school district recently won a statewide award for technology leadership from the Minnesota Technology Information Education Services, which was created in 1967 to provide technology and information resources to school administrators, educators, and students. It is now known solely by the acronym TIES, and is currently a self-sustaining collaborative of 46 school districts that offers its members software for school administration, technical support, discounts on purchasing hardware and software, Internet services, and professional development designed by educators to increase/improve technology integration. For example, TIES has developed enterprise-wide programs to manage student information data (grading, attendance, scheduling, and reporting), financial systems that HR departments need, including payroll and personalized learning systems to track students throughout their K–12 experience, etcetera (see http://www.ties.k12.mn.us). This organization also selects and recognizes technology leadership annually, and the Technology Leadership Team at IGHCS won this award in 2010. Second, Simley High School has been named one of America's top high schools by *Newsweek* magazine for 4 consecutive years, and in 2011 the *Washington Post* ranked Simley the 15th best high school in Minnesota. Third, this small school district, along with several other small districts we studied, appears to be representative of the vast majority (about 86%) of school systems in the United States that educate between 2,500 and 4,999 students annually (see Table B at http://nces.ed.gov/pubs2001/100_largest/discussion.asp#gc). Fourth, the superintendent of the Inver Grove Community Schools, Dr. Deirdre Wells, has a reputation in her state, as well locally in her district and region, for being a technology leader. Along with the rest of her technology team, Dr. Wells has been recognized for taking "giant steps to prepare its students for the 21st century," as described on the TIES website:

The district is challenging old perceptions with data and trying new approaches with technology. Guided by data, decisions are transforming learning and making it more personal for students. The team provides close support for administrators and educators in using data. All schools use TIES online personal learning plans to shape instruction. With this new technology, robust data help us to identify a personal path toward personal success and academic achievement for each student. . . . Classrooms use iPods, interactive whiteboards, student response systems, and many more technologies. Students have a greater variety of ways to learn—and to express what they are learning. Staff share their classroom ideas with each other via blogs and Moodle, spreading the excitement of their work. Even the building and grounds department uses data and technology to significantly reduce energy costs. The [Technology Leadership] team has had a central role in supporting and implementing challenge-based learning, as well as action research projects exploring the effectiveness of iPods and iPads in Kindergarten readiness, reading fluency and foreign language fluency. Through technology, all Inver Grove Heights students, their parents and the community have greater access to information and online learning. Over 1,200 parents access the SchoolView online portal to see grades, attendance and other student information. From home, families also have online access to district libraries, as well as over 40,000 Atomic Learning video tutorials. A wide variety of assistive technologies enable the district's special needs students to bridge the digital divide. Many of these tools are used throughout the student population, including text-to-speech and animated video. In these ways and many others, the Inver Grove Heights Technology Team has helped the district make great strides to increase opportunities and accessibility for student learning. (http://www.ties.k12.mn.us/ Technology_Team.html)

Implementation Process

In talking with many teachers, administrators, staff, and the chair of the school board, it appears that since Dr. Wells arrived in 2005 there has been an ongoing push to add, upgrade, and integrate more technology in the schools, to improve many of the district's policies and systems, and to build a new middle school, among other initiatives. While both the district and the parent-teacher groups in the schools had put desktop computers and SMART Boards in many classrooms in previous years, and had done their best to regularly upgrade and add to the computers that both teachers and students were using, as a result of Dr. Wells's leadership the district has finally gone wireless (including making the high school parking lot a wireless access point so that anyone in the community can use it), and is working to put more technology in the hands of the students by purchasing handheld, mobile devices such as iPods and iPads. Dr. Wells recently led a change in the district policy so that students can use their cell phones during breaks and use their own technology during class to search for information if the teacher allows them to. In the past few years, Dr. Wells also designed a new and somewhat innovative idea for offering action research grants to teachers who want new technologies. Dr. Wells described how things have progressed during her tenure at IGHCS:

> And I really just sort of made it a personal goal to expand the horizon for people here about what technology really should be in schools. And I didn't even realize I was doing it . . . I think it probably wasn't until maybe the third or even—you know, this is finishing my sixth year here—that I really realized, sort of unconsciously, what I was doing. . . . But after that somehow, somewhere in my mind it just sort of jelled that, you know, there are some other things we could do here, too. And I just have this vision that we're not providing students the resources they need to be twenty-first-century students. And I've been harping on that now probably for the last two and half years. . . . And about a year or so ago, maybe even a little longer, I did some interviews with some students, and by this time there were SMART Boards in classrooms, and I talked to the students, and the students said, "Yeah, those SMART Boards are nice, we never get to touch the technology, teachers touch the technology." And I thought, "Well, that's the end of that, no more SMART Boards as stand-alone devices." So I said, "You know, I think the SMART Boards are okay, but our staff use them as sort of just an expensive whiteboard. And I'm really not thrilled about that, so I'm going to say that from now on any funding we get around here we're going to put the money in some technology that's actually going to go in the hands of the students." And that's when I started the idea of these action research projects. And I said, "You know what? If you guys want to go farther with this, I'll get you some iPods, the iPod Touches, but you'll have to write an action research project." And so the first action research projects were born here and that was basically in an attempt to have them link the technology to the standards. In other words, it wasn't going to be a toy, it was going to be something that you were going to be able to give me some indication that you were using it for student achievement and some sort of measurable change in the classroom . . . and now, I think we're on the fourth rendition of the action research project guidelines. So, I still have this

long-range vision that every kid in this system is going to have access some way somehow to some sort of personal technology, whether it's their own or whether it's something that the district has provided.

Leadership Practices

What we heard from teachers and administrators in IGHCS, as well as from others who are not employees of the district, were descriptions of this superintendent as a dynamic leader, one who is thoughtful but quick to take action, works with her team to try out new ideas right away, and encourages collaboration within the school district, within the TIES collaborative, and with other districts across the state. They also said that she studies how things are working, uses data for looking at special projects as well as the general curriculum, and encourages others to look at data as well. In fact, the chief executive officer of TIES told us that IGHCS is the most data-driven of any district and always takes a systemic approach. She said that

> [Dr. Wells] uses data to establish a need for change and then creates a sense of urgency for change, especially with regard to how they can use technology in various ways to leverage change in the district and push it into the twenty-first century.

Teachers in IGHCS told us they appreciate the fact that both Dr. Wells and their building leaders listen to them; are willing to take risks and let them try new things; push new technology tools; model ways to use new tools for instruction, assessment, and data analysis; and also work to help them acquire new tools and get permission to use new Web 2.0 tools that might be blocked in most districts. Teachers in IGHCS also told us they feel their leadership is supportive and understanding, values and sees the need for professional development, and willingly goes the extra mile to help them try out new ideas they have to improve student learning.

As an example of the support that leaders in this district try to provide, the director of Secondary Education in IGHCS, who also functions as the principal at Simley High School, told us that he has done and continues to do all of the following to raise money for technology: organizes 5K runs, garage sales, and black light dances and uses the proceeds to purchase technology; partners with local restaurants and the points program at Best Buy to be able to purchase more technology; and charges a fee to any group that wants to use the high school building, which goes straight into their technology fund. He has also purchased a set of iPads as part of the summer school supply budget knowing that this technology could then be used all year long. And at Simley High School they are also moving away from purchasing textbooks toward using these funds to create digital curriculum that can be easily updated, as will be described in more detail in the section about changes in teaching and learning at IGHCS.

Technology and Technology Support Structures

According to the director of technology and her only tech support person (they were looking for a second tech support person at the time of this study), this district currently has 70 SMART Boards located in about half the classrooms across the district's five schools. All the Advanced Placement classrooms in the high school also have SMART Boards thanks to a grant applied for and received by their principal. There are five older Macintosh labs at the three elementary schools and two PC labs at the high school as well as 64 older Mac computers in four common areas of the middle school. There are ten class-size and three smaller new labs at the middle and high school, all with dual-boot (Macintosh OS and Windows) available. Each school has one or more mobile laptop labs. All secondary teachers and office staff have newer iMacs with dual-boot capabilities, and elementary teachers now have brand new iMacs. Simley High School and IGH Middle School have 2-year-old iMacs that are dual-boot machines so that teachers can choose to use either PC or Mac applications or both. There is also video conferencing equipment at each school so that teachers can use this equipment for collaborative conferencing between schools, both within and outside the district, for virtual field trips, and for communicating with content experts around the globe that are available in a local community setting. In addition, all teachers have either a laptop or desktop in their room. Many classrooms also have a student computer in addition to the teacher computer. The administrators all have iPads.

The technology in IGHCS is used by teachers for instruction, but also for assessment and for managing data. For example, the teachers all have access to a TIES-created tool called i-Cue that they use to take attendance. However, this same tool also provides class profiles and allows teachers to create personal learning profiles for each student that are color coded with arrows that indicate up or down changes in the previous 10 days. The data domains included in i-Cue are attendance, behavior, grades, tests, and graduation on track. These data are automatically updated when quarterly grades are posted, when standardized tests are taken, and when any discipline issues arise. With this tool teachers can monitor not just attendance but also behavior, grades, tests, and whether or not the high school students are on track for graduation. The district plans to use these data to make individualized plans for students who do not already have IEPs, and might normally fall through the cracks, so that they can be continuously monitored and targeted for whatever intervention is needed. So, while TIES has developed this technology, the leadership at IGHCS has jumped onboard to make use of these and other tools that TIES offers its members.

In addition, the students in IGHCS who do have IEPs are making use of many different kinds of assistive technology devices and software programs, and the teachers are aware of how Universal Design for Learning (UDL, see http://cast.org) includes technology as one of the ways to make the curriculum accessible to all students (e.g., word prediction and text-to-speech software, plus numerous applications [apps] available on iPods and iPads, and also recorders and flip videos). In IGHCS this is managed, modeled, and pushed out to teachers by the assistive technology specialist who has a background in special education, a master's in instructional technology, and 20 years' experience in this district. "Assistive technology specialist" is not a leadership position or job title we heard about in any of the other schools and districts we studied; however, it is a prominent position in this district and the person who holds the position is a part of the district's technology leadership team.

Professional Development

Professional development related to technology use and integration for teachers in IGHCS is also available through their relationship with TIES. Three times a year a catalog full of seminars, workshops, and webinars about multimedia, web tools, interactive whiteboards, and other technology integration products and tools is made available. Most of these offerings are free to teachers in TIES member districts, are available either online and/or face-to-face, and are taught mostly by other educators who cover a broad range of topics at a variety of skill levels from introductory to advanced. Also, TIES puts on an annual conference in Minneapolis each year and teachers from IGHCS both attend and make presentations at this technology conference. There are also several other resources available through TIES, including on-site professional development in the district if requested, hosting and software for developing classroom and school websites, and a website that links to multiple technology resources for teachers and those who support technology in the classroom called InforMNs (Innovations for Minnesota Schools), which has been in place since 1993. Teachers in TIES member districts also receive discounted rates to use online software tutorials from Atomic Learning, so there are many options available to IGHCS teachers, staff, and administrators who want to learn more about technology integration, specific tools, and instructional strategies like digital storytelling and project-based learning.

Though small in number, the technology staff at IGHCS offers some professional development and assists with preparations for others who lead technology-focused professional development. For example, building principals at the elementary schools lead technology PD during half-day grade-level meetings that occur 4 times a year. And core groups of teachers were provided with SMART Board training a number of years ago, as well as training by Apple about challenge-based learning. Since then the district has used a trainer-of-trainer model to get new people up to speed on using their SMART Boards, and some of the teachers have formed User Groups for themselves. For example, there is currently an active SMART Board user group and an iPad user group, and they decide when and where they are going to meet and set their own agenda.

Changes in Teaching and Learning

Lots of "experiments" are going on in IGHCS with the 500 or so iPods and iPads that have been purchased recently as part of the district's push to get technology in the hands of the students. For example, the action research grants have been focused on a variety of goals, including increasing reading fluency in Kindergarten and 1st-grade classes, exposing pre-K children to new technology by listening to stories recorded by senior citizen volunteers, trying out numerous applications (apps) to improve 3rd-graders' math skills, and increasing both listening comprehension and speaking fluency in Spanish classes at the high school. And in Language Arts, math, and science classes at the middle and high school level, students are using iPods and/or iPads for skills practice, accessing tutorials, reading online articles, doing real-time research, and for improving their written communication skills. In addition to the 1:1 laptop configuration for students in the Alternative Learning Program (ALP) described in the opening vignette, next year several high school classes move to a completely digital, paperless curriculum designed to focus on 21st-century skills, including communication, collaborative group work, and problem-based and challenge-based learning. So while we observed mostly in the middle and high school in IGHCS, we saw many examples of how the iPods and iPads are currently being used, but we also saw that this is currently happening mainly in classes where teachers have applied for and received action research grants.

As an example, one of the math classes we observed at IGH Middle School looked at first like a traditional math class with students completing warm-up problems by hand and then the teacher going over each question to review what they had learned in a previous chapter. This was followed by students completing problems about exponents on a certain page in their textbook while the teacher circulated around the room to encourage and assist where needed. All students had calculators but only about half the students used them. After this the teacher went over their homework, which meant that the students checked their own work as the teacher read the answers aloud. However, what happened next looked and sounded quite different from typical math classes: The teacher asked the students to line up to check out an iPod so they could look at videos loaded on them until they got to what she called the "blue box" activity where they needed to stop and do the problems on paper. Most of the students proceeded to do this independently, although the teacher did have to assist four or five students in getting to the right place to see the videos on their iPods. All the students had their own earphones, so the class was quiet and focused on their iPods for about 15–20 minutes as the students listened, watched, and worked diligently on the "blue box" problems. The teacher circulated to see who needed help, and some of the students helped one another when asked. When finished with the videos, the teacher instructed the students either to play some of the math games on their iPods or to start on their homework. The teacher also mentioned that some of the videos would be on her class website so that the students could review them at home if they needed them. At the end of class everyone checked in the iPods fairly efficiently, although the teacher did count carefully to make sure everything was accounted for. Later the teacher told us that she really likes to use the iPods because it helps with pacing. That is, some students need more or less time to understand what is on the videos, and more or less time to practice and learn the material. Therefore, having additional material, like math games on the iPods, allows more time for those who need it and gives the faster workers something to do. Of course this is nothing new for teachers because students always finish assignments at different times, but these students seemed more engaged when continuing to use the iPods, and therefore the slower workers were not distracted by those who finished earlier because both were still using the iPods.

In another class at the middle school, a social studies class with many of the same students who were in the math class just described, we observed the students lining up to get iPads from the cart and then quickly accessing an article the teacher had posted to her blog with a free tool called Edublogs that she has been using since the fall. After the students finished reading this article, they used their iPads to respond to the questions the teacher had posted on her blog. While the students were typing, we observed that either the keypads on the iPads don't encourage good keyboarding skills, or the students didn't have good keyboarding skills to begin with, but that this did not seem to slow most students as they typed in their responses to her higher-order questions with good speed. This teacher also told us she loves using the iPads, in this case for teaching the social studies curriculum, because she can find current articles about places they are studying from free and reliable news sources like the *New York Times* or from Scholastic.com, and she is able to keep the students up-to-date on current events that relate to their social studies curriculum.

At Simley High School we observed an 11th-grade English class using iPads so that the students could contribute to online book group discussions. Although this was a rather large class, the students were involved in responding to questions about the different books they were reading that the teacher has posted on Edmodo, a free Web 2.0 tool that allows teachers to organize students into groups and give them assignments and surveys that are either prepared ahead of time, which this teacher had done, or created on the fly, which this teacher also did when he saw a need. The class time we observed was spent writing and reading responses that other students in their book club group posted to the questions their teacher had posed about the book they were reading. Throughout the class some students were observed either reading their books or writing on the iPads while the teacher was circulating, posting new questions, or making comments to the various groups, which he could monitor in real time. He also quickly created a poll for the students to take on Edmodo. This teacher had also located articles, charts, and videos related to the books the students were reading, which he included as part of their book club discussion assignment on Edmodo. The poll he created on Edmodo for students to respond to was about whether they preferred face-to-face book club discussions or online book club discussions, and whether or not they liked having the questions about their reading prepared ahead of time or not. And, although these are questions any teacher could ask orally and get a show of hands to gauge their response, doing the same thing online eliminates socially desirable responses or students voting the same way their friends vote because they can respond privately and anonymously. Book club discussions can also be carried out face-to-face, and in fact this class had been doing just that for a few weeks before they switched to trying out online book club discussions, which they will very likely experience when they go to college. And, the same goes for responding to the teachers' questions online; this can be done by hand but by using a course management tool like Edmodo the teacher can monitor in real time what students are saying and not have to wait to read each individual's paper to know if they are on the right track, or if they need redirection, different questions to discuss, or clarification about the questions posed to get them on track.

In a 12th-grade English class we observed that the teacher used a variety of devices, but mainly iPods and laptops for several different activities that the students were completing during a unit on advertising. The day before the students used flip cameras to take pictures of advertisements around their school, and then discussed different kinds of advertising ploys on Edmodo. During the class we observed, students were answering different questions and/or doing different tasks in small groups at centers the teacher had created. Most tasks required students to access Google or specific websites to find answers to questions or to complete certain tasks, and then use Edmodo to post their group's responses to the questions/tasks before moving on. This teacher told us that she also teaches what is called a "hybrid class" at Simley High School. That is, during first and last period classes, students come to class several days a week, but on other days they do their work online and do not have to be physically present unless they slip below a "B" average. If they start getting "C" grades they have to come to class daily to do their work and get individual help on days when others are working online. This teacher and the administrators at Simley High School told us that such hybrid classes are becoming more and more popular with seniors, and that students are scoring higher in their hybrid classes than in their regular face-to-face classes, and that they are covering more material. In fact, the number and variety of hybrid class offerings is increasing to the point where the administration and the teachers are trying to figure out how to schedule them for both first and second, and sixth and seventh periods in the future.

Another innovative way of using technology that is emerging at Simley High School and which is supported by the leadership is something called "inverted instruction" or the college model, which we first heard about from the superintendent and later the director of secondary education, as well as some teachers. As it was described to us, "inverted instruction" at Simley High School means that the students prepare for class at home by watching videos of lectures (vodcasts), and/or doing required readings, and/or listening to annotated presentations their teachers have prepared. When they come to class the time is not used for lecturing or reading, but instead for discussions, debates, labs, group work, problem solving, project work, or other things where the students are actively engaged and talking with one another and their teacher, rather than passively listening to a lecture or doing individual seatwork. Inverted curriculum is most often found in the fields of computer science at the college level and for science education at the high school where, for example, conceptual physics is offered to 9th-graders, chemistry to sophomores, biology to juniors, and Advanced Placement physics to seniors (see the STEM Academy case in this book for an example of this), but what they want to do at Simley is really inverting instruction (see http://mast.unco.edu/programs/vodcasting/index.php), which is similar to what many students experience at college. However, in the IGHCS district, the goal of inverting instruction is to create more time in class for problem-based and challenge-based learning so that students are more actively engaged in their learning while at school. And while this pedagogical model may not be suitable for every student, it may be a good option for those who plan to seek post-secondary education—a high percentage of students attending Simley.

Noteworthy Outcomes

Many things we learned from our study of Simley High School and the Inver Grove Heights Community Schools are noteworthy. Among them are the importance of having leadership that is willing to use data, and to push, model, try new things, and take risks with technology to benefit students, teachers, and the community. And, while this very small school district and its leadership team have been recognized for effectively using technology for making data-driven decisions and trying to transform instruction, it is happening slowly and in pockets because of limited funding for technology. As the director of secondary education and other administrators in this district told us,

> You have to have the vision, know how to do things yourself so you can model it and know the capabilities, and then feed the people who are interested to create an environment where others want to do things themselves, it's a mind-set, and it's finding the way to get it done.

He also told how his perceptions were changing with regard to getting technology into the hands of the students:

> You know, I was convinced a few years ago that SMART Boards were the new tech. And, boy, it would be nice to have one in every classroom. It is interesting how my perception about that changed over time. I think we've spent quite a bit of money. I mean we went from having no SMART Boards in our high school to having about forty in three years and ceiling-mounted projectors—all by hook or crook, finding ways to raise the money. It is a nice tool, so don't get me wrong, but I would love to go to one-to-one computing. I just think that's the way to go to have something in the hands of each student . . .
> so I probably would do that differently, and I would probably invest in personal computing devices like iPads, iPad 2s, laptops, mobile labs. I think mobile labs are the way to go. I used to be convinced that each department should have their own lab, but I am not so convinced of that anymore. I think that computing has gotten so personal for people that they are moving to using their own computing devices without the need to go to a lab. You know the [nearby] university, it was in the paper recently, built a big lab and no one is using it . . . so think about what that vision is, getting wireless so students can bring their own devices to school, *they have them*, so bring them to school. . . .

What is also noteworthy is that the leadership in this district is doing everything it can to "feed the people" who want to integrate technology into their classrooms, finding ways to purchase technology for their students, all the while holding them accountable through the use of action research grants that require that data be collected so they can determine if the technology is helping the students. And finally, what is noteworthy in this district is its collaboration with TIES and with other districts in the area to leverage limited funds by working together to get things done. In fact, we left Inver Grove wishing that every school district in the country had access to something like TIES, which provides so much to its member districts because they are a collaborative.

Challenges

As has been mentioned several times, one of the challenges in this district, as in many other districts large and small, continues to be limited budgets. While the IGHCS leadership at all levels (school, district, and school board) is committed to getting more and more technology into the hands of students, the tax structure and the district's demographics make this a challenge. This then leads to another challenge when limited resources are used to seed special projects, such as the action research grants described earlier. Although we believe these action research grants are noteworthy, and understand that applying for them is a rigorous process, nevertheless the unintended consequence, and thus a challenge, is one of potential inequity. That is, teachers apply for and get the action research grants for class sets of iPods or iPads, for example, but there is no guarantee that additional funds will be available for other teachers in that department or grade level to get the same technology for their students, even if the pilot project is found to be successful. In fact, this is a dilemma that every school and district faces when there is not enough funding to provide 1:1 devices for all students. It is also a dilemma when some schools have active and/or affluent parent teacher organizations that can raise funds for technology, while others do not. And, in reality it is also a dilemma in districts where there are Title I schools that can use their funds for technology, but where not all schools are Title I. Generally speaking, the digital divide is present in IGHCS, and it is probably present in most school districts in this nation.

An additional dilemma is that when funds are tight, progress toward ubiquitous technology integration will be slowed way down and students may start to disengage in schools where there is very limited use of technology compared to what they are used to accessing at home. In today's work world, and even in most of today's homes, people not only have access to computers but also find them necessary to do their jobs, or to manage their family finances, to communicate with others, to shop, to plan vacations, to access entertainment, and so forth. Such access should be the case in schools as well, but it is not, and the questions we should ask ourselves include: What if we only had three or four pencils to share among a class of 20–25 students? What if we had to go down the hall to a special room to use pencils? Or, What if every student in our schools, large or small, had some kind of smart, handheld device available to use 24/7? This is the frustrating dilemma for many students, parents, and teachers, like those in IGHCS who wish there was enough funding to make this happen quickly instead of slowly.

Lessons Learned: Key Factors for Success

Despite these challenges, there are many lessons to be learned from the leadership of the schools in Inver Grove Heights that are valuable for other small districts about leadership and planning for getting technology into the hands of students. We also learned some good lessons about funding technology when resources are very limited and the importance of building a strong infrastructure and maintaining partnerships to keep technology initiatives moving forward. Based on our interviews with faculty, staff, and administrators in IGHCS (N=17) and classroom observations at Simley High School and Inver Grove Middle School (N=10), these are the lessons we think are valuable for others:

- Having a vision and a process for getting technology into the hands of students are where every school and district leader has to begin. Then, you have to work tirelessly to fulfill that vision, as we learned from the leaders of IGHCS. It is also important to have all of your leadership team onboard so that everyone is working hard to integrate technology into their schools. Further, the leadership should be modeling ways to use technology in front of faculty and staff whenever the opportunity arises in public or private settings. To accomplish their vision of getting technology into students' hands, this district opens the school media center and student common areas early and closes them late, and has made the high school and district parking lot into a wireless hotspot so that students, parents, and community members can get access to the Internet if needed.
- Planning for ways to achieve the vision of getting technology into the hands of students leads to changing policies, including cell phone policies, so that high school students are now allowed to use their personal technology devices in classrooms for legitimate research and/or communication purposes, as directed by the teacher. At the high school, students are also allowed to use their phones during passing times, which they appear to be handling well.
- However, when your goal is to put technology in the hands of the students rather than just the teachers, it means not buying

more interactive whiteboards if they are not being used to their
fullest potential. It also means using all available systems to
manage data of all types, including monitoring students so that
teachers can provide differentiated instruction, remediation,
and enrichment opportunities, as well as using data to monitor
healthy eating habits in the cafeteria, the HVAC system, and
other systems needed to run the district.

- To support their vision, and to support planning and
  professional development as well, this district is a member of
  Minnesota's TIES organization and makes good use of the
  resources and services provided by this collaborative. If there is
  not anything like it in your region, it is definitely worth looking
  into and encouraging schools and districts in your region to
  establish a similar organization for collaborative projects.

- We also learned helpful lessons about many creative ways to
  fund technology purchases when district funds are limited. For
  example, the leadership in this district made use of building
  funds, grants, textbook funds, fund-raisers, rental income,
  community and business partnerships, and even proposed a
  bond issue to purchase technology. The main lesson learned is
  to think outside the box when it comes to funding technology.
  Furthermore, being a part of a collaborative like TIES was also
  a way to save money in many areas–professional development,
  record keeping, infrastructure, finance, etcetera.

- When funds are limited, a unique way to figure out the best
  next steps for technology integration that will work in your
  context is allowing teachers to experiment and try new things
  in their classrooms that are supported by action research
  grants. Such mini-grants are focused on studying the effects
  of integrating technology, and they require teachers to collect
  and analyze data about the educational outcomes of using the
  technology purchased for these projects. These mini-grants not
  only help the leadership in determining next steps; they are
  also excellent professional development for the teachers who
  undertake action research projects.

- Another way to save money in this district includes trusting
  teachers to evaluate online learning tools and unblocking them
  when requested. This allowed teachers to take advantage of the
  numerous free Web 2.0 tools available for instruction, including
  tools like Moodle and Edmodo, which serve as learning
  management systems, free blog and wiki tools found online,
  OpenOffice and Google tools, as well as the many other tools

for teaching that are available on the Internet for all content areas. And for some teachers, downloading free or cheap applications and podcasts to use with iPods or iPads was also a way to save money that had previously been spent on expensive software licenses. Further, allowing teachers to find and use free digital curriculum also resulted in expanding the curriculum to include more than just textbooks as learning resources.

- Related to this, professional development in this district is viewed as a necessity for all teachers with regard to integrating technology into the curriculum, whether the participants are pioneers leading the way, or those following the lead of others. In this district, professional development provided by TIES was mostly free to members, but teachers also did a lot of peer-to-peer sharing within their buildings and started up their own user groups, comprised of teachers from across the district who were interested in learning more about and sharing their successes with tools like interactive whiteboards and iPads. This district also joined with other districts in the area to offer professional development for teachers in the summer, which was another cost-saving measure.

- Making sure the infrastructure is in place to support growing uses of technology is also an important lesson learned in this district. For example, the increased use of online testing required increasing bandwidth on the district's network so that online testing days did not preclude other teachers from using technology for instruction. Making wireless access a top priority in all buildings, as well as in common and public areas, in order to serve the students and the school community was another lesson learned.

- Creating a positive culture by doing whatever it takes to encourage and support teachers who are willing to use technology and then celebrating their successes is another lesson from this district. One example of this is purchasing dual-boot computers so that teachers can choose to use PC or Mac software tools, whichever they are more comfortable using. Also, giving positive feedback to teachers who are trying new things helps create a positive culture around technology use and leads to teachers experimenting with 1:1 technology in their classrooms. Creating a culture of innovation that includes moving more toward using a digital curriculum to replace textbooks, which will eventually save money, was also a lesson learned.

CHAPTER 6

Creating a Culture for 21st-Century Learners

The Case of Chesapeake High School, Baltimore County Public Schools, MD

Vision: All students will apply the knowledge, skills, values, and behaviors learned through participation in a rigorous STEM-based education in order to realize their maximum potential as citizens and become more productive individuals in the global economy, thus keeping the United States high in global competitiveness.

Mission: To provide an environment that fosters high standards for academics, relationships, and goal setting through a rigorous STEM-based culture.

This is the case of a STEM magnet school with a unique curriculum that uses technology to provide students with authentic learning experiences designed to prepare them for 21st-century careers. The superintendent of this large school district in Maryland received a Technology Leadership Award from the International Society of Technology in Education (ISTE). He selected this magnet school for us because it showcases what purposeful, intentional leadership can do to create a 21st-century education for students whose families live in an economically depressed area. This is also a case of what successful partnerships with local businesses, industries, and universities can do for a school in transition.

At the time of this study this diverse high school of about 1,075 students had 14 laptop carts (all PCs) spread among departments, as well as document cameras, interactive whiteboards (IWBs), and content-specific technology, as needed in business, technical, and science classrooms. All teachers had laptops, and there were flip video cameras, MP3 players, and class sets of clickers to use with the IWBs available for checkout from the school media center. This school also has a $3 million Virtual Learning Environment (VLE) similar to the Applied Physics Lab at Johns Hopkins University.

The librarian at Chesapeake High School (CHS) invited us to attend the final showcase event of a professional development certificate program offered by Johns Hopkins University, taught by Baltimore County Public Schools (BCPS) faculty, and focused on technology integration. During the event approximately 25 teachers from all over the district gathered to share their final technology integration projects with their classmates. The CHS librarian had been co-teaching this mainly online professional development class and was excited for us to see what the teachers in the class had accomplished. Because much of the class had been taught using virtual tools, these teachers seemed quite happy to come together, enjoy pizza, share their projects, and celebrate all they had learned. In watching their presentations and chatting with them we learned how well supported the teachers in BCPS feel about having the opportunity to learn and explore the potential uses of educational technology in their classrooms. And, during their presentations they focused mainly on how their students had reacted to and become involved in the various technologies they had learned to use in this professional development course.

District Context

Baltimore County School District, the 26th largest in the country, serves 103,180 students in 174 schools, has 8,850 teachers, and typically has district-wide scores that are in line with Maryland's average test scores. Currently the BCPS student population is 51% African American, 41% White, 6% Hispanic, 1% Asian, and < 1% Native American. In addition, 35% of the students receive free or reduced meals, 13% receive special education services, and 25% are designated as "gifted and talented." Dr. Joe Hairston, the district superintendent, explained to us how the district has changed during his 11 years in this role. In 2000, the district was classified as having 29% poverty and being 36% diverse; in 2011 those numbers were up to 42% and 54.3%, respectively.

One of the reasons we sought out a school in the BCPS district is because Dr. Hairston won a Technology Leadership Award from the International Society for Technology in Education (ISTE). However, it is also important to understand the type of leader Dr. Hairston is in order to understand the school he selected for us to study, Chesapeake High School.

When Dr. Hairston first became the superintendent in 2000, his decisions were based on a careful analysis of the way in which the district was functioning at that time. He asked for a report on the state of things, but did not want an evaluation; rather, his goal was to obtain a snapshot of the district's strengths and challenges. We asked questions about the decisions he made—to become a totally PC school district, for example—and he encouraged us to assess these decisions through the lens of his Transition Team report (Gemberling, Peterkin, Rohr, & Sneed, 2000) that he calls his Blueprint for Progress. Dr. Hairston specifically asked for the transition team to focus on key areas (curriculum, instruction, and student assessment; business and facilities operations; and human resources) and to provide recommendations to him. He also asked the team to identify "hot spots" or issues that needed immediate attention. When we asked why he wanted this report before he accepted the position of superintendent, Dr. Hairston explained, "It is called intelligence gathering. Why would anyone go into a project without gathering intelligence first!"

In examining this report, we immediately recognized the wisdom in his recommendation to us because steps taken over the past decade were clearly designed to help address the challenges identified in 2000. The transition team recommended restructuring and pulling in some dispersed functions under the superintendent's oversight; it also suggested making explicit that the primary goal of the entire district was to "meld abilities and responsiveness of the area and central offices into one unified force to support teaching and learning in the school system" (p. 40). Based on this "intelligence gathering" Dr. Hairston created a blueprint for progress that is updated regularly and has as its center the goal of student achievement; it also includes specifics about standards, quality instruction, and individual accountability (www.bcps.org/offices/super/pdf/Blueprint-for-Progress.pdf). He said, "I am a reformer, a real reformer," and in examining the results of changes made during the past decade in BCPS, it appears he is quite correct.

Based on a belief in world-class standards, quality, and performance, this blueprint is a product of both Dr. Hairston's own experiences during more than 25 years in education and his careful analysis of the district's needs; he told us that everyone has goals but what is important is that our "behavior matches the goals and everything aligns and contributes to meeting those goals." The supervisor of the Office of Instructional Technology said that each time someone has an idea or suggestion, the same question is asked; namely, "Show me how this activity supports or leads to our goals."

Dr. Hairston also told us that he has a simple system for operating within a community; that is, rather than telling a community what he wants, he uses his intelligence gathering to determine what the community values and wants and then helps move things in that direction. Further, each time the blueprint for progress is revised (including every time there is a change in national or state policies), it is co-developed with educators and community members. Dr. Hairston's point is, "It's their community and they get to decide what they want. They all want the best for the children." Ten years and many blueprints later Dr. Hairston stated with pride, "Now rather than having a system of schools, we have a school system."

School Context

Dr. Hairston's reasons for pointing us to Chesapeake High School are a story much like the rise of the Phoenix from the ashes. Prior to 2006, this school was considered to be in distress. One educator described it as follows: "When you walked down the halls, you did not get the impression that good teaching and learning was going on or that most people wanted to be here." Then in 2006, CHS became the first STEM (Science, Technology, Engineering, and Mathematics) Academy in the state of Maryland as a result of funding from the state, county, and district. When the opportunity to create this STEM school came along, Dr. Hairston told us he only considered Chesapeake. He said, "People thought I was crazy but I had done it before, and this was where it should go." He explained that it was the lowest-performing high school in the district: Students and teachers did not want to go there, it had worn out four consecutive principals, and the area had high poverty, high unemployment, and was drug infested. While other schools may have thought they deserved to be transformed into a STEM school, they did not get to make that decision.

Five years later Chesapeake High School STEM Academy is a very successful comprehensive magnet high school located in the southeast area of Baltimore County. As a comprehensive magnet high school, all students zoned to attend CHS are automatically part of the magnet programs. Incoming 9th-grade students from around the county can apply to this magnet academy through the BCPS Office of Magnet Programs, and nearly 300 do apply annually. However, because families from the community now support CHS instead of looking to send their children to other high schools, only 30–40 students from outside the area are admitted to CHS each year. Nevertheless, the school population of approximately 1,075

Academy of Science, Engineering, and Mathematics	Academy of Arts, Multimedia, and Communications	Academy of Business and Information Technology	Academy of Leadership and Humanities
Project Lead the Way Pre-Engineering Environmental Science Mathematics	Photography Interactive Multimedia Journalism/Communications	Information-Technology Programming Business Management Marketing	Criminal Justice Marine JROTC

students is reflective of the diverse school district, although 49% of the students at CHS receive free or reduced meals.

The curriculum at CHS is unique, and the students choose from ten magnet pathways within four academies of study, including a nationally accredited "Project Lead the Way Pre-Engineering" program. The school has also established partnerships with Johns Hopkins University and with two nearby aerospace companies, Lockheed Martin and Northrop Grumman, which provide opportunities to both students and teachers during the school year and during summers. Each student selects one of the following STEM academies and then picks a concentration within that academy for further focus.

Implementation Process

Once the location of the STEM magnet school was determined, many decisions were made quickly. Maria Lowry was the choice for principal, which appears was a wise and appropriate decision. Speaking about Mrs. Lowry, Dr. Hairston said, "She was principal of the feeder school, and brought that prior experience with her. Students and the community knew what to expect of her and already had a relationship."

Mrs. Lowry was quite ready to take on this challenge of creating a STEM school culture in a location that was in need of significant commitment. She brought with her a number of staff who had worked with her before and selected others who were known to possess the skills and knowledge needed for this transformation. One assistant principal, for example, made the transition from middle school to high school, having worked with Mrs. Lowry before. She explained, "So I have worked with her. That middle school was a magnet for technology and STEM and I knew she would bring that to Chesapeake, too." She went on to explain that students from the feeder school were going to know exactly what to expect in terms of culture, expectations, and consistency. Among the praise we heard over and over from the faculty with whom we talked at CHS regarding their leader included "visionary, makes things happen, is all about the students, advocates for us, reaches out into the community, brings in resources, sets expectations but doesn't micromanage, encourages us to try new things, very supportive, approachable, values family life, believes in collaboration, empowers us, and capitalizes on our strengths." One teacher remarked, "I would go anywhere she goes. She rocks; she has the ability to make her ideas happen." Another concurred: "She perseveres–she is all about the students."

As a part of developing the STEM Academy at CHS, Mrs. Lowry asked all teachers to re-apply for their position because the district had decided that a reorganization of CHS was necessary in order to move forward with the STEM initiative. The understanding was clear to all; those who elected to stay would need to be committed to supporting the STEM goals and to becoming part of the new culture of the school, which included having high expectations for all students. Mrs. Lowry explained,

> I asked for and received the ability to have all teachers on the staff re-apply for their position; some chose to move to other schools and many stayed. They realized that things were going to be different but they wanted to stay. It allowed me to have teachers who wanted to be here and step their teaching into the new model of what Chesapeake could become.

One teacher who was eager to stay said,

> I actually attended Chesapeake! The population of students is very diverse because of the magnet program but there are still quite a number of students from poverty. So for me, I had some loyalty–this is where I grew up. When I first started things were different but each year now I have seen such changes.

Another teacher who remained said, "I have always worked with this type of population and I enjoy working with this type of student–those who may not have all the support at home, or structure, and that is why I stayed."

Leadership Practices

Mrs. Lowry's background was as an elementary teacher, then as an English and science middle school teacher; she also had a personal interest in technology because of her own family members. In fact, she told us that she comes from a family that is interested in technology, and that "It was fascinating to watch my children finding information; it opens doors for students. So, when I was asked to start the magnet school at the middle school level, I really wanted to make sure that the technology was an integrated approach." That was just the first step, however, and regarding her leadership style, she is very clear:

> Surround yourself with smart people; everyone has a different skill set. I look at it as if I can give them an idea, how do you think we can make this work? My job is to clear the path, get everything out of their way, and provide them with the resources. I don't want to give them the plan, but rather throw the idea of "Wouldn't it be great if we could . . . ? How do you think we could make that happen?" Let them build it; the only way they can do that is if you get everything they need. The first is the reorganization, so they have the right people on the bus with them.

She also is very clear about how she has structured departments and the responsibilities of the chairs. "The teachers within each department have to respect their chairs, not to do things because Maria said you have to," she explained. She wants to give autonomy to each department but also expects responsibility for what happens in the department: "If I go into a teacher's room and the room is in disarray, the students are sleeping or not engaged, and good teaching is not going on, then I am more upset with you [the department chair] than with that teacher because it means you have not been in that room."

We asked teachers and other staff to discuss what a leader needs to do to support their efforts and their observations of the ways in which the school is working. One teacher said,

> Maria sets the expectations, and tells you what to do but does not micromanage; it is up to us. I have worked for some principals who did micromanage and always looking over your shoulder; she encourages you to try new things, try something different and let me know how it worked.

Several teachers mentioned characteristics that a good leader must have and they stated emphatically that these are seen in Mrs. Lowry's leadership. First, they want to feel safe in trying things and in making mistakes; in this school they know they are rewarded for trying new ideas. They know they can come to her with ideas, and they say she is "very supportive." One teacher said, "It's not often she turns something down, and if she does there is a good reason."

The teachers noted other characteristics that a leader should have and that they see in Mrs. Lowry. Examples include being very hands on, involved in everything, encouraging people to try new things, and being supportive of getting you what you need to do your job. One assistant principal said that the most important things Mrs. Lowry does is to model consistency, fairness, and more consistency. Another assistant principal mentioned that Mrs. Lowry is very willing to find and use resources (people or information) in the district to help solve problems. "She is not afraid to say she does not know something and to find out who does."

Staff members recognize that their principal is passionate about the students but also about them, their families, and their balance in life. One teacher reported, "Leadership is teamwork, that is what supports my work. Someone who says, welcome and what are your ideas?" Another teacher said, "I want for nothing; they will give any teacher whatever they need. It is unheard of to hear [the] administration asking, What do you need or want?" Teachers also appreciated that there is no new focus each year but rather a clear path to how things build from year to year. We learned that it is common for Mrs. Lowry or others to ask, "What do you offer to the school? What are your strengths? Would you mind helping others and sharing with the others?" Another teacher explained that "Maria came into a faculty meeting before the winter break and said, 'Leave your books in the car for a few days,' and I have never had a principal say that to me!" All in all, we learned that this principal is caring, collaborative, and definitely a believer in distributed leadership.

It is of interest that Dr. Hairston and Mrs. Lowry share some ideas of leadership. For example, Mrs. Lowry stated, "You create a vision and stay the course. Stick with the people who have stuck with you." She expects teachers to follow the chain of command so that everyone "understands we are all on the same page, keep the lines of communication open up and down and around." Her hope is that no teacher would ever come to her with a problem that "I have not heard of before from the chair or whomever." To her, if one person has a problem, the entire organization has a problem. Mrs. Lowry's model goes even further; she tells her staff, "When you come to me with a problem, come to me with some solutions. Show me you have thought about it; don't come to me and just hope I can fix it." In asking Dr. Hairston the same questions, he said, "Don't leave the dead mouse on the desk!" and talked about his belief that you have to correct mistakes with dignity, that you cannot fear failure, and always seek to "Do the right things right." Dr. Hairston said, "I don't fear mistakes—I do try to avoid them, but if I make them, then just admit it and do what is right for the kids. It is not about me."

Curricular Changes and Technology Integration

In addition to establishing a core set of curriculum goals for the school, in that students select a pathway and focus when they enter, a significant number of other changes occurred under Mrs. Lowry's leadership. For example, gifted and talented (GT) classes are now in evidence, as is the growth of Advanced Placement classes. One teacher said, "We had seven Advanced Placement classes [with eighty-four students taking exams] when she came, and now there are nineteen different classes [with over three hundred taking those exams]; she is all about the students." We heard this same statement many times during our interviews. The Advancement Via Individual Determination (AVID) program has been put in place and each student involved must take at least one Advanced Placement class. The STEM coordinator stated, "When Mrs. Lowry arrived there were limited GT classes. Now we put students with potential in these classes, and they have really lived up to the expectations."

Another new program that has had a positive impact is the AdvancePath Academy for credit recovery, held in a room outside the building. The courses are entirely self-paced, and the program includes four academic teachers and one or two assistants. This program allows students who might not have succeeded in traditional high school to shine. Some of the students were not able to get up early or had to work, so now there are two sessions to choose from to meet their needs. Also, some students don't like to work with others and in this environment they can work individually. The goals of this program are to improve student achievement as well as to assist in the smooth running of the traditional classes.

Curriculum changes have also included building a professional television studio, adding pre-engineering courses, and business classes that use only authentic activities that engage the students with skills they will need in their future careers, including the formation of a student-run credit union branch that is open to all students and staff at this school. In the first year of transforming into a STEM magnet, there were 27 students in engineering classes with perhaps only one or two girls; now there are over 200 students in that pathway and one-third to one-half are young women. An additional goal is moving to a completely electronic portfolio for all students from the time they enter CHS until they leave, "so they can see and understand how they have grown and developed, because students don't always see what they have learned," said Mrs. Lowry. She continued, "When they are seniors they will have some choices of what to keep and use over time."

It is also important to recognize that while this is not a 1:1 device school, all teachers have laptops, and all departments have access to mobile laptops. The core departments (math, science, social studies, and English) have two carts each, and there are a total of 14 laptop carts in the building. Classrooms also have document cameras, interactive whiteboards, and content-specific technology, such as a science lab with muscle grippers, respiration belts, EKG monitors, pressure cuffs, and digital microscopes. In fact, CHS teachers reported that when they teach summer school in other schools they are astonished at how much technology they have in relationship to those other places. More than that, one teacher said, "When we teach summer school in another building, we show up and say, How can we teach without our tools?"

The library media specialist joined the school after its first year and has seen changes in her role as she supported technology use and the focus on STEM in the curriculum. She explained, "My philosophy is—I don't know all the answers but I know where to find them and help you." She explained that now she maintains a Google Docs spreadsheet so that teachers can check out the devices she stores, such as flip video cameras, MP3 players, class sets of clickers for their interactive whiteboards, and so on. Now teachers can reserve equipment as they are planning, over the weekend, or on the fly.

Both the principal and the librarian explained that they are seeing changes in student engagement and interest results because of the ways in which the teachers are integrating available technology into their classes. For example, students who may not normally participate in class are adding to online group discussions, other students are working in groups with students they may not have worked with otherwise, and students now have choices to demonstrate their knowledge. It is not unusual, Mrs. Lowry said, "to see students around the building working collaboratively and totally engaged." One teacher added,

> If you only offer one way to assess a student, we know that some students will not succeed in that way; why bother, just go ahead and give them the D! But if we offer more ways to show their learning we can help many more succeed.

Technology Support

Students do not always enter the school with the requisite technology skills for required educational activities, although they certainly know how to use their game machines with 60 buttons and their smartphones. One teacher said, "We still get freshmen who cannot open a file and save it, or use MS Word, and they learn these things, but then the new freshmen surprise me because they again don't know those things." As a result, all students are required to take a one-credit course in technology education as a graduation requirement. This course is taught by the school's Technology Education department in ways that emulate real-world technology skills. However, all teachers in the building are also responsible for assisting students with acquiring the skills necessary in order to effectively use all the technology tools available to them.

The supervisor of the Office of Instructional Technology explained that Dr. Hairston's decision to switch to a totally PC-based district, in order to make the district more aligned with business and industry, was a challenge.

However, once accomplished, this switch did simplify the support of local schools, including CHS. The district also provides a variety of programs that support communication, such as Edline, but he explained that "Dr. Hairston would prefer if we could build our own programs." So there are several initiatives in the works to do this. Currently, Edline is the grading and web communication system that facilitates interaction with parents, and one teacher said "Some parents do email with me through Edline." As an example, she explained that she had assigned a project over a break and "probably had fifteen students email me through Edline and ask questions. I think it is much easier than if they had to look up my email address, etcetera."

Because all the students take 1 year of technology courses and the students seemed engaged during our observations, we asked about other technology-related initiatives. One technology teacher told us that he developed a way to encourage students to develop games and simulations as part of what they do, and in fact there are competitions for student-developed learning games in BCPS with the award-winning games slated to be produced professionally. For example, he imagines building quizzes or pre-assessments and then embedding an engaging story line for physics. He wants students to figure out ways they can control the character, make choices in how the events play out. He started a graphic adventure club that meets during lunch and after school. His hope is that the computer will be able to assess students' learning while they are playing the game.

In general, the technology at CHS is maintained jointly by the technology integration specialist, the librarian, and the BCPS personnel, although there are many teachers at CHS who have the expertise to troubleshoot and manage new hardware and software that they request. For example, the teacher who runs the after-school Robotics Club maintains those machines with the help of students in the club. He is also the lead teacher for Project Lead the Way, a nationwide STEM curriculum that is currently being provided to 250 students at CHS (www.pltw.org).

Changes in Curriculum and Technology Use

Project Lead the Way (PLTW) is part of the CHS engineering academy, and the teacher for this program has formal training in all aspects of it. PLTW teaches students about industry standards, but the teacher wanted more of a partnership with engineers, especially given the school's relationship with two nearby engineering and high-technology companies. However, he did not have people from this industry just come in and talk; instead he established a way for the engineers to work with students to design a remotely operated vehicle (ROV) that, once made, could be made cheaper and faster. The students in the Robotics Club, which he developed, recently attended an international robotics competition. Although they did not win, CHS sent several students and this teacher to the event in 2010 and 2011. They already have plans for 2012 to involve the school's art and business classes to help in designing graphics and publicity for their next competition.

Mrs. Lowry explained the changes she has seen in teachers and technology over the past 5 years:

> I used to see a lot of packets, paper packets where the kids would have to go through the packet, with their textbooks, fill in the information. I would say, well, I am glad you got the packet done but tell me what you have learned about genetics, and they could not put into words what they have learned. Now we are giving them some control over their learning, and they have more background and deeper understanding.

One of the assistant principals related how teacher planning has changed with respect to technology. All observations are preceded by a pre-observation meeting; she explained that "I ask why they are doing things in this or that way, and they now clearly understand, have reasons for their decisions, and realize that they are making decisions based on engagement, outcomes, past experiences." She also explained that in the past, someone would have said they were going to use a wiki, but not really know why or how. "But now they are being intentional and purposeful about it. They can reason out what the best tool is to reach objectives, and explain why it is part of the lesson." Another assistant principal said, "The staff is relatively 'young' in terms of faculty members. They are willing to try new things, whatever works, and they are comfortable with the technology."

A teacher explained, "She [Mrs. Lowry] does not want us to do it just for technology sake, but she wants us to delve into the lesson to ask will this make it better and how will it make it better." Another remarked, "People find the best ways to teach their content; you see teachers discussing different things. There is a lot of informal PD [professional development] that allows teachers to share how they used a new tool to accomplish an educational goal." A social studies teacher remarked,

> I find I have fewer behavior problems when we have the laptops out; I have done a social studies WebQuest, and they can use the technology; even if we use the clickers they are engaged. Not every school has the technology we have, and it is millions of dollars, so it is unfortunate that every school does not have the same opportunity we do.

Mrs. Lowry also told us, "I see differences in the teachers' planning, too; they have to chunk things, rethink the way they can teach the content, include more group work, less 'hearing' from teachers and more student interaction." The teachers we talked to seemed to agree with her. One explained that the first year "we had a summer session dedicated to planning, so we were able to really think through and sort of reinvent the curriculum." One science teacher said, "It is almost as if you have your strategy toolbox, and your content toolbox, and then you have your technology toolbox, so it is always something to think about, but you know what is in those boxes and can add new things."

Perhaps the jewel of this school is its Virtual Learning Environment (VLE), which was built with $3 million from the county government funds, in addition to other funding sources, to offer a virtual learning experience similar to that of the Applied Physics Lab at Johns Hopkins University. One individual, the manager of Administrative Technology Support for Virtual Learning & Special Projects, spearheaded the development of this project, with the support of Dr. Hairston and Johns Hopkins, which developed the software for the VLE with a National Science Foundation (NSF) grant. Once again, when the decision to build the VLE was made, it was clear that the location for it would be Chesapeake High School. The VLE space is hexagonal and is flanked by six 92 inch Promethean boards connected to high-end gaming computers. There is also a connecting room with 30 high-end computer stations, each with three screens, for small-group project work. Importantly, before they designed and developed the VLE, the VLE manager told us, "We did a lot of data collection to figure out who would benefit under what circumstances" and concluded that every student at CHS would get time in the VLE and opportunity to work through the interdisciplinary curriculum.

The VLE manager explained that the simulation software used in this lab focuses on Mount St. Helens; it simulates geospatially correct conditions. Students are given science and math problems to solve in collaborative teams; for example, a new eruption might be about to occur and the students must determine how to safely evacuate the area based on the speed and direction taken by the clouds of ash and gas from the eruption. Now, in addition to supporting science and math concepts, several CHS teachers are developing ways to integrate English and social studies content knowledge and applications into this simulation. One of the teachers involved explained,

> Through the many challenges built into the tasks, the student teams are required to make a proposal for a good emergency evacuation plan. This builds their skills in logical reasoning in a real-world application way, but they are doing this within the context of this virtual experience.

The VLE manager has not stopped with the building of this VLE, however. He has gone to the next step of collaborating with the gaming community to develop other game-like activities for hard-to-teach concepts. The first

Virtual Learning Environments at Chesapeake High School

example, Biomes, requires applying new information to play the game so that it engages learners but also pulls in the other aspects of the world today. As a first step, everyone agreed that the Biomes simulation was successful; the next step was to see if high school students might build their own simulation games for learning, too. In fact, almost 300 students from two schools volunteered to work in teams to develop new learning games, not just for the high-end gaming computers but for more typical computers. The VLE manager explained that he secured Race to the Top funding to support the development of the best of these virtual environments. He explained that it is no longer good enough to teach social studies in a classroom, but that the technology "changed our instructional approach so it is now blended; we don't just teach social studies or biology but we teach how social studies relates to biology and to math, and so on."

Professional Development

It is clear that teachers and others at CHS feel exceptionally well supported when it comes to learning opportunities and other resources. One teacher summarized,

> We have so much PD so it is not just the technology; they ask what you want and there are all types of training. And we get good opportunities; a number of us were able to go to the Learning and the Brain conference in San Francisco last fall—maybe others in other schools get to do that, too, but not likely as many as we were able to send or to other conferences.

Teachers reported that Mrs. Lowry starts professional development programs, advocates for each department, and looks for funding from a variety of other sources. Additionally, about 20% of the teachers are still under mentoring support that is given to all novice teachers in their first 3 years of teaching; it is clear that ongoing professional development is important for these novice as well as experienced teachers.

The professional development at CHS appears to be both formal and informal, and offered at both the school and district levels. The tech integration specialist offers "just-in-time" professional development (PD) for teachers, which he thinks works best. He has also created a lot of 3-minute how-to videos showing the teachers how to use various tools to help them build their expertise. And the administration surveys the teachers regularly to see what PD they need or want before offering sessions at several levels: entry, some experience, very experienced. Teachers also share new things they are doing in classrooms at departmental and schoolwide meetings. Furthermore, the district has content area offices with specialists who support professional development in a variety of ways. As one teacher said, "Technology is more and more a part of those activities." These offices pay for memberships in content area professional associations, support travel to state and national conferences, and develop districtwide PD programs. One teacher said, "The district offers a lot of opportunities and we are encouraged to attend. Our library media person keeps a wiki that is the professional development calendar so that we always know what is available for us to attend or learn."

Perhaps one of the most innovative PD projects is a certificate program, developed in conjunction with Johns Hopkins University, which is focused on leadership for technology integration and pedagogy. Teams of teachers from a school take five classes together; most importantly, the teams must include a principal or assistant principal so that a critical mass is created within a school community and the leadership is on board. The principal at CHS, who now teaches one of the classes in this program, explained that this program has been one of the most successful she has seen, and over the course of the past few years, about 20 BCPS schools have gone through the program. Significantly, everyone involved can see how this type of program leads directly to the accomplishment of district goals for student achievement.

Noteworthy Outcomes

Changes in the school are "remarkable," according to those who have witnessed them. Dr. Hairston summed up what he celebrates at CHS as follows:

> We have literally changed the lives, beliefs, and value system of human beings on the positive side. And we have to remember in America that the system is driven by beliefs and values. We have human beings who now believe that there is a future for them. That's powerful.

In addition, one assistant principal said, "We set forth to make a change and we did. We are on track in changing the culture and on a scale of one to ten we are on a seven or eight now." She credits consistency in all aspects of planning and building the culture. "Did everyone get the same discipline? Do we expect the same behavior in an assembly? Does each student taking a particular class get the same rigor?" She also said, "Before we started, there were perhaps forty-five hundred discipline referrals in a year, and now on average, we have eleven hundred."

Changes have occurred in the teachers and their practices, too. One explained, "Now the kids expect the technology and quick transitions; your planning has to be completely different, rethinking how to design a lesson." An administrator said, "So many of our teachers now started teaching here, and this is just a habit of mind that they have. It is not that it is rethinking for them; it is just what they do." The administrative goal appears to be to encourage that exploratory mind-set; but as one administrator said, "They might fall on their face but that will be okay, too." It was explained that this is a standard understanding of the administration. One teacher commented,

> At first teachers did not want to risk taking the chance to use technology during an observation, but they set the tone that trying is

okay, and problems occur in all situation but it is okay. How do you get back up, move on, re-teach, or figure it out? They are willing to let you take a chance.

Another teacher said, "The teachers are letting go of the control in the classroom and letting the students be more responsible for finding information, solving problems rather than giving them the answer right away."

Other teachers explained that students are engaged, attendance is up, and "students' beliefs about their futures are different, but the real mark is 'spirit.'" Students are wearing Chesapeake-named clothing and hats, and show their pride to be here. They join sports teams and after-school clubs. Students appear to know what is unique or new about the school. One teacher said, "It is really interesting to hear one student say, 'Well, we don't have this new thing' and other students will say, 'Yes, but we have this and this and get to do that.'" Another teacher reported, "More kids are going to college; students are getting into colleges that are more challenging. This year some are going to the University of Maryland, Cornell, and Bucknell. At first, maybe ten students went to a four-year college!" While test scores are moving in a steady and positive trajectory, everyone agreed that they are not where they want to be just yet. Dr. Hairston explained that the challenges have been many, but overall the district's longitudinal data show success when other districts with BCPS's demographic rates have a downward trend. He said, "Chesapeake is absolutely part of that success." Mrs. Lowry said, "More students are leaving with solid goals and plans for their future rather than just 'getting through high school' as their goal."

The Chesapeake community is extremely proud that it has made AYP, which prior to the start of the STEM initiative was not accomplished. The number of students taking the Advanced Placement tests is one metric to gauge improvement in academics at CHS, and the number of students doing internships and attending post-secondary education institutions are other achievements to celebrate. Furthermore, teachers comment on the positive trajectory of behavior, attendance, and participation in sports or after-school activities, and definitely in the wearing of Chesapeake clothing. One assistant principal said, "I watch that aspect grow from the first return to school activity until the end of the year." A teacher said, "Mrs. Lowry reaches out to the community, changing the expectations and vision of the community about Chesapeake." We mentioned that it appeared she wants for her students exactly what she wants for her own children, and she quickly agreed. She also says that everyone—teachers, support staff, and the community—also want the best for the students at Chesapeake. One assistant principal said that the positive results come from "consistency, expectations, and exposure to new models."

Everyone gets involved in supporting the new commitment to post-secondary education, and when students are taking the PSAT, seniors have the option of visiting an institution of higher education. One assistant principal explained that some parents refuse to pay for Advanced Placement exams, probably because "they may not really understand what it is about or whatever." But the county offers some waivers and CHS takes as many as they can. When that is not enough, they "work and raise money to make sure everyone can take them. Even teachers pitch in because it is important."

Challenges

Chesapeake High School still struggles to reach the average for high school test scores across the state of Maryland, and was about 10% below this average in algebra, English, and biology in 2010. Nevertheless, over these 5 years, it seems clear that a lot of things have changed and there have been many successes, so we were curious what Mrs. Lowry learned during this time. She explained,

> You always start out with a mind-set of getting people involved and input. Sometime you are working in a time frame that does not let you get input and that will bite you every single time. One of the things I learned [from mistakes] was that we would ask teachers for their input and then never tell them what the results were! But you have to give them the results, and you may get a result that is not the one that you were hoping for, but you have to deal with it.

We were also curious what she identified as those tasks she still needed to accomplish. She described:

> I want to do more with the lesson-study process, and increase the interdisciplinary aspects of our curriculum. If you want to be a STEM school, you have to have the crossover. Start small and work your way out; when teachers see that you can do it, you see the results, and they want to get on board.

Lessons Learned: Key Factors for Success

As a result of positive changes at CHS, as well as thinking about ways to tackle unmet goals, there are many lessons to be learned from the leadership in BCPS and Chesapeake High School. Furthermore, we believe the key factors for success at CHS that we describe below are relevant for other secondary schools, even if they are not STEM-focused or magnet schools. Based on our interviews with faculty, staff, and administrators in BCPS and at CHS (N=18) and our observations throughout this school (N=10) and in the VLE, these are the lessons we think are worth considering:

- Having a clear vision is essential, but so is testing every new idea against that vision. This school's vision includes wanting the same things for each student as you want for your own children; if your vision is equally ambitious, then the pathway to realizing it mirrors what you would want for your own children.

- Engaging the community when planning new initiatives or making changes was a key factor in the success of this school and this district, as was partnering with local universities, businesses, and industries.

- Incorporating everyone's views and opinions when establishing goals and priorities was important to the leadership in this school and the district. But this must then be followed by establishing clear expectations for meeting those goals. To do this requires finding the right people and then trusting them to accomplish the tasks set. In other words, you have to give your professionals what they need to do their job and get out of their way so they can do it.

- However, it also means leading by example, working toward your goals rather than changing them every year, and being consistent. In other words, if you say you will do something, then you have to do it! It can also mean admitting mistakes and making adjustments when needed, and doing so with dignity for all.

- The kind of culture that develops from this type of leadership includes expecting the best from teachers, staff, and students while still holding them accountable. It also means celebrating every success. At this school the leadership celebrates the pride of the school community when each student gets accepted to college, passes an Advanced Placement (AP) exam, attends the robotic competition, or whatever the teachers say their students have accomplished. Of course, this means knowing every student in your building.

- Supporting students by removing obstacles they may confront is part of the culture of this school. For example, if students cannot pay for Advanced Placement tests, then the leadership seeks the few free tests offered to the district, or raises money to pay for those tests, rather than leaving it up to families who may not have the ability to support such expenses.

- Supporting teachers as they explore ways to integrate technology into their curriculum, encouraging trial and error, and celebrating when they try new things is also the culture of this school. Relatedly, the leadership at this school encourages teachers and other staff member to participate in professional development and certificate programs, and supports them when they are getting advanced degrees to the extent that the leadership is willing to team up with teachers who are seeking professional development.
- This school is all about providing a real-world, career-focused curricula, which connects to two key lessons learned that are worth reiterating: First, it is important to support teachers as they explore new things and celebrate their success in doing so. Second, this works best when the leadership expects the best from teachers, staff, and students *and* holds them accountable.

CHAPTER 7

Deliberate and Focused

The Case of Mooresville High School,
Mooresville Graded School District,
Mooresville, NC

"Go wider, go deeper" and "Every kid every day."

This is the case of a small school district in North Carolina with a highly successful 1:1 digital conversion that now includes an Apple laptop for every student in grades 3–12. The superintendent of this award-winning district had purposefully phased in 1:1 laptops using an efficiency model. The district ranks 99th out of 115 in per-pupil expenditures, and is tied for third with one other district in the state, with 88% of students in grades 3–8 scoring proficient on end-of-grade exams in math and reading. Further, this district is one of only six districts in the state to make every one of its AYP targets.

At the time of this study this district had about 5,300 students, with 1,545 attending the high school. Over 4 years the district rolled out over 5,000 Apple computers so that now all students in grades 3–12 have their own laptop. The K–2 classrooms have carts of laptops or iPads, and there are interactive whiteboards in most elementary classrooms. The district's technical staff of five people manages the district's wireless network, 20 servers, and the learning management system (Angel). There is also a help desk and an instructional tech facilitator at every school. The high school offers a help desk elective and these students staff the help desk at their school as well as in other schools in the district.

During the focus groups we held with parents, we heard the following story:

> Just this week, as my wife and I entered the gymnasium for a basketball game at the high school, my daughter's math teacher stopped us and told us that she had failed a math quiz that day and he was concerned. We listened and told the teacher that we would spend the evening reviewing the material if she could retake the quiz the next day, to which he replied, "Sure, I can do that."
>
> No sooner did we finish talking to this teacher than we turned around and saw our daughter entering the gym with her cheerleading squad. We stopped her, hugged, and then talked briefly about what her math teacher had just told us. The rather shocked look on her face, and the fact the she hung her head so that her chin touched her chest, told us that she suspected that she had failed the math quiz that day and that she was rather shocked that we knew it before she did. We talked about our plan to study after dinner tonight and told her she could retake the quiz tomorrow, hugged again, and went our separate ways.
>
> I am telling you this because it is an example of the caring nature of teachers in this school and district—and we have three kids in three different schools—and the power of having teachers who can immediately check quizzes, tests, and other assignments that students complete using Angel, the school's learning management system. We think it is great that they can immediately pinpoint who needs help and do something about it, and we know that if we hadn't run into the math teacher at the game, he would have emailed us, because our daughter did not usually get behind in her work or fail quizzes. And the teachers know that as parents we want to assist our children as long as we know when they need help.
>
> We have high expectations for all our children attending Mooresville's schools, and we believe the teachers also have high expectations. The communication has been great with this digital conversion. Teachers know they can email or call, and we have access to parts of Angel so we can see how our children are doing. Our kids can email their teachers and even chat online with them. We love being able to be so involved, thanks to the technology and the digital conversion.

Context

While most districts in North Carolina are countywide, Mooresville Graded School District (MGSD) encompasses just one small, tight-knit community populated mainly by blue-collar and middle-class families employed by the car-racing industry, working in the corporate headquarters of a large home-improvement company, or commuting to jobs in nearby towns. In fact, the town of Mooresville is located only 30 miles north of the state's largest city, Charlotte, and is also close to a recreational area, Lake Norman. With just seven schools, MGSD is a very small school system compared to others in North Carolina. The total student population of about 5,400 students is 73% Caucasian, 15% African American, 7% Hispanic, 3% multi-racial, and 2% Asian, with almost 40% eligible for free meals. There is one high school in Mooresville, with about 1,535 students enrolled, one middle school (7th and 8th grade, with about 880 students), two intermediate schools (grades 4–6, each with about 600–700 students), three K–3 elementary schools, with about 500–600 students each, plus one advanced technology and art center that serves selected high school students. About 400 certified staff serve these students. As the principal of Mooresville High School (MHS) described the district and his school,

> It's this little—it's kind of what you read about or you see in old movies. I mean it's this high school in this one town where the town revolves around the high school and the whole town shuts down on Friday nights and our kids are—you know, our great athletes are treated like rock stars around town. And I mean our community really takes care of our kids.

In recent years the population of Mooresville has become more ethnically diverse, and at MHS the percentage of students eligible for free or reduced meals has grown from 31% to 40% in the past 4 years. Furthermore, test scores have increased so that the composite rate on all end-of-course exams required of high school students in North Carolina moved from 68% proficient in 2006–2007 to 88% proficient in 2010–2011, which is a staggering accomplishment envied by others across the state, region, and country.

These statistics are among the reasons we included Mooresville High School and MGSD as one of our case studies of exemplary, award-winning schools/districts. In addition, MHS was named for the second year in a row as one of only 52 Apple Distinguished Schools, and the district has been featured in several videos produced by Cisco, Discovery Education, and SAS software. The main reason for these many accolades is that in the winter of

2007 MGSD began what they call their "Digital Conversion" so that by 2011 every student in grades 3–12 had his or her own Apple laptop. Furthermore, this district is touted by many groups and in several publications as a model for how a wide-scale digital initiative can change not only the way in which students learn and teachers teach, but also the way in which this can be accomplished in a district that ranks 99th in the state (out of 115 districts) in per-pupil expenditures ($7,463 per student). And in the same time period, MGSD tied for third place with one other district in the state for student achievement, with 88% of all students in grades 3–8 being proficient on end-of-grade exams in math and reading—up 15% in the past 4 years. Furthermore, Mooresville was one of only six school districts out of 115 in the state of North Carolina to make every one of its AYP targets in 2009–2010.

Leadership Practices

The high school principal, Todd Wirt, was recruited to MHS from another, much larger school district in the state at the beginning of the digital conversion in 2007. Over the past 4 years, his leadership team, along with the full support of both veteran and new teachers and staff at MHS, has worked hard to improve not just access to and use of technology at MHS, but also the rewriting of curriculum guides using the principles of Backward Design (Wiggins & McTighe, 2005). This is so that all teachers in each particular content area are aligned and following the pacing guides, creating common assessments that are given every 4.5 weeks, which are then used to make immediate changes in their instruction, to target individual remediation needs, and to get more students into Advanced Placement classes. This was done while also working to improve the climate and culture of the school based on the ideas from a program that Mr. Wirt brought to the school called Capturing Kids' Hearts (www.flippengroup.com/education/ckh.html). As a result of all this work on curriculum, assessments, and school culture over the past 4 years, some other statistics about MHS of which the staff is rightfully proud include an increase in the graduation rate from 64% in 2005–2006 to 91% in 2010–2011, making MHS's graduation rate the second highest in the state. Further, the actual dropout rate at MHS decreased from 87 students in 2005–2006 to just 39 students in 2009–2010, and there was also a drop in the out-of-school suspension rate of 64% over this same period. Further, daily attendance currently averages about 96%, and the college-going rate is now 86%, up from 74% in 2006–2007.

    The goal of this principal was to make MHS "a good school for every kid" as he described the hard work everyone put in to get where they are now:

It made us spend more time in our content and it also made us flesh out some things that we were teaching that were getting in the way of improving performance. And then off of those [curriculum guides] we've written our own formative assessments that we give every four-and-a-half weeks. I mean when it boils down to it, that's been maybe the single most important factor in improving performance. I mean we give an assessment, we get the data back the next day because we give it online. So that night–I mean as soon as the kids are done you have the data and it's broken down by standard, by objective, by ethnicity. So it's all broken down immediately. . . . And then there would obviously be the technology integration here. I mean to go from a school that had an older PC desktop in every classroom, data projectors here and there, mostly overhead projectors, to a full one-to-one, that has taken some time to evolve. I mean we're obviously in a much better place now than we were in year one. I mean year one for us was triage. I mean it was–there was a lot of coaching, it was try something new, it was just trying to get people to take the next step, you know? And I remember all the time, I said, "Just try something new this week, try one thing new this week." And teachers always wanted me to quantify it. How much do you want to see us using it? And I never would. You know, I mean they wanted me to but I never said it.

Implementation Process

According to the MGSD website (www.mooresville.k12.nc.us):

During the winter of the 2007–2008 School Year, MGSD started Phase I of the Digital Conversion by placing laptops on carts at the high school in all English classes, and giving all certified staff laptops. In addition, all K–2 schools were outfitted as 21st Century Classrooms with the SMART suite of technologies (Board, Slate, and Response System). In the fall of 2008–2009 Phase II was implemented and all Mooresville High School (MHS) students (all 9th–12th-grade students in the district–approximately 1,550 students) and half of the districts' 4th–6th-grade students at Mooresville Intermediate School (MIS) (approximately 850 students) received laptops for their use 24/7 for the entire school year. Phase III came in the fall of 2009–2010 when all 4th through 12th grade students received a laptop and all K–3 grade classrooms received the SMART suite. In the fall of 2010–2011 Phase IV was implemented and laptop carts were placed in 3rd grade. And, because of the success of having laptops on carts in 3rd grade, in Fall 2011 all 3rd graders in MGSD received their own laptops.

This rollout was originally seeded by a $250,000 grant from a local corporation and ongoing costs were partially offset by the use of building funds for technology when a new intermediate school was built, by creating a self-insurance program for the laptops paid by students' families (currently $40 per year), and by a change in policy so that funds traditionally used for textbooks and other instructional materials (globes, maps, encyclopedias, etc.) could be used for technology. In addition, careful allocation of local, state, and federal funds, accompanied by grants and donations, made this initiative sustainable, as did the creation of a foundation to raise funds through community events like an annual golf tournament (to pay the laptop insurance fee for those who cannot afford it), and also an annual summer technology institute attended by school districts from around the state and the country that is also a money maker for MGSD. Ultimately, under leasing agreements with Apple, the cost of a laptop and software for 4 years ranges between a $1 per student per day and about $200 per student per year. Ultimately, the model created to support the Digital Conversion is what the MGSD superintendent calls the "efficiency model" that takes advantage of leveraging many efficiencies and savings in various areas to free up funds to support the 1:1 laptop initiative and other technologies that are used throughout the district. And while the schools in MGSD are not completely paperless or without textbooks, they have greatly reduced costs in these areas by using more and more digital material for learning, and the district recently made a profit re-selling 2-year-old MacBooks and other discarded equipment.

District Leadership

Dr. Mark Edwards, the superintendent in Mooresville, was recruited from another state to come to Mooresville in 2007, largely because of his experience leading a very successful 1:1 initiative in a much larger school system in Virginia, but also because of his vision for what was needed to provide a 21st-century education for Mooresville's students, his ability to build consensus among multiple constituents (e.g., teachers, staff, parents, school board members, and corporate partners), and the fact that he could build on lessons learned in Henrico County:

> Whether it was making sure that we engaged the community with
> thoughtful dialog, whether we looked at the infrastructure with great
> detail, teacher preparation and planning, so the whole planning
> component, down to deployment scheduling with minutiae, to dealing
> with discipline issues. So, we look at the whole spectrum of deployment
> implementation challenges and detailed that out.

Among the descriptors we heard from many teachers and administrators who described Dr. Edwards as a visionary leader, they also said he was strategic, motivational, a big picture person, like a coach, a master at fund-raising, straightforward, goal oriented, lets you know where you stand, gathers information, makes informed decisions, etcetera. In fact, when the MHS principal talked about Dr. Edwards, he said,

> It's all about leadership, I mean, it starts with him. And it's been a really clear vision from the very beginning that, you know, it would be a full digital environment, that we would be the top-performing district in North Carolina and one of the best in the country, that we would be a model for technology. I mean he said that before we ever rolled out a laptop. And he has not wavered from that since day one. . . . And I think that's where, you know, Dr. Edwards' vision . . . that it hasn't just been a fun tool, it's been a tool for engagement, because it's always been about performance, and it has to be about performance when you're asking the community to spend that kind of money. I mean it's all about return on investment. Education is no different than the business world when it comes to that. And certainly he's been able to say [to] Lowe's, you've given us a quarter of a million dollars, well look what it's done for the performance. We've gone from ranking thirtieth as a district in the state to tied for fourth [now third at the end of the 2010–2011 school year].

In talking with many people in MGSD we learned that the digital conversion was a "driven initiative–from top down, but adopted from bottom up" and managed through very careful planning with everyone at the table, complete transparency along the way, and also with everyone on message once a decision was made. Of course, Dr. Edwards did not do any of this alone, and is supported by a small, hard-working staff that includes several veteran-to-the-district curriculum leaders and finance people who are all on board with the digital conversion, as well as some new hires, including a chief technology officer (CTO) who understands both the curriculum and the technical side of things, and an executive director of instruction, who worked with Dr. Edwards in Henrico County, where he was principal of a very successful high school.

Throughout the implementation process there were monthly parent advisory group meetings, student focus groups, community meetings, plus regular meetings with vendors and industry partners including Apple, Cisco, Angel Learning, and the local cable company, as well as weekly meetings of leadership teams at both the district office and the schools. The school board that hired Dr. Edwards remains supportive, but as we were told, it helped that there was a leader who "could sell ice to Eskimos" and get everyone on board, all the while using data to drive instructional decisions. Finally, all this "happens in an atmosphere where teachers understand that it is okay to make mistakes, but they at least have to try things, and where everyone understands that things may fail but that is okay. This message has to come from the top and teachers have to believe it." When we asked Dr. Edwards what things he was proud of achieving so far, he responded,

> Well, first and foremost is the access and the opportunity created for students and for staff. We had a serious digital divide, an economic divide, a racial divide, and with no real means to address it other than hoping that traditional means would work. And now I hear almost every single week some parent or someone telling me that this is the first time that they feel like their child has a level playing field or that they have the opportunity. . . . The second thing is that it has translated to outcomes. It has really translated to achievement and, you know, a lot of people would say, "Well, that machine didn't," and I'd say, "Of course not." But the composite of the tools, the opportunity, and then the relevance, I think those are kind of the triangle that really has driven it. The kids know this is real. They know this is about their future. They see themselves using this tool, so the relevant piece just kind of drives it. . . . And, I think it has translated from the teachers' standpoints in terms of accountability, again, having the precision with intervention, the use of data that we have not had before. . . . So, we've blended the twenty-first-century hardware, software tools with the twenty-first-century scientific part of teaching, using data for precision intervention. So our results across the board by content area, by grade level, the fact that our suspensions have been reduced by, you know, they've been reduced by sixty-four percent. Now again, it's had to do with the culture . . . that we've created a culture of learning for adults and that there's a level of collaboration that was unheard of and that exceeds any experience that I've had.

Technology Support Structure

One of the unique things about the digital conversion at MGSD is that tech support is provided by both district- and school-level personnel and also by high school students. At the district level, the CTO has a staff of five people to handle the wireless network, the learning management system (Angel), other infrastructure, plus over 20 servers. There are also eight tech support personnel spread out at each school site to keep all the technology working at each site. But high school students who take a help desk elective course that teaches them how to troubleshoot and do minor repairs offer technical support as well. Some of these students remain at the high school for this elective class and staff the help desk there, but some of the older students actually drive to other schools to help staff their help desks. The teacher who created the help desk course told us they use a project-based learning approach to help interested students learn how to troubleshoot both hardware and software problems encountered by other students or teachers. New students come into this elective each semester, and each year the course evolves; however, due to the decision to purchase Apple products for the digital conversion, everyone believes the number of problems with potential viruses and required upgrades is minimal.

Professional Development

Professional development at MGSD has been extensive throughout the digital conversion, and continues to be a priority, even as the teachers become more proficient and are building a culture of sharing ideas for technology use with each other. Each school has one dedicated tech facilitator in addition to help desk personnel, and that person's job is to educate and support teachers as they integrate various programs and other tech tools into their lessons. The basic expectations placed upon the tech facilitators by their administrators include helping teachers to change their lessons, letting teachers move at their own pace but increasing expectations each year, conveying positive appreciation for the changes being made, and in some cases pushing some teachers to move ahead. To accomplish their responsibilities, some of these tech facilitators still offer classes regularly, but most have gone to a flexible schedule that allows them to work with teachers in their classrooms—including setting up new programs or equipment, modeling, troubleshooting, offering moral support, and being another adult who can help students. They also provide professional development in small groups, or one-on-one, in order to introduce and demonstrate something new to a grade, or department, or at school-wide meetings as requested. Using ten early-release days spread throughout the year, all the tech facilitators have moved from large group instruction to smaller group, choice sessions for offering workshops during planning periods about twice a month based on ongoing needs assessments. The MHS principal calls this a YMCA schedule, as he describes it here:

> We had done a needs assessment and I said, "Okay, now I want you to create a schedule that looks like the YMCA. I mean on Monday you can come down here and get this, and on Tuesday at these times you can get this, and I want it all to be voluntary." I mean because we were already using early-release days and staff meetings to present really

great things that were going on . . . [so] I would go to a classroom and say, "Hey, why don't you present that at the next staff meeting and just pique people's interest?" And they would say sure, and "I want to know how to do that." And I would say, "Great. On Tuesday at this time you can go see [the MHS tech facilitator] and learn how to do that." And we made it completely voluntary. And we planned that out in February of that first year, and I think that first month voluntarily we trained like forty-nine people. . . . [And] this year we had ten days where we get out at 12:20 PM and that's when we do professional development to keep us from doing it in planning periods or after school. And it's been really key, and we'll differentiate it. I mean that's one thing we learned pretty quickly, too, is that teachers are just like kids, you know, and the ones that are struggling get frustrated when they're in the class with the high flyers, and the high flyers are equally frustrated, you know? . . .
And now when we get a needs assessment we've got this population that wants something around this general topic, but we'll have multiple things going on at one time.

The tech facilitators also take a leadership role and teach during the Summer Institute, which is overseen by the district office. According to everyone we talked with the teachers like the Summer Institute the best, followed by appreciating individual help. However, teachers are now sharing and teaching one another so that outsourcing professional development isn't needed in times with tight budgets. Further, even the administrators get professional development during the Summer Institute, and they also come to the early-release sessions.

Changes in Teaching and Learning

While we arrived more than halfway through the third year of the digital conversion at MGSD, most of the high school teachers were in their second year of teaching with laptops, except for the English Department, which was in its third year. At the intermediate school (grades 4–6), which we also visited, the teachers had been teaching in a 1:1 laptop environment for over 2 years as well, while the middle school was in its first year of the 1:1 laptop initiative. At the high school our research team observed in 14 classrooms, while at the middle school we observed in 15 classrooms, and at the intermediate school we did 28 observations. As a result we saw what can happen in just a few years with a well-supported implementation of a 1:1 laptop initiative in a district with solid leadership, buy-in from all parties, strong tech support, and ongoing professional development. We also saw that much more has happened in MGSD than just putting laptops in the students' hands because we also heard and saw the results of doing curriculum realignment, creating and using formative assessments, and then making data-driven decisions based on those assessments. Following are some examples from our observations at the high school.

In one of the first classrooms we observed 12th-grade English students giving presentations on the final chapters of the book they were reading using the presentation tool in Google Docs so they could collaborate in groups outside of class time to create their presentations. The teacher told us that she had modeled what she wanted them to learn and include in the presentations by presenting the first ten chapters herself before letting them work in groups. She also told us that she loves using Google Docs because the students will use it in college, and because presentations allow students to practice public speaking, which is another skill they will need for college. Furthermore, of all the books they read this year in her class only one had to be purchased because the others were freely available online. After the last presentation, students were told to put their answers to the study guide questions into the drop box on Angel, and that they would have a discussion board question to do for homework, which is also the kind of assignment they would experience in college. This was one of our first observations, but as we heard over and over again in this district, the use of the laptops had increased communication between teachers and students, as well as between students and students, and also extended the school day, as the MHS principal described:

> I mean one thing technology has done is our kids communicate more than ever with their teachers, maybe not as much face to face but they're constantly communicating with teachers, whether it's—you know, like for instance, when we were out during snow days waiting to take exams, we had teachers online and they've got fifty-five kids online with them doing a biology review. Yeah, that's cool, right? So then—or at night, you know, the night before a test a teacher will say I'll be on tomorrow night from seven to nine on this discussion board, hop on if you have questions. And then what it leads to, a kid will email their teacher ten times in two weeks, then all of a sudden it's like they've somehow developed this relationship in a cyber way. So now all of a sudden they feel more comfortable talking in class or going up to talk to their teacher after class. And I just think the kids think teachers care. . . . And it's easier for a teacher. I mean it's efficient to be able to go on a discussion board for two hours at night after they've put their kids to bed and made dinner for their family, and not staying after school or that sort of thing, to go home and say hey guys, I'm going to sit here while I'm watching my favorite show. If you've got a question,

pop it on and I'll answer it. It's easy for a teacher and it's cool for a kid
to talk to their teacher that way.

In a science classroom we observed a veteran teacher who taught chemistry and physics using the laptops in a variety of student-centered ways that had the students working hard and being fully engaged during the entire period. To our surprise this teacher had the students watching a BrainPop video about matter and the atomic model as their warm-up, and then answering the quiz questions when they finished. While we thought BrainPop might be a bit juvenile for high school students, the content presented was not, and the students gained background knowledge for future work on this topic in an engaging manner. They viewed BrainPop individually using their earphones before moving onto a vocabulary activity that, once completed, was loaded into Angel so the teacher could assess it. The teacher had to explain how to do a screen shot of the vocabulary quiz, but mainly she moved around to help individuals, encouraging students to check answers, make corrections, and get 100. She told them this was an easy way to get 100, and encouraged mastery. Later, this teacher told us their scores on state-mandated, end-of-course tests in her discipline have gone from 67% proficient to 91% since having the laptops, and that she feels laptops are what has made the biggest difference for two reasons: (1) she can encourage mastery and (2) after each assessment she can pinpoint precisely what students need to work on when they use Study Island [standards-based assessment, instruction, and test preparation software programs for K–12 students]. After these two warm-up activities the teacher directed students to folders on Angel with information she had compiled for them and directions to learn about different scientists who had studied atoms, electrons, and protons, etcetera. In groups of three the students got together to plan who would read the articles and websites and view the Discovery Ed videos with the goal of creating a group presentation to show what they learned about these scientists who had made discoveries about atoms, electrons, protons, and so forth. Throughout this lesson we did not see a textbook, or any pencil or paper, for that matter, as all the resources needed for each task were available in other formats and online.

Later the principal shared with us that this teacher had almost been on the verge of leaving education when the digital conversion began, but

> now she—I mean she knows more of the latest websites and free
> and cool tools than anybody in our building. I mean she presents at
> conferences. Her class is, you know, collaborative-based all the time,
> or you walk in her room and she's carrying around some tablet and the
> kids are manipulating stuff. She's got this great website she uses where
> she can project it and every kid can log on and they manipulate the

equation from their desk . . . so to see her transform from somebody that was ready to quit, and go through a process that was hard—I mean it wasn't like her job got easier. It got harder, and now she's a model for it and she's getting her master's to be an administrator now. I mean she's gone from ready to quit to ready to lead change.

We also observed numerous other uses of the laptops at the high school, middle school, and intermediate school, including students using Google Earth in a combined science and social studies lesson about plate tectonics, and also for a mapping activity. In several classes students were working on a "challenge-based learning project" (CBL), which is Apple's term for a version of problem-based learning (PBL), which requires students "to draw on prior learning, acquire new knowledge, and tap their creativity to fashion solutions" that can make a difference for their school or community. CBL and other interdisciplinary projects make extensive use of the Internet for information gathering, and the use of a variety of tools for data analysis and presentation was not uncommon in the classes we observed. At the middle school, we also observed students creating ABC books about the U.S. Constitution and our system of government, using Citation Maker 2 or Citation Machine to cite their sources, as well as students doing writing, peer editing, and annotating of texts as a part of their assignments. At Mooresville Intermediate School (MIS) we observed students reading eBooks about science topics, working independently on skills practice in math and reading/Language Arts, finishing vocabulary work and completing graphic organizers before loading them into the drop box on Angel, and also participating in online chats or contributing to a wiki. In all the schools we also saw that students were reading and writing/keyboarding all the time, were often able to choose what to read, and were almost always able to choose the tool they wanted to use to present what they had learned (e.g., iMovie, Keynote, GarageBand, a wiki, etc.). There were also tutors, parent volunteers, and community volunteers in evidence in all the schools.

Noteworthy Outcomes

Based on what we observed, we felt there was clear evidence across the district of student-centered learning and the students being very focused and working independently while teachers mainly provided appropriate learning materials, and guided, facilitated, scaffolded, encouraged, and assessed their learning. In every classroom students were engaged and using their laptops for a wide variety of tasks. At the start of classes we often observed students watching short videos to either introduce or refresh their learning about a topic that they would then discuss as a group, or taking a quiz online, or posting their answers to problems or questions to Angel, or using Google Docs, the discussion board feature on Angel, or a blog to write responses to questions their teachers had posed. Students all had earphones to plug into their laptops and used them when needed, and in some classes teachers allowed students to listen to music as they worked independently. We also saw students working together on projects in small groups, working alone to read electronic books or doing work they then uploaded to Angel to be graded, following along with the teacher's Keynote presentation, or presenting to each other using Keynote, iMovie, or GarageBand, which were all readily available to students on their MacBooks. We also observed students using Study Island, iStation, and PLATO for remediation and practice at all levels, and we observed students in the library at the high school participating in advanced and college-level classes offered online by the state's virtual public high school and a nearby university. Also, since the laptops made ongoing, formative assessments easy to give to students, and even easier to grade for teachers, we observed teachers using these data on a regular and routine basis to track what their students were learning and to adjust their lessons accordingly. As mentioned previously, one teacher at MHS told us that her test scores have gone from 67% proficient to 91% since she has been using the laptops, and that she feels the laptops are what has made the biggest difference because she can encourage students to check their answers and redo their work until they get 100, and because she can encourage and expect mastery.

Also, one of the librarians told us that their Angel LMS was very helpful and was actually changing the bounds of the school day because students and teachers could communicate after school hours. This librarian and several teachers also told us they have changed the way they teach, that the textbook is not so important for some classes, and that both teachers and students are collaborating more. And not only are teachers not teaching the same way, they are using email and Facebook to support one another as they plan and find new ways to integrate technology into their lessons. High school students are more engaged and willing to perform and are more involved in their education, and thus there are many positive outcomes—high test scores, better graduation rates, more kids going onto post-secondary education, more scholarships, and so on.

Challenges

According to the superintendent of MGSD, among the challenges when leading a digital conversion where over 5,000 laptops are being deployed is understanding that "your strategic plans have to flex and evolve, and that they have to be dynamic because everything is constantly changing." Having the right people in leadership positions is also crucial. In addition, he also told us that "it takes a voracious appetite for the unknown and having the will and determination to keep moving forward."

Dr. Edwards also felt the need to "create a sense that bringing the school district into the twenty-first century is moral obligation," and that this needs to come from the community as well as from the schools, so everyone has to be involved and educated. In order to sustain such a sea change you have to get buy-in and change the culture of the community, which takes time, patience, and a willingness to include and educate community members. One way they did this in MGSD was to establish a standing Parent Advisory Committee, to be sure every parent was aware of the planned changes, and then connected, which the technology provided and the district supported by partnering with the local Internet service provider to offer reasonable rates to families. As Dr. Edwards told us,

> You know, one of the things is creating a sense of moral obligation, and it has to come from the community. It has to come from the teachers. And that it's not some jargon on a strategic plan but . . . it is truly a commitment as part of, a big part of the team and the family. And so, you know, all those pieces. And then ultimately the dynamic nature of the whole venture—content is constantly changing . . . and . . . when I look at the tactical and the strategic lines for deployment, you know, you look at a plan and you look at benchmarks for the plan, but I guess that one of the revelations is that it's all dynamic and evolutional. And I think one of the takeaways that I really think has relevance for education in general is that competency is evolutional. You know, we've had teachers who were perceived as highly competent, highly capable in the last century, and in this century it's a struggle because it's a new world. It's a different world. Students are different. Their needs are different. The instructional dynamic has changed. So, part of the planning and the differentiation of professional development, you think, all right, you got to teach everybody to use the laptop. Well, that's the easy first step.

Therefore, another challenge is that once the laptops are rolled out everyone has to understand that it is a process, because as the high school principal told us "every teacher was a first-year teacher, that first year." In MGSD they quickly learned the need to differentiate professional development for teachers. Teachers also had to work at letting go and not feeling they had to know everything, which was helped by conveying to teachers that they could take a risk, that they could ask for help, and that students could help one another, and help teachers as well. As an example, one story we heard from the MHS principal drives home this point:

And then as a teacher you have to be willing to give up control. I mean I can't tell you how many times in the last two years I've walked in a classroom with a competent teacher that says guys, I've got this—like, for example, I was in a biology class last year and we had visitors here. It was ironic, but we were in a biology class and this teacher said, "Hey, guys, I want to do a rap about cell division and I want to record it on a podcast in GarageBand," and she said, "I think it sounds cool," but she said, "I have no idea how to do it." And within two minutes, two or three kids stood up, presented GarageBand to the class on here's how you do it, these are the steps you go through, and in forty-five minutes they had it done and they were posted in Angel. You know, I mean— but it takes a while for a teacher to get to the point and say, "Hey, I've got this idea. I don't have a clue how to do it, but let's figure it out together." But again, that's engaging for a kid.

So, building a culture where it is okay to say "I don't know" or "I need help" and understanding that you don't have to be in control is something that has to happen. But that takes the support of leadership that is willing and wants teachers who are not afraid to allow kids to participate more, to do more exploration, to be more student-centered, and to let kids go ahead. When that begins to happen, students gain more confidence, the technology lets them participate more in their learning, and teachers and students begin helping one another. So now, several years into the digital conversion at MGSD, teachers are not afraid to allow kids to participate more, to make choices about how they will show what they learned, to do more exploration, and to let kids go ahead and pursue things that they are interested in learning. The outcome is that you can clearly see that teachers definitely are more student-centered, and students are more engaged, and learning and mastering more.

Nevertheless, future challenges and areas where the leadership and the teachers at MGSD still want to do more include finding ways to make more global connections, even though they already use Skype to connect to other schools and to experts outside of school; creating more opportunities for students to do more problem solving; and experiencing challenge-based learning on a more regular basis. And most importantly, even with close to 90% of students showing proficiency, the leadership and the teachers in MGSD still want to find ways to meet the needs of the remaining 10%, close the gaps for all their sub-groups, and continue their pursuit of "every kid every day" so that students are more engaged, more connected to school, and like school more.

Lessons Learned: Key Factors for Success

There are many lessons that can be learned from the digital conversion in MGSD that are valuable for other schools and districts, large or small, and these lessons seem especially valuable because they are based on over 3 years of experience with a 1:1 initiative. Based on numerous interviews (N=43), focus groups (N=14), and observations (N=57), these are the lessons we think are most valuable:

- Starting with a clear vision is important, but so is including all constituents in regular planning meetings in order to develop the vision, the mission, and detailed plans for proceeding. In this case, this meant including parents and students in the planning process by having a parent advisory group and a student advisory group.

- Distributed leadership was evident in this case because there is a purposeful plan for building a cadre of future leaders inside the district, which includes supporting teachers and administrators who wanted to get advanced degrees, and paying for at least part of their tuition. The resultant benefits to the district include sharing what these future leaders are learning, and ultimately having the right people in place doing the right jobs.

- Very careful planning for the digital conversion in this district was evident in many ways, and planning is a key lesson learned. One example was making sure that teachers had access to new technology and new software before the students did. Another example was staying on message consistently throughout the entire digital conversion process by using multiple methods to inform all constituents each step of the way about what would be happening with the rollout of laptops to students. Being flexible and able to overcome and regroup when there were glitches, or technical difficulties, was also built into the planning process, which is another lesson learned.

- Having a plan for how to fund and then sustain a digital conversion in this district was another key part of planning. This included identifying multiple sources of funding (foundations; grants; and reallocation of local, state, and building funds), and changing policies so that textbook funds became instructional funds that could be used for hardware and software purchases. Successful planning also required that the chief financial officer was included in all the planning from the very beginning.

- The lessons learned about technology infrastructure from this district were particularly valuable because they are the result of several years of success with their 1:1 laptop program, and because of the statement above about having the right people in place doing the right jobs. This was especially true with regard to having a chief technology leader who understood curriculum and instruction as well as the technical side of things, not just one or the other.

- One of the reasons for continued success had to do with the technology staff taking metrics on software usage to guide purchase of future licenses. They also made use of parent and student surveys to get additional input about technical services.

- Related to continuous self-assessment, ongoing professional development based on the results of regular needs assessments is an important lesson to learn from this case, as is the resultant menu of professional development opportunities differentiated by level (e.g., introductory to expert) offered during early-release days and summers so that teachers don't have to stay after school or use their planning time to continue learning.

- Selecting and maintaining a robust learning management system (LMS) was crucial in the success of this district because it expanded the boundaries of the school day for students and teachers and allowed educators to gather materials to create lessons and formative assessments. Having a robust LMS allowed teachers to assess, pinpoint, and monitor the progress of students on assignments, quizzes, tests, and other formative assessments. This district also made use of software that allows principals or another administrator to monitor the laptop of any student at any time during school hours, which is valuable for many reasons in a 1:1 school district.

- Changes in school culture and in the curriculum were apparent in this district and seemed to come from conveying the message that while it is okay to start slowly, teachers must continue to try new things and not be afraid to allow students to participate more, do more exploration, go ahead and pursue their interests so that teaching can become more student-centered. Such change also appears to be the result of having administrators who are perceived as being encouraging, supportive, enthusiastic, energetic, committed, warm, visible in classes and in the community, good at growing their teachers, and understanding and valuing family obligations. The district's culture also included fostering digital citizenship, encouraging students to be responsible with technology, and having Internet access 24/7.

- Along with changes in culture, other changes to the curriculum in this district included changing instruction so that it is data-driven, aligned, and focused on students using 21st-century skills. As a result of having ubiquitous computing and a strong LMS, it is common practice in this district to use data to target needs for review and remediation for individual students in order to help them achieve mastery. In fact, the leadership in this district is not willing to settle for even 90% success when the remaining 10% still need attention and assistance, and they feel they have both the technology and the culture available to achieve this goal.

- Collaborating with parents, families, and community members also is a noteworthy lesson learned from this district. The benefits of having good communication, holding monthly technology nights for students and families, and making sure that the leadership is involved beyond just showing up at school resulted in school and district leaders not being perceived as making decisions in a vacuum. The lesson learned from this is districtwide and communitywide support for the digital conversion.

- Finally, celebrating successes both within the community and telling people outside the district how these successes were accomplished is another lesson learned about how success breeds success.

CHAPTER 8

Using Data for Continuous Improvement
The Case of Science, Technology, Engineering, and Mathematics (STEM) Academy

To create a rigorous and supportive academic program which will prepare 100% of our students to earn acceptance into the college of their choice and where they gain the necessary skills to successfully earn a college degree.

This is the case of a STEM-focused charter school in Colorado that has successfully focused on preparing a diverse population of secondary students for college since 2004. Every student having a laptop has been a part of this school's model since its inception. The development of a rigorous, college-prepatory curriculum and unique school culture, plus its assessment system and use of data is also remarkable. This school was selected because it has received numerous grants and other accolades for its success in having 100% of its students accepted at 4-year colleges.

This high school of about 400 students was the first public high school in this state where every student was provided with a wireless, networked personal computer. When a similar-sized middle school had opened a few years later, computers had been provided on carts. Currently every student is provided with a laptop or tablet computer to use at school and take home. Every classroom has an interactive whiteboard and data projection system. Due to the ongoing costs of sustaining 1:1 technology, STEM Academy is working toward a cloud computing environment so that all data, software, and support systems will reside on the Internet rather than on individual computers and servers in the building. This school also has a robust learning management system that supports its assessment system, teacher planning, and communication needs.

One story that stays with us is about the many ways the head of the middle school at the STEM Academy (a pseudonym, as is the location and all names) compares his school to Starbucks. He described the way that each store is organized to demonstrate what is important, and to encourage those who enter to understand the purpose of the place and the roles played by various people. In particular, he mentioned that Starbucks encourages you to sit, relax, and be mindful of your goals. He asked, "But why aren't schools on a physical space set up like that? Why aren't classrooms set up like that, where the first thing you see are the values? Or the first thing that, like for me, after school, when we dismiss, how kids hang out is really indicative of what kind of . . . the intentionality of the process." He wonders why we are still set up on a seven-period day in most schools. If math is important, then students need 90 minutes of math a day, he reasons; and if they are behind, they need 3 hours a day. He believes that if reading and writing are important to students' learning, then each student needs 2 hours of that a day. And more than anything, he notes that if every teacher in your school is not the one you would want to be teaching your own children or grandchildren, then something needs to be done to help them become that teacher. He reflected, "Why do we have these concepts? Why do we have morning meeting? Why do we have silent hallways?" He is convinced that these things make their school the success it has become.

Arriving at STEM Academy, we found ourselves entering an amazing, modern space that looks nothing like a typical school. The original STEM high school opened in 2003, and the middle school was built, connected to it, and opened in 2008. On our first day, no students attended because it was the end of the second trimester; the day was devoted to analyzing the results of end-of-term tests, then using those data to adapt future curriculum and instruction accordingly. Nevertheless, the sensation of STEM, even without students, was still intense and energetic; and as it turned out, our ability to gather information about the school and its culture before observing the way everything works together for the students was beneficial.

Context of the District

STEM Academy is a charter school that is one of several in a large, metropolitan district with almost 80,000 students and 4,555 teachers. This district's mission is to provide all students with the opportunity to become contributing citizens in our society. The district reflects the deep diversity of the region, which has changed over the past several decades; it currently serves students who are 58.4% Hispanic, 14.6% African American, 19.8% White, 3.3% Asian, 0.7% Native American, and 3.1% classified as "other." The total percentage of students eligible for free or reduced meals for the 2010–2011 school year was 72.49%. The district has identified 11.41% of the population as gifted and talented. English learners represent 31% of the student population; Spanish-speaking students (including non-ELs) comprise 40% of the student body. The top five languages spoken by students in this district are Spanish, Vietnamese, Arabic, Russian, and Somali.

Currently, the district has 162 schools (73 elementary, 16 K–8, 16 middle schools, 12 traditional high schools, 4 K–12 schools, and 11 other types of schools) plus 30 charter schools. As part of the state's initiative for charter schools, these institutions receive public funding but may opt for waivers from some types of educational mandates; they also have their own governing boards and set their own enrollment quotas. It is a requirement, however, that their population be chosen through a lottery and that the ethnic diversity of each charter school be representative of the district's diversity.

Demographics, History, and Culture of STEM Academy

STEM's charter states that at least 40% of students should qualify for free or reduced-price meals (i.e., are from low-income families). However, it was explained that the governing board's goal is to increase that percentage to 55% eligible for free or reduced meals, because the school's mission includes providing a diverse student body with an outstanding liberal arts high school education that includes a science and technology focus. Currently, 35% of the students at STEM Academy are White, 29% are African American, 25% are Hispanic, 7% are multi-racial, 2% are Asian, 1% are classified as other, and about 50% are eligible for free or reduced-price meals. Students come from about 50 schools in the area, predominantly public schools, but also from parochial and private schools. In addition, as part of its mission, STEM Academy intends to prepare 100% of its students to earn college degrees and aims to create a community of learners and a school culture that fosters both academic and personal success for its students. Test scores at STEM are among the highest in the district and in the entire state, so STEM is achieving its many goals. For example, the first set of students graduated in June 2008, and by the end of November of that school year almost 90% had been admitted to a 4-year college; now they are extremely proud that 100% of STEM Academy graduates in all four of its graduation classes (2008–2011) have been accepted to a 4-year college.

One of the founding organizers, Mr. Johns, has a background in engineering, previously served on the State Board of Higher Education, and now serves as treasurer for the STEM Charter Management Organization (CMO). He was interested in the school's development and has been deeply involved since its inception. Through a synergistic and timely turn of events, state funding came available to create public magnet schools for math, science, and technology. Soon the organizers were also able to garner an $8 million grant from a technology foundation; together these funding sources helped support the creation of STEM Academy. The goal was and continues to be the creation of a diverse liberal arts high school with a science and technology focus that prepares all students for a 4-year, post-secondary education without needing remedial academic support. Another guiding goal is to develop an innovative model for education that will ultimately redefine the American high school experience. The STEM campus on the outskirts of the metropolitan area that we visited is now the original, and five more STEM campuses were in the planning stages at that time. Several months later we were informed that three of these schools opened in the fall of 2011.

The current CMO started with a large planning group that included people from local foundations, businesses, and organizations. The board continues to include business CEOs, high-technology individuals, faculty from the state university's School of Engineering, and members of a state organization designed to improve health and wellness, access to early childhood care, and K–12 education.

It is important to understand the trajectory of this school and the model it has created. When STEM started in 2003 as a high school serving students in grades 9 through 12, it quickly realized it had a challenge. About 100 of the first 135 students admitted through the lottery system tested either at or below the 7th-grade level in terms of their skills. Given the school's goals, the faculty spent an enormous amount of time and effort in remediation, and it soon became apparent that they needed to start at the middle school level in order to help students be successful earlier in their academic careers. After a year of planning, the middle school opened in the fall of 2008.

A charter school always needs to think about its interaction with the public schools in the district. In this situation, that is especially important. When the original high school building was being developed and planned, the governing body was about $5 million short of the required total. As part of the school district, it was able to participate in a bond issue, so money became available to complete the original building. According to members of the STEM governing structure, the district and STEM Academy continue to have a symbiotic and complementary relationship; one reason for this may be the successful model developed for STEM education. For example, a K–8 school in the district was also focused on science and technology, but the community worried its students would lose that focus if they went to the traditional-style high school. It sought the type of curriculum that STEM provides, and so, in collaboration with the city's public schools, STEM: Flow Middle School opened in 2011 to its first class of 6th-grade students. Over the next 3 years, this campus of STEM will add one grade per year, and most interestingly, after the full complement of 6th- through 8th-graders is established, Flow will open as a complementary high school. Like the original STEM Academy, the curriculum at STEM: Flow Middle School will have a college-preparatory focus, but it will emphasize developing core liberal arts skills in reading, writing, mathematics, and science. Similar to other STEM campuses, this school also will have a highly structured classroom environment with clear academic and behavioral expectations, and will focus on preparing all its students for the challenges of college. Also, STEM: Dream Farm Middle School and High School opened in the fall of 2010 and fall of 2011, respectively, as part of a large community-development project. And while science is paramount, the focus at STEM: Dream Farm will be on preparing students for professions in the medical sciences. To further that goal, the governing board has developed a partnership designed to help populate a new program at the state university that leads to a BA/BS/MD degree. In the spring of 2011, the school district approved sites for two more STEM campuses that will open in the fall of 2012. When full enrollment is reached in all five schools they will serve over 4,200 students, which will double the number of college-ready graduates in this district by 2020. Given these developments, we selected STEM Academy for one of our case studies because we felt it was important to look carefully at its leadership, curriculum, culture, use of technology, and overall educational environment, which it has accomplished in intentional ways. Clearly, STEM Academy fit our criteria for exemplary, award-winning secondary schools that have used technology as a lever for school improvement.

Culture and Curriculum at STEM Academy

The culture of STEM Academy is guided by six core values that can be observed in all aspects of the school environment: Respect, Responsibility, Integrity, Doing Your Best, Courage, and Curiosity. These values are posted in each classroom and around the school building, and everyone knows that a goal for STEM is that its graduates will be responsible and engaged citizens who are prepared to be leaders in the future. The culture of these schools also communicates to students that learning important content, concepts, and skills is more important than grades earned. STEM Academy intends to prepare 100% of its students to earn a college degree, and does everything possible to make this happen for each student.

Equally important to the culture and organization of the school is the commitment that parents and students are required to make in order to attend.

Each parent promises to support any after-school remediation for academic challenges, after-school study hall for students who have not completed their homework (termed a College Prep, or CP), or a Refocus for students who have broken any of the rules (preparation, dress code, punctuality, etc.). The school also celebrates students' academic efforts and demonstrations of core values in weekly meetings of the entire school community. Teachers reflect that the deep understanding each student has about these expectations eliminates the need for arguments and disagreements, and even negotiations. If a student receives an after-school Refocus or a CP there is no discussion about it. Following is a chart (Table 8.1) posted on the walls of every classroom that describes these two basic features of STEM's guiding rules.

Both the middle and high school on STEM Academy's original campus share common standards, curriculum, and expectations for the students. Parents and students must sign an agreement that students will attend after-school sessions as necessary, and struggling students are required to attend summer school designed to assist their individual needs. The curriculum is demanding and has several aspects that are unique to these schools. Besides having a 1:1 laptop program, students know from the beginning of their time at STEM Academy what rules and regulations are in effect. The middle school students wear uniforms, and there are no bells in either of the buildings. Students and teachers understand and follow the daily schedules. In addition to the regulations, all students quickly learn the habits that are expected of them in each classroom. For example, all middle school teachers

Table 8.1. Example of informational chart found in each classroom

Refocus	How to Avoid College Prep
Talking in the hallways	Make sure to have all things required during morning check
Any type of food, gum, candy in the school	
	Bring all supplies to class
Being late to school twice in a week	Bring IRB/Lit Circle book to all classes
	Be sure to place MLA heading on assignments
Being late to class once in a week	Make sure all assignments are neat, legible, and complete
Inappropriate language	Organize binders, backpack, locker, and other materials
Inappropriate behavior	
	Come to CP prepared with all materials and be sure to complete all assignments correctly during CP

use the terminology SLANT to remind students to: Sit up straight, Lean toward the speaker, Activate your thinking, Nod in agreement, and Track the speaker. Students enter and leave the classroom in an orderly manner and know where they should be at all times, even without bells. Over half of the students use public transportation to attend STEM and thus, if they stay late for a Refocus, CP, or an after-school club meeting, they have to arrange their own way home. Overall, the staff reiterated to us in many ways that students and their families have to want to be part of this school when they apply.

Every student is assigned to an advisory group of about 12 students and one teacher. A typical day begins with a meeting of the advisory group where it is the responsibility of the teacher leader to check that all homework is completed and that students have their materials and any other requirements ready for the day. Furthermore, the advisory teacher is also the person who interacts with the families of students in his or her advisory family, and with other teachers if a problem arises.

When students are suspended, they are held accountable for the academic work they miss, have to write a formal apology, make a public apology at a schoolwide meeting, and ask for admittance back into the community. Students are very involved in monitoring their school's norms and expectations, and someone might say publicly to a fellow student, "You know, you have been up here too many times, and I don't think this is real and perhaps you really need to think about what you are doing and why before you come back into the community."

It is also very important to recognize that every student has a rigorous, integrated, and personalized plan to succeed; there is no remedial track at STEM Academy. Every student completes the same core curriculum, or a challenge course in each subject, and overall the curriculum exceeds what is required to enter any 4-year, post-secondary institution in this state. In fact, on the website for STEM Academy it states clearly that the curriculum is designed to ensure that all students will meet state standards in math, science, and English and that every student will earn acceptance to and graduate from a 4-year college. Therefore, students who fail a quiz or test, or who just need extra support receive mandatory teacher tutoring. In general, all subjects are evaluated against the most rigorous of standards; for most content they use the ACT college-readiness standards, especially for math and English, and they continue to explore the best standards for science and history.

Student schedules are also unusual for a typical middle or high school. At the middle school, each student's schedule is designed to provide what that learner needs. Because they enter via a lottery, many students may arrive without strong academic skills, which must be remedied. We heard many times that if a student is not succeeding, it is the school's responsibility. The school does not blame the student in any way. Further, if a student arrives with an Individualized Education Program (IEP), then the administrative team determines how to best serve that student in getting the skills he or she needs up to speed.

The high school also has a strict set of requirements for its students; for example, physics is taught in 9th grade, chemistry in 10th grade, and biology or earth science in 11th grade, so that by 12th grade they can take either physics and engineering or biotechnology. Furthermore, every student has to pass precalculus to graduate. Because the goal is for all students go to a 4-year post-secondary institution, and many students enter not believing they can possibly go to college (interview with the high school principal, 2011), one of the requirements for all 9th-graders is to research and identify four colleges or universities they might want to attend. Additionally, all 9th-grade students spend 1 day on the state university campus and actually work on an engineering activity. In fact, there is an entire department at STEM Academy that assists students and their parents in understanding the process of applying to and paying for college, finding scholarships, and celebrating success. Other examples of unique academic requirements include:

- Senior projects—a capstone experience over 2 semesters in which students identify and investigate an issue, create a product of some sort, and then present it to a panel of experts. One teacher explained, "Many schools have their students do a senior project but here it is close to the way it is done in independent schools. All students do it and unlike other places, a supported core class is devoted to it."

- Eleventh-grade internship—all 11th-grade students must participate in an internship on Tuesday and Thursday afternoons; typically these internships are completed at a nonprofit or at another organization. Prior to the beginning of the internship, students go through a Junior Achievement program to learn how to act and what to expect. STEM also provides training for the organizations willing to take STEM interns so they are prepared for working with the students and understand the requirements and responsibilities on both sides of the arrangement. The students must then document what they learn.

Teachers at STEM Academy

One thing both the middle and high school leaders agree on is hiring of the best possible individuals to staff the schools; it is common to have national searches for administrators and faculty. By many measures, the faculty and administration are highly qualified and hardworking; many teachers have followed alternative paths to licensure and a large number come from the ranks of Teach for America. One newly hired teacher knew of STEM, and had actually taught summer school here. However, he still needed to go through three interviews and staff members actually traveled to his previous location to observe him for a day. Most members of the faculty are available before and after school to work with students who are not performing well; there are English and math seminars that take the place of electives for students needing extra support; and there is a mandatory tutoring program for students who are struggling.

Hiring excellent teachers is a good first step, but supporting them takes a purposeful plan of action. One first-year teacher reported receiving the type of support that seems ideal. She said, "I meet at least once a week with my head of school or department head, and I have had the opportunity to observe a lot of excellent teachers." STEM educators explained to us that they are evaluated using a "360-degree" model. This means that a peer, the department head, the dean of the school, and sometimes the head of the school all provide significant feedback. They also use surveys to get feedback from students. One new teacher explained that in his previous school he was given high ratings and considered to be an exemplary teacher, but he knew that this was not really accurate. He wanted to really improve his practice and become a great teacher. He stated: "The system here really helps push my practice further." When he sat down for his first review the feedback was very clear and included definable things he could improve. He explained it was "[t]his and this is good but let's talk about what can be improved." He said that he also received an email with a rubric of clear expectations for teaching at STEM, and for each item below a certain level the observer had included detailed recommendations. It is worth noting that our interview took place in February of his first year and by then he already had three formal (and many informal) reviews; of the formal ones, two were observations of 45 minutes (half of a class period) and one was for a complete 90-minute class period. This teacher stated that he really appreciated the high expectations and accountability for teachers and students at STEM.

In general the teachers reported that the "leadership supports you as a teacher" and they provided several examples of this. A humanities teacher explained,

> In a traditional school as a humanities teacher, I might be responsible for a hundred and forty students but here it is broken up so that they hired two people and I am responsible for about sixty-five. It is a big difference. Grading load, catering to my students, I don't think I could do it with that many.

The teachers also described the ways in which schoolwide systems outside of the classroom support their efforts. For example, everyone knows the rules about doing homework or discipline; as one teacher reported,

> It is all known that it is not my job to chase down a student and try to make them do something. It is clear and known that I just send an IM [instant message] to the director, that student is notified, and the homework is done. Our job and focus is on teaching.

Another teacher stated that he might not be the one supervising the College Prep or Refocus that he assigned a student, so the student does not feel singled out by one teacher. "My relationship with the student is important and preserved," he explained.

While the goal at STEM Academy is to teach in a rigorous manner and to maintain strong accountability, teachers state that "To back that up we must support the students. So students in my family [advisory] come to tutoring with me every Thursday." Students are also supported in succeeding in many other ways. Teachers explained that every lesson has three levels of differentiation, as does every homework assignment. One said that even seats in the classroom are differentiated. "It would be hard to meet the expectations if we did not do the back work to support the students." Everyone expressed the view that in order to accomplish this, no one person has all the answers—that much can be learned from others.

The middle school head described the process for finding good teachers, interviewing them, and then giving them what they need. For example, he talked about the year he spent planning the school and visiting a remarkable school in New Jersey where their math scores are the top in the entire state. He was impressed and so, "The first thing I did, I hired my two math teachers, I told them to take two days off, meet me in Newark and we just hung out at the back of the classrooms, just so that we could take whatever their matriculation was and play that through in our school."

Leadership Practices

The leadership teams at the middle school and high school work together but also have their individual goals and styles. They see their role as helping maintain the culture and expectations of the school, doing this in positive ways, and doing things that enable the teachers to do their job in the classroom. The middle school head explained his philosophy of leadership:

> You know, I think leadership style is really important to consider. Like, I don't micromanage anybody. I don't come in with a clipboard and

say, Hey, these aren't on the walls and da, da, da; you want people to own any issues academically, own interventions, own culture . . . and building in time for those, right. Like, our teachers will sit down every week and say, Hey, we have a problem with a seventh-grade girl bullying, how are we going to address it? It's not me telling them, you all need to fix this problem. It's, like, they're going to be reflective enough to know that. And also, I want to empower them to fix it, because really, if I came down, I'm going to fix it at a seven out of ten. If people—enough people are buying, it's going to—the dividends are going to be higher.

At the high school, the current head previously had been a classroom teacher at STEM, the head of his department, and dean of students, and is now serving as the principal. He stated, "But I felt like I knew what made us successful. I've tried not to change the things that have made us successful, but I've tried to add kind of my vision and my leadership around instruction and other things." He also recognizes his strengths, and draws on others in their areas of capability to support the school's mission. He said, "But I think my expertise and my passion is instructional leadership, and so that's what I spend more time on than other things. And then I leverage our deans and other people to do maybe more of the cultural heavy lifting." He summed up the focus of the school by stating,

But I think the other reason is that they [our students] actually really are prepared to succeed other places because of what we have taught them and what they have learned. They go somewhere else and whether it's easy, whether the rigor is easier, or whether just the circumstances have changed and they have a fresh start, and maybe they have a little bit less homework. I mean, I think there are some of those structural issues that also conspire to help them. But I think in general they're also just, they were prepared here, and they realized what it took and what it means to study and do your homework and learn and really be prepared, and they ultimately were successful. And I think that's good.

Overall, the focus of the school is on the team, according to the high school principal. He embodies distributed leadership in the sense of how individual strengths and abilities are used. He stated,

[Our success is due to] the incredible team we have. It's not me. It's not one person, or role, or another, next door. . . . It's all of them and it's all of us, but it's every person. I mean, you know, it's the history teacher doing things at an absolutely outstanding level, and it's the math teacher who, you know, writes an assessment totally different for struggling ninth-graders, and then there's, you know, the Level I assessment where the questions are scaffolded much clearer in the first trimester so that those students who are having a really hard time adjusting to the ninth grade have ultimately a chance to pass or be close to passing that first trimester so that second trimester maybe they're farther into the game.

Assessment System and Uses of Data

From the first moment of our visit it became apparent that the use of data is a hallmark of STEM Academy. One of the primary uses of technology is to support schoolwide assessments and to help teachers efficiently analyze and act on weaknesses found in the data so they can design lessons to address them. The first day of our visit was the second of 2 days without students at the end of the second trimester. During these teacher workdays everyone was focused exclusively on the analysis of second-trimester data, reflection on the progress of students as groups but also as individuals, and planning for ways to improve practice and encourage the students to understand their strengths and areas of needed improvement. On the following day, when students returned to their classes, we observed many teachers spending the first part of the period sharing data from both individual and class assessments, discussing areas of needed remediation, setting goals and establishing priorities for the third trimester, and also celebrating their success and progress. Such systematic and almost daily review of data is highly valued at this school, and very important to all the teachers. One chemistry teacher stated:

> Some places in public schools looking at data is scary, and evaluative, so that if your kids don't do well, it is that you are a bad teacher. But here, because we look at it all the time and it is part of the process, no one gets mad at you if your data is not good; it is just a starting point.

Another science teacher explained, "In my feedback, I was not being transparent enough in my use of data, or was not having data drive my instruction enough." As a result, he came up with a way to display the data from regular assessment using a whiteboard, and provided feedback to everyone in the class quickly. Now he says,

> The students and I now know exactly what we are doing and how we are doing. I will keep hitting the three standards we were low on;

every day we give them a quick assessment. I take data from bigger assessments but also daily assessments.

Another teacher stated, "I've learned more about education in the six or seven months working here than I did in the seven years previously. Just about their use of data, has taught me a lot." Yet another teacher reported, "I came from another school where the use of technology was only for attendance and report cards, so this is very different where we look at data deeply." She went on to explain that trying to use data takes a lot of time to really drill down, but she feels that now she has the time to do this.

Many students also track their data on a daily basis in the data tracker. As one science teacher explained,

> For example, a unit six data tracker has all the activities, lessons, and standards for each unit. Students look at their levels for a particular standard, code it [green for ninety percent, yellow for seventy to ninety percent, etcetera] and they follow how they are doing. So, I might say, turn and tell your partner everything you know about standard six point three, for example. For a unit review, I can do a differentiated unit review for what each student needs to revisit; so it is really student-driven and there are no surprises.

Technology and Technology Support

When STEM opened its doors with a ubiquitous computing environment, thanks to a technology company's donation and grant of computers and related equipment worth about $1 million, it was the first public high school in this state where every student was provided with a wireless, networked personal computer. Every classroom in both the middle school and the high school also has an interactive whiteboard and data projection system. When the middle school opened, there were computer carts for the 6th-, 7th-, and 8th-grade students. However, since then the leadership for STEM has realized they have a funding conundrum; so STEM Academy is working toward having a cloud computing environment in the near future. In this way, all data, software, and support systems will reside on the Internet rather than on individual computers and servers in the building, which will save money and ensure that all schools, students, and educators are using the same state-of-the-art technology.

The director of technology told us, "I'm responsible for everything that plugs into a wall that doesn't cook or cool food," and his role is expanding daily. He originally came from industry and high-technology companies, but now loves the school and his role supporting its mission. As the director of technology, he actually works directly "with school directors to ensure assessment, data analysis, instructional practice, and alignment of the curriculum." He explained that it is not acceptable for an outage to occur during school time because students may miss an entire class period. The demands are quite extensive, "more than most companies. . . . So everything has to just stay up and the network is designed that way." He also explained the unique aspects of the original STEM campus with respect to technology support, which includes sharing help desk and other personnel. "The standard school model seems to be to pay a teacher a stipend to also do that. It wouldn't work in this environment. . . . I would rather have another teacher in a classroom than spend twice as much on my IT guys," he stated.

To help with costs, STEM collects an "insurance" premium of $150 a year from each student's family and then charges for damages when something breaks, sort of like a deductible that varies for different types of damage. If students damage a keyboard, families pay $25 to replace the keyboard, but the actual fees are based on what is broken and on what the family can pay. The director of technology explained, "We spend the summer reconditioning the computers and then we deploy a new image at the beginning of each year. We use Windows deployment services for all of it, and have five different images because at any time we have five different types of computers."

STEM Academy has experienced challenges in finding an appropriate and rigorous learning management system (LMS). The schools now use Promethean's ActivProgress as well as "Compass, an in-house tool that's really a Swiss army knife in our environment" and they would like to develop their own systems.

While teachers make most of the decisions regarding which software, websites, or other technology applications will serve their own and their students' needs, the administration has made some of the decisions at that level. For example, teachers talked fondly about the previous LMS, although they recognized that eventually the new one might prove to be more appropriate for all the data analysis they and their students do. The director of technology for STEM further explained:

> The one advantage that Learning Cube has is they have Promethean behind them and, I mean, they are the five-hundred-pound gorilla in any of the education technology aspects just overall. But they still don't even get it because they look at it that they've got this website with three million users who then go download things for their boards. What they [the producers of the Learning Cube] don't understand is that a fifteen-minute glitch of that website has zero effect on their customer base [in businesses]. A fifteen-minute glitch

that stops digital proctoring from occurring shuts the classroom down and you've lost a class period.

Teaching and Learning

Although some uses of computers are mandated at STEM Academy, for the most part it is department chairs, teachers, and students who decide how, when, and where to use the laptops. The STEM view of educational technology as described on its website is:

> Technology should empower and enable, and never replace or reduce the central human role of the teacher in a liberal arts education. The role of a liberal arts education is to enable and facilitate the creation of leaders who value community, individuals and the creation of a truly human society. Technology must serve this end.

Teachers all have a tablet or laptop computer, and are encouraged to start each lesson with a "hook," which is often a video clip, a piece of software, or other technology, but they are not required to do so. They are, however, encouraged to make sure that students are actively involved with the content, perhaps following an outline, or using the response systems, or another program; and each lesson must have some measure of accountability, often several times during the 90-minute class session. However, according to the director of curriculum, there is still room for improvement:

> Many teachers have become exceptional at using the technology for assessment and have learned to use a video as a hook to engage learners, but the other uses of the technology for curricular enhancement and to differentiate still have a way to go. Some teachers are doing really well taking advantage of the affordances of the technology; for example, math classes often use Geometer Sketchpad, and science classes often use Probeware.

Professional Development

Professional development (PD) and the unique culture at STEM Academy is not just something to which teachers pay lip service; rather, both PD and school culture are purposeful and intentional foci of the governing board, the administrators, and the teachers. Several teachers mentioned the annual retreat where they discussed planning, environment, and culture, and where teachers have a chance to get to know one another both personally and professionally. Teachers commented to us that while some schools have a few days of preparation for a new school year, at STEM this takes 2 full weeks, and they are paid for this additional time. Also, it should be noted that new 6th-graders get a summer orientation, half days for 5 weeks, to learn about STEM's systems and culture along with learning some science content by using experimental methods.

Beyond getting everyone ready for a new school year, in-house PD by and for teachers is taken seriously at STEM. New teachers receive additional training before school begins, as well as after school every 6 weeks, so they can learn how the culture and systems work, as well as how they can use data to guide their planning and teaching. Some years, a book is selected to focus the professional development for the year. In 2010 it was *Teach like a Champion* (Lemov, 2010). Everyone read and discussed this book and made it a priority to integrate the suggestions made by Lemov. In 2009, *Brain Rules* by John Medina was selected. Several individuals mentioned that these two books are used now by everyone to guide instruction and environment. In addition, teachers told us that they provide PD for one another in addition to that offered by members of the leadership team, and teacher sharing is a regular event at meetings. In addition, a new rubric for the evaluation of the teachers' practice was created to provide feedback to teachers and to assist them in improving their practice. Further, as attested to earlier, teachers at STEM Academy do not seem to feel threatened by the careful and constant review of their students' data or of their teaching practice, which for them serves as an individualized form of professional development. In fact, they readily explained to us the types of internal support they get as part of the school's focus on data analysis and student outcomes. One new teacher stated,

> I have friends who are also in their second year and they have two days without students but it is all spent catching up. Our time without students is spent in planning ahead, examining our data, and working together to improve practice.

Noteworthy Outcomes

By all accounts, STEM Academy has been successful at meeting its goals. For example, based on the district's performance framework from 2008, STEM was the only high school rated as "distinguished." The 11th-grade students at STEM averaged a 3.75 point pre-post gain on their ACT tests during an 8-month period, and 100% of STEM's first graduating class of seniors were accepted into 4-year colleges or universities, a remarkable result that has continued. STEM Academy graduates also have the second lowest level of remediation needed at colleges in this state. Over 1,000 students applied to the lottery for 140 seats in the next 6th-grade class at STEM. Given the diversity of the population at STEM, and the reality that large proportions of its students are first-generation college students, this school takes notable pride in these results and is clearly a school that many students want to attend.

However, some students do leave because the rigor of STEM is not right for them, although this is not frequent. The middle school head stated:

> I don't like to lose kids, because if we lose kids, we're not doing our job. It is one thing if you lose kids because the family moved to California. It's another thing, like, if it's a fit issue, like, if it's a fit issue, that's our fault, not the kid's.

Just as losing students is considered unfortunate, this individual did not like to have teachers leave, "But I don't lose teachers. I think if you lose teachers, you either don't hire well or you don't work hard to keep them." However, many teachers at STEM do move up in the organization to take other positions, or they move into the management of the organization, rather than leaving the school system.

As we conducted our study many respondents were discussing the coming school year because the new 9th-grade class starting in the fall would have gone through their entire middle school years at STEM Academy, and the expectation was that these students would excel beyond any previous group of students. In fact, with these students ready to enter the high school, the curriculum was already being revised because many of the students will have had some of the courses prior to entering the high school. So, for example, precalculus has been a graduation requirement to date, but that will need to be "bumped up," which is a very exciting prospect for all the administrators and teachers, one they consider to be both a success and a challenge.

Challenges

Individuals we interviewed expressed to us their excitement as well as the challenges of reaching the goal of opening more STEM schools; while some things benefit from economies of scale, others may stretch the limits of what can be accomplished in the ways they want it to work. For example, finding and preparing expanded numbers of teachers and administrators is an ongoing requirement, so it is a challenge to be constantly recruiting high-quality people and then getting them socialized into the expectations and the culture of STEM Academy. In addition, salaries are not as high as they should be compared to other schools and for the long workday expected of STEM teachers.

A related challenge that teachers mentioned had to do with work-life balance issues. Many young teachers were starting their careers at STEM, and for now they saw this as a wonderful place to work. A few did mention, however, that as they began to establish their families this may prove to be too demanding a place to work.

Other ongoing challenges include aligning the curriculum with various sets of standards across grades 6–12, providing literacy support for students who need it, and meeting the needs of the students who come to STEM with IEPs. Some students and teachers told us they would also like to see more opportunities to include the arts in the curriculum. Some teachers also expressed the need for more technology support for those who are not as ready or confident as others to integrate the laptops into their teaching. For example, not everyone is using the interactive whiteboards as interactively as they could, and this is primarily because they are not yet comfortable. They said they worry, "If this stops working in the middle of the class, how do I restart it?"

Challenges at the CMO level are related to expanding STEM to eventually include five campuses. These challenges include moving to cloud computing, finding and hiring good administrators and teachers, and fund-raising, which is a necessity for STEM, as it is for most charter schools.

Lessons Learned: Key Factors for Success

There are many things to be learned from STEM Academy because it has been extremely successful in meeting the goals it established as part of its charter. Further, we believe that many of these lessons are useful for public, public charter, and private schools that also want their graduates to be college ready. Because this school's mission, culture, structure, instructional strategies, uses of technology, focus on assessment data, and professional development are both unique and palpable, there is much to glean from STEM Academy. Therefore, based on our interviews with administrators and teachers (N=13) and classroom observations (N=12), these are the lessons we think are valuable to share:

- Having a clearly articulated mission and vision to work toward in order to establish specific goals, and working toward them every day in every way, are two lessons learned from this case. Planning and being forward thinking is another lesson learned from STEM Academy that we also recognized in other schools and districts.
- The leadership in this school believes student diversity is a positive, and that never giving up on a student is a virtue. In order to fulfill these values and achieve their mission, the

lesson learned from this case is that schoolwide expectations must be clear, owned, and demonstrated by all—teachers, students, parents, and school leaders. Further, public display of these values and mission is an important acknowledgement of their importance.

- From this case we learned that to achieve the mission and vision of your school you have to construct systems for everything—school culture, expectations for behavior, structure and pacing of lessons, assessments, use of data, graduation requirements, etcetera. Then you have to revisit your systems annually to make them work better each year, and you have to continue to question everything so that every detail (culture, programs, space, uniforms, rules, time, etc.) is well thought out and fits the goals of the school.

- To make these systems work, you have to be strategic at all times, especially with networking and hiring. You have to find the best and the brightest teachers, and you have to connect with and build relationships among all constituents—students, teachers, staff, and parents.

- To continue to develop your staff, you have to do regular observations and provide honest, constructive, usable feedback. For example, this school uses 360-degree evaluations that are consistent, repeated, and supported by peers, department chairs, and administrators. Further, feedback comes with support to make necessary improvements. And this school also builds in time during teacher workdays to discuss assessments and revise teaching plans.

- Professional development at this school is kept relevant by keeping it in-house, and nearly all of it occurs during regular school hours. With regard to technology PD, this school uses in-house videos to share what teachers are doing with technology in their classrooms.

- With regard to technology infrastructure, this school has spent a lot of time finding the right learning management system (LMS) to support the level of assessments and data analysis they need. Also, this school standardized the type of computers, operating systems, and software that is in use on the laptops that were provided by the school. However, like some other schools we visited, this school is moving to cloud computing to reduce costs and minimize downtime.

- Most of the learning principles used at this school are based on brain-based learning. For example, the content of the curriculum is spiraled; therefore, the content standards in the curriculum are revisited and retaught throughout the year in order to consolidate earlier learning. Teachers plan and teach in several short-time segments within the larger block of time for each content area in order to keep students focused. Teachers also incorporate lots of visuals in their lessons, and almost always use technology in some way. The pacing of lessons is very brisk and there is no downtime. Teachers also plan for and offer numerous opportunities for students to interact with one another in class daily, and they assess knowledge in every class every day in some way, using what they call "mastery checks." They then give students nearly immediate feedback following these numerous formative assessments.

- Assessment data are used by teachers to plan for remediation and reteaching weeks, as well as for differentiating assignments and homework, especially during reteaching weeks.
- Another lesson learned is that a set of core values is as important as the content that is being taught. In this case, the fact that 100% of the students and staff live by the mission of the school is an important lesson related to the success of this school. Those core values are respect, responsibility, integrity, doing your best, courage, and curiosity.
- This school has a unique, consistent, and palpable culture that is manifested in the school's goals and core values. For example, being willing to take responsibility for one's own learning, because they (both teachers and students) understand the rationale and purpose behind this value is a lesson worth aspiring to achieve because of the school's success. Part of this culture is never giving up on a student, which is supported, for example, by providing teacher-advisors for small groups of students called "families" and also by celebrating successes on a regular basis (another lesson we learned in many other cases).
- Related to both culture and the curriculum, in this school both students and teachers track their progress on meeting specific objectives in each course. Academic achievement is assessed daily and weekly, as well as at the end of each trimester. Students are provided with feedback nearly immediately following assessments (a benefit of a robust LMS), which provides valuable information that is authentic and unambiguous about ways for both teachers and students to improve.

- Part of the classroom teaching culture of this school also includes using a variety of classroom management strategies to get and keep attention. In addition, the schedule for each period of a class is on the board for students to see and teachers to follow, and students are reminded how much time they have to complete each task during a lesson. Again, the brisk pace in every class is reflected in the schedule to keep students on task through the period.

- To support the rigorous curriculum at this school, students receive tutoring and other forms of extra help every time it is needed. If they do not complete homework or need to be corrected in class for inattentiveness, they receive mandatory time [as remediation] after school, which they and their parents agree to when they matriculate to this school. The school also adjusts schedules for needed remediation during the day for students with IEPs, as well as to make time for internships and senior projects.

- Because every student at this school is prepared to attend a 4-year college, helping students access information about applying to and paying for specific colleges begins in 9th grade. This serves as both a motivator and a reality check for students and their parents, and is also another example of the value placed in this school on building relationships among students, teachers, staff, and parents.

CHAPTER 9

The Value of Partnerships
The Case of New Tech High School,
Napa Valley Unified School District, CA

"If not us, then who? If not now, then when?" –Goethe

This is the case of a small high school with over 15 years of experience with 1:1 laptops, project- and problem-based learning (PBL), and a unique curriculum that includes mostly interdisciplinary and co-taught courses purposefully designed to prepare all students for work and life in the 21st century. This site was selected for several reasons, including the fact that it received top state honors as one of California's Distinguished Schools in 2009, and because it is the original site for a specific model of secondary education that has been replicated over 60 times across the nation. In fact, across this network of schools, 98% of its graduates are accepted to at least one post-secondary institution.

This small high school of about 400 students in grades 9–12 started by providing desktop PCs for every student, and today the wireless network supports 450+ laptops being used daily for research, communication, collaboration, writing, analyzing and manipulating data, and creating final projects for PBL units that are the core of the interdisciplinary curriculum. Most students bring their own laptops to school, but about 120 netbooks are loaned out for $8 per month to students who can't afford to buy their own laptop. This school uses a custom-built learning management system to keep the environment as paperless as possible, and to track student performance, among other things. Due to the expense of sustaining a 1:1 program, when a new high school was built in this district, money was put into infrastructure, providing wireless access, and cloud computing so that the students could bring and use whatever computer devices they owned–PC or Mac laptops, netbooks, iPads, iPods, etcetera. They call this the college model.

As we were escorted around New Tech High School's relatively new Leadership in Energy and Environmental Design (LEED) gold-certified building in Napa, California, we couldn't help but be impressed by how knowledgeable our two student guides were about their school building, as well as about the school's curriculum, core values, and culture. They were obviously very proud of their school, and we were impressed by their poise and willingness to answer our questions with complete candor. As these two students explained some of the many "green" features of the building, they also told us that students had been on the planning committee for their newly renovated building and worked with the architects to make the school functional for them as well as energy efficient and sustainable. One thing they told us that they really fought for was the open commons area that is the heart of the building and where we saw many students gathered together in small groups or working on their own—all with their laptops open. Our guides told us these students were either working on group projects for a class or were doing independent studies. They also told us proudly that any student in their building could walk away from their computer, or leave their backpack anywhere in the school, and it would still be there the next day. With their school's motto being "trust, respect, and responsibility," this was an example that told us they really lived their motto and that this was a unique high school with a strong sense of student stewardship.

As we observed various classes through large plate-glass windows that allowed us to see entire classrooms from the commons area, we were amazed at the size of the rooms and the many activities going on in each one. We knew that this school, the original of all the New Tech High Schools, used project-based learning as its main pedagogy, so we didn't expect to see students passively listening to teachers lecture. However, we hadn't envisioned what it might look and sound like in a room with 50–60 students and two teachers. As we stepped inside several classrooms, the atmosphere looked and sounded like a think tank with no cubicles where everyone was interacting in teams. In almost every room we entered the students were clustered around tables and either standing or sitting in office-style chairs with wheels and high backs. Most students either had their computers open or were looking at a classmate's computer screen. Our guides explained that it takes a little time for freshmen to get used to working in groups all the time, but they also assured us that their teachers were always there to guide and help students learn to resolve conflicts that might arise. However, the guides also told us that there are team leaders for each project and team norms are established by each group for each project. We also observed that the teachers had learned strategies for managing large groups, such as using a microphone when they needed everyone's attention for something or holding small workshops for students who may need to dive deeper into specific topics.

Context

New Tech High School (NTHS) in Napa, California, was established in 1996 to meet the goals of community leaders in business and education for a new kind of school to prepare students for work in the 21st century. Some of the main features of this small high school, which currently serves about 400 students in grades 9–12, include integrated use of technology in every class, using project-based learning to deliver the curriculum, and students working collaboratively in a school culture based on trust, respect, and responsibility. Napa's New Tech High School is a school of choice, but not a charter school, that draws students from more than five high schools in Napa County. One hundred students, 50 boys and 50 girls, are selected annually by lottery for each class. The NTHS principal told us they had just admitted 108 students from a pool of 150 applicants for their next freshman class.

Students attending Napa New Tech are ethnically diverse, increasingly low income (about 33% qualify for free or reduced meals, up from 12.5% just a few years ago), and about 50% will be first-generation college students. About 44% of the students are ethnically diverse—22% Hispanic or Latino, 12% of mixed race, 5% Filipino, 3% African American, 2% Asian—with the remaining 54% reporting as White. At the time of this study both the principal and the part-time assistant principal had been at NTHS for 3 years. The principal, an experienced administrator, told us he always seeks to make important decisions by consensus, believes in continuous improvement, and models distributed leadership. Before coming to Napa New Tech, he had been a teacher and assistant principal and had opened another New Tech High School in Sacramento, California. The assistant principal had been a middle school teacher before going into administration.

The Napa Valley Unified School District (NVUSD), of which NTHS is a part, is comprised of 32 schools located on 28 sites serving approximately 17,000 students in grades K–12. There are three large, comprehensive high schools in NVUSD, and one alternative high, plus New Tech. There are also six middle schools and 20 elementary schools in this district, which has a mix of small-town, suburban, and rural housing. In recent years NVSUD has seen several superintendents come and go, and the district has been mandated for school improvement based on low test scores for the past 4 years

due to about a third of the schools not meeting standards. The current superintendent is very supportive of NTHS and is committed to expanding this
model to other schools in the district. Future plans by the NVUSD for such
expansion are based on an initiative called SC21 (see Student Centered 21st
Century at www.sc21napa.org) and the added support of a new foundation
that is a collection of interested educational and business partners, NapaLearns, at http://napalearns.org. The goal of NVUSD and these organizations
is to expand PBL and technology integration into all the K–12 schools in
Napa Valley so that all students will be prepared for living and working in
the 21st century.

With support from the Bill and Melinda Gates Foundation to support the
replication of this innovative high school through the New Tech Network,
Napa's New Tech High School has grown from a once very small school of
about 200 students in 11th and 12th grades in 1996 to be one of the New
Tech schools in a network of 87 New Tech High Schools serving 9th- to 12th-
grade students in 16 states. Today NTHS, as it is known, is housed in a new
LEED gold-certified addition to its original footprint (a renovated elementary school) funded by a large local bond issue. This bond issue also provided funds to build American Canyon High School, a comprehensive high
school for about 1,400 students that will follow New Tech's model of using
interdisciplinary, technology-infused, project-based learning that promotes
collaboration among students and teachers.

Napa New Tech was selected for this study because it was the initial model
for all the New Tech High Schools across the country, because of its long history with ubiquitous technology use, and the fact that the New Tech model has
been replicated many times across the nation. Napa New Tech was also one of
only 261 middle and high schools to receive top state honors as one of California's Distinguished Schools in the spring of 2009, and it consistently makes
AYP. Napa New Tech is also an interesting case to include in our research
because of continued attention from organizations like the Gates Foundation,
the William and Flora Hewlett Foundation, and Carnegie, plus continued local
support from the business community in Napa Valley. And, the fact that Napa
New Tech High School has been in operation since 1996 makes it an exemplary case for what a 21st-century school can be.

Students at NTHS are taught by 16 fully credentialed, full-time teachers,
and one part-time, fully credentialed teacher. Teachers typically collaborate
to teach classes of 50–60 students in large rooms that easily allow group
work. For example, each grade has one English/Language Arts and one
history/social studies teacher who pair up to co-teach and integrate their
content standards. For example, 9th-graders take a global communications
class, which includes American literature and performance/public speaking; 10th-graders take World Studies, a class that combines world literature and world history; 11th-graders take American studies, which includes

American literature and American history; and 12th-graders take a political studies class that combines English, government, and economics. Science and math courses are also integrated in innovative ways, are co-taught, and are project- and/or problem-based. For example, a biology and a PE teacher co-taught a BioFitness class we observed, and the geometry and digital media teachers also co-taught in one large room. The Napa County Office of Education provides two instructors to teach the Regional Occupational Program (ROP) courses on campus, such as digital media; and Napa Valley Community College also offers courses on campus (e.g., high-level math courses like trigonometry and calculus, or psychology, advanced digital media, criminal justice, etc.), which is helpful because students must earn 12 college credits in order to graduate. As with most small high schools, sports and music programs are not offered, but students can and do join sports teams and take music or foreign languages at a nearby high school (other than Spanish, which is offered as an elective at New Tech). Art and drama courses are among other electives offered at New Tech.

Among the other graduation requirements at NTHS is the New Tech Professional Digital Portfolio, which is based on the school's learning outcomes rather than on test scores or the usual collection of resumes and work samples. This digital portfolio is started shortly after entering the school in 9th grade, and is web-based so that colleges and employers can view it. Another difference at Napa New Tech from most schools is that grades for projects and for all classes are based on eight student learning outcomes, including Technology Literacy, Citizenship and Ethics, Critical Thinking, Collaboration, Career Preparation, Written Communication, Oral Communication, and Curricular Literacy. Additional graduation requirements include a senior-year internship of at least 50 hours, as well as 20 hours of community service during junior year and 10 hours of school service during sophomore year. Scores on California's required tests, including the high school graduation test, are well above the district's and state's average in English/Language Arts, science, and history/social studies, but not in math. However, NTHS has made AYP every year.

School Culture and Climate

When Napa's New Tech High School opened in 1996 after a 4-year planning process, the vision was for a school that would prepare students for a technologically rich work environment that would require 21st-century skills, including communication and collaboration skills, problem solving and critical thinking, and innovation and creativity. The curriculum for this public, non-charter, small high school was designed to be interdisciplinary, project-based, and technology infused. Originally Napa New Tech was only for 11th- and 12th-graders, but was expanded in 2004 to include 9th- and

10th-graders. Today the school's culture, which is based on trust, respect, and responsibility between and among the staff and the students, is palpable. At Napa New Tech students, teachers, support staff, and administrators are constantly working together to improve themselves and their school. Walking around, one readily observes students and staff conversing respectfully with one another about projects they are working on and the things they are learning. You also see students taking excellent care of their environment in various ways, students being trusted to leave the building for lunch, and students self-monitoring as they work together in the commons area, knowing that classes are in session all around them. Students also told us stories about being able to leave their laptops and backpacks anywhere in the building and not worrying that they wouldn't be there when they returned, of going on a school field trip to a science museum and being trusted to be on their own until lunchtime, and of being in a school without cliques where everyone is friendly to one another, a by-product of working together in shifting groups on projects. One veteran teacher elaborated on what the students seemed to be telling us about their sense of ownership and pride in their school:

> The longer they have been here they come to own the school, or take ownership of the process here. They begin to have a certain pride because we've been trusting them all this time, and they feel an obligation to be trustworthy. So we have fewer problems as they go through, and they will, they'll say "knock it off" to the other students when they need it.

Students also talked about Freshmen Connection activities they are responsible for leading, which include every new student being assigned an older student as a mentor. Their teachers also talked about students doing a lot more peer tutoring given impending losses of staff due to budget cuts in the district. We witnessed a leadership class at Napa New Tech with over 30 students taking this elective, in which each student was engaged in planning and leading at least one school event or community-service project. These activities ranged from planning a school dance or a poetry slam to leading a fund-raiser for children with leukemia to planning a clean-up day at a local park. The two guides we described in the opening vignette for this case were members of this leadership class. There are also other electives like art, drama, critical thinking, current events, environmental science, literature and film, three levels of Spanish, video production, and yearbook, as well as after-school clubs at Napa New Tech that can be started by any student. In fact, the commons area at Napa New Tech is busy after school with student study groups and club meetings until the principal or assistant principal is ready to close up the building for the night.

Leadership Practices

The leadership at Napa New Tech is quite flat and distributed among the staff and students. As one teacher told us,

> We do have administrators but the relationship is much different from other schools. It is much more a flat hierarchy. It's not that we don't have different roles, but we all have a voice. And it's not just show, we really do have a voice. I feel really comfortable being honest with the administrators and I really feel as though they trust me as a professional. . . .

The principal told us that he believes in consensus building, but he does make some decisions about things such as building maintenance and the schedule for assemblies and testing without seeking consensus. He also makes some personnel decisions, but teachers told us they are very involved in the hiring of their co-teachers, in curriculum changes and course decisions, and in revising the school's learning outcomes. The principal described his views as follows:

> We're trying to make this the best school possible. We're the flagship for the New Tech Network, which now has eighty-seven schools. We're trying to be a district role model. We're trying to grow into becoming a center for teaching excellence, where we work on professional development. . . . The biggest issue is giving up control, which doesn't mean you don't have a say, it doesn't mean you're not involved. But you can't control everything. And a lot of times what you need to do is even—you don't think it's a good decision, or it's the right way to go, but you still have to try it. We've had a couple of those, but the reality is, if the—when you're working in consensus, it's a two-way street. I think some principals fail with consensus because it's consensus right up to the point where they don't get their way. . . . Leadership, now you have to give up that ultimate authority, that ultimate control. You have to persuade people and you have to have a way of building consensus and coalition.

As a consequence of their leader's style, everyone at NTHS feels that they have a voice, including the students. As described earlier, the students are trusted to lead all the tours for the thousands of visitors this school hosts from all over the world, including tours for the families of potential students, the press, potential funders, educators who want to see how New Tech works, and researchers like ourselves. The pride in the voice of these student leaders is palpable, and while students told us that they may have given up having a football team to root for, or a homecoming dance to attend in order to come to NTHS, they feel they have gained a strong work ethic, the ability to work with others, presentation skills, critical thinking, and ease with using technology as a learning tool. One of the best stories we heard about students' having a voice was shared by the NTHS principal, who told us what happened when the Napa Valley district superintendent came to New Tech recently:

> So we're rounding up students at the last second. So I grabbed everybody and people were going, "You're putting 'him' in there?" And I go, "Sure, what the heck, John's been here before, he knows the school." So this kid didn't say a word and finally John, the superintendent, said, "You haven't said a thing." And he goes, "Well, sir, you have to understand, I hate school. I just plain hate school, but this is by far the best school I've ever hated."

Implementation Process

As mentioned above, the leadership at Napa New Tech is distributed across the school among both staff and students, but this school is also supported by key personnel from several foundations and organizations described earlier: New Tech Network, NapaLearns, and SC21. These groups are all involved in the dissemination and advancement of the New Tech model of technology-infused, interdisciplinary, project-based learning to other sites. We interviewed one of the early principals of NTHS, Mark Morrison, who started up two different foundations to spread the New Tech model to other districts and is now working with the local K–12 schools to infuse the New Tech model into all schools in Napa Valley. Realizing early on the ongoing need to raise significant funds annually to support New Tech, Mr. Morrison, along with Scott Stewart, established a nonprofit group called New Tech Foundation, and soon received Bill and Melinda Gates Foundation funds to replicate and support this model across the country. A new superintendent came to Napa and started the Student Centered 21st Century (SC21) initiative to help teachers learn to do project-based learning in other high schools through professional development opportunities in NVUSD. This superintendent also shepherded through a very large bond issue that included funds for the new LEED-certified addition to New Tech High School and to build a large comprehensive high school, American Canyon High School, which will eventually have every student using laptops and learning with a project-based learning curriculum. Knowledge Works Foundation recently incorporated New Tech Foundation, after which it evolved into New Tech Network. Mark Morrison came back to NVUSD to try to sustain the goals of SC21 and infuse them into all K–12 classrooms in the district. Finally, similar to the original New Tech

Foundation, NapaLearns was recently established by the local business community, which includes many local wine growers and vintners, to involve all the public school districts in Napa Valley because they want to see all students prepared for work and life in the 21st century.

Curriculum and Assessment

The interdisciplinary curriculum at NTHS is innovative and never static. Teachers are always developing new projects and tweaking ones they have taught in previous years. The school's eight learning goals (Technology Literacy, Citizenship and Ethics [aka Work Ethic], Critical Thinking, Collaboration, Career Preparation, Written Communication, Oral Communication, and Curricular Literacy) are the criteria for how teachers assess each project they develop. Teachers select four to five of these outcomes, weigh them for each project, and develop detailed rubrics that they share with the students at the beginning of each project. For example, teachers might determine grades for a final project based on allocating 20% to work ethic, 10% to collaboration, 10% to critical thinking, 10% to written communication, 10% to oral communication, and 40% to mastering the content knowledge for a project that might last for 2 to 4 or more weeks and require both individual research and writing and group projects and presentations. The students submit their work and track their progress in a learning management system called ECHO, which is the learning management system developed by the New Tech Network for use in all 87 New Tech high schools around the country.

The students not only use ECHO to submit assignments and collaborate with one another; they use data from project assessments to set personal goals and try to improve themselves based on the scores earned and the feedback they receive on each of the learning goals. Examples can be seen on the students' digital portfolios located on the school's website (http://newtechhigh. org). For example, we noted that one student wrote the following under the learning goals section of his portfolio about citizenship and ethics: "I have an 80% work ethic. I work with my team members and get work done. I also do my individual work. I have done my school service hours and school service hours are when you do work for your school. Most of my hours have come out of helping our president in making a garden." Students at Napa New Tech are quite self-directed with regard to improving their percentages on each learning outcome, and some strive to earn more than 100% on some of their learning goals. In addition to the students, teachers, administrators, and parents are able to connect through ECHO, making this program available to the community instead of just a storage device for resources.

Of course, as with any high school student, those at NTHS also must take standardized tests annually. They take California Standardized Tests (CSTs) as well as the PSAT and the SAT. As mentioned earlier, Napa New Tech was one of 261 middle and high schools to receive top state honors as one of California's Distinguished Schools in 2009, so named by the California Department of Education. To qualify for this honor, schools have to exceed state and federal accountability measures and earn schoolwide standardized test score averages above 720. In addition, in order to qualify, schools must also show progress toward closing the achievement gap—a term used in California to describe discrepancies between the lower scores of the English learner (EL) population and the higher scores of their native English-speaking peers at their school. While only eight students at New Tech are currently identified as ELs, there are about 60 students who previously received ESL services and are on watch.

Despite good test scores, which seem to validate the efficacy of project-based learning for the teachers and students at NTHS, we also learned from the administration that 80% of New Tech students are finishing college, compared with a national average of less than 50%. However, the New Tech Network is equally concerned about meeting its own internal benchmarks, which include their own learning outcomes, having high attendance, and using student surveys, as well as using the National Student Clearinghouse (www.studentclearinghouse.org) and College and Work Readiness Assessment (www.cae.org/content/pro_collegework.htm) data, and the results of the Youth Truth Survey (youthtruthsurvey.org) as measures of success—at least until more robust computer-adaptive measures of critical thinking and other 21st-century skills are developed. In fact, the results of academic and other success indicators from all the New Tech High Network Schools around the country are very impressive. As cited in a report of their 2008–2009 data:

- In 2008–2009, 85% of the reported NT seniors applied to one or more colleges. Among these students, a total of 98% were accepted to at least one post-secondary institution. The acceptance rate for students who applied to a 2-year college was 100%, while the rate for those who applied to a 4-year college was 85%.
- NT schools displayed high rates of attendance and low dropout and suspension rates in 2008–2009. Overall, 26 of 28 NT schools (or 93%) had attendance rates between 90 and 100% in 2008–2009. Almost two-thirds of the NT schools had a 0% dropout rate across grades in 2008–2009. Only five schools had a rate of 1–2%, while three sites had a rate higher than 2%. Almost half of NT schools had a 2008–2009 suspension rate between 0 and 5%. An additional 40% of the schools had suspension rates between 6 and 10%.
- Results were analyzed from each NT school's reading, math, and science state tests. Proficiency or pass rates were compared

to comparison schools for 2008–2009 and 2007–2008. Reading achievement was strong at grade 9 but decreased somewhat in upper grade levels. Overall, 89% of NT schools outperformed the 9th-grade reading rates of their comparison sites. In contrast, slightly lower rates were evident in 10th- and 11th-grade reading—between 63 and 67% of NT sites surpassed comparison schools.

- In Algebra I, 50% of the NT schools surpassed comparison school rates. Also, 38% of NT sites outperformed comparison schools in Algebra II, while 43% did so in geometry.
- The majority of NT schools performed well in life science and biology and had lower achievement in chemistry. In life science and biology, NT schools outperformed comparison sites at high rates (75% and 69%, respectively).
- The majority of NT schools showed growth across multiple subject areas from 2007–2008 to 2008–2009. The highest growth rate was evidenced in life science, with 83% of NT schools demonstrating a higher proficiency rate over the 2-year period. The next highest rate was in geometry at 75%, followed by 10th-grade reading (67%), and chemistry (67%).

Technology and Technology Support

Since they have been using computers at Napa New Tech for over 15 years, both the teachers and students appear to use them naturally as a tool for teaching and learning, and everyone appears to be very tech savvy. When we asked teachers about how things are working now that every student is using their own personal computer, we didn't hear any concerns. In fact one teacher told us,

It's actually been working really well. . . . We used to have all desktops, and I much prefer them having their own laptops. There is much more personal responsibility for the equipment they are using, and they are much more careful. Obviously they own it, they answer to their parents. And they are better able to stay more organized by using one device.

She also told us that the biggest challenge is bandwidth. When a teacher wants the entire class to go to one web-based application, it makes the system run slowly, so they don't do this often. And although we did not see much paper at all around the school being used by teachers or students, which is an added "green" benefit of ubiquitous computing, we were told that they are still using textbooks as well as web-based resources.

Students carry their laptops around with them at all times because they use them to do research, to communicate, to collaborate, to write, to analyze or manipulate data, and to create final products and projects for the PBL units that are the core of the interdisciplinary curriculum in every class. Students are taught how to use new hardware and software in specific classes, such as Adobe Premiere in the Digital Media class, different kinds of probes and simulations in their science classes, and Geometer's Sketchpad in math class. They also learn how to evaluate sources found on the Internet in just about every class, because students are doing so much research. In fact, there is no longer a basic technology class offered for 9th-graders because they come in with more than basic skills, and they readily teach one another as needed. With their new learning management system, ECHO, teachers are using technology more and more to assess students, to evaluate and record the results of formative assessments, and students are using ECHO to track their progress on the learning goals as described earlier.

At NTHS the support for technology infrastructure, including the wireless network and all 450 laptops at Napa New Tech, is in the hands of one person who is the network administrator on site. All the computers have tracking devices in case of loss or theft, but this and serious hardware failures seem to be minimal. Of course, the network administrator has to keep all the servers running and the wireless hubs working so that at any given time all 450+ users in the building can be online or using the newest version of their learning management system (ECHO) developed by the New Tech Network. Most students bring their own laptops to school, but about 120 netbooks are loaned to students who can't afford their own for an $8 per month donation.

On a related point about technology support, Mark Morrison (former NTHS principal and now director of Secondary Education for NVUSD) told us in a phone conversation before our visit that they have figured out that the cost of providing laptops to each new group of entering students every year is prohibitive in today's economic climate. Therefore, in building American Canyon High School they put their money into infrastructure, providing wireless access and cloud computing, and told the students they could bring and use whatever handheld computer devices they owned—PC or Mac laptops, netbooks, iPads, iPods, etcetera. Students have to have OpenOffice or Microsoft Word installed on their devices, as well as Adobe Reader and Flash, but these kinds of programs come on computers you can buy at Walmart, or any other place students may buy them, and the programs can be downloaded for free.

This move to wireless and cloud computing and students using their own technology surprised us, given how many schools and districts around the country have selected particular computer models for their 1:1 initiatives. However, cloud computing and the use of personal computing devices seems to be working, and may be the future of schools and districts who want to maintain 1:1 computing. Of course, as in any 1:1 initiative, students need to be educated about the ethical use of computers and the Internet, and even at Napa New Tech and American Canyon (another school we visited, which will be discussed below), students are still not allowed to use their cell phones, which is a policy that the principals with whom we talked thinks will be changing very soon. As the NTHS principal said,

> We've not yet had the conversation with the staff about giving up control of cell phones and it's going to be tough, because they're still kids. They're incredibly social, who knows what the conversations and the texting will be about and especially in this environment, with these kids. They're so good at it [but] eventually those are going to force us to just deal with cell phones at all schools, because it's so much cheaper and more flexible. . . . It's just there and, you know, IT directors are going to have to deal with it. And the teachers will have to give up control of knowledge and to some extent, control of process, to give flexibility to kids. . . .

Professional Development

Throughout our time at Napa New Tech we actually heard very little talk about professional development (PD). In fact, PD for integrating technology into their classrooms was not mentioned by anyone during our visit to NTHS. However, we did hear about PD for problem-based and project-based learning, especially for newly hired teachers, and ongoing professional development related to the SC21 initiative, which we assume includes PD about technology integration into project-based learning. There also seemed to be a focus on differentiating instruction and using various assessments at the district level, but at NTHS it seems that much of their learning has been on the job and/or from their co-teachers over the past 15 years that they have had 1:1 computers/laptops at NTHS.

At the new American Canyon High School, which we also visited, learning to do project-based learning required most of the veteran teachers who were hired there to make adjustments in their typical teaching practices, including finding ways to integrate technology when students might be using a wide variety of personal computing devices. However, these teachers told us that they do get what they feel is adequate time and professional development about PBL through the SC21 initiative, and also through opportunities to visit Napa New Tech to see PBL in action. Furthermore, the format for professional development about PBL is always done using the PBL format, so teachers learned PBL by experiencing PBL themselves. In addition, some teachers get the opportunity to attend the New Tech Network conference held each year, or at least get the benefits when their project-based learning facilitator passes on new things.

Changes in Teaching and Learning

As mentioned previously, the curriculum at Napa's NTHS, and at all the New Tech high schools around the country, is interdisciplinary and project-based, and increasingly problem-based—especially in math classes. Project-based learning at NTHS was originally based on the pedagogy developed by the Buck Institute for Education (see BIE at www.bie.org), which defines project-based learning as an "extended process of inquiry in response to a complex question, problem, or challenge. Rigorous projects help students learn key academic content and practice 21st-century skills (such as collaboration, communication, and critical thinking)." In addition, BIE's website states that rigorous project-based learning includes the following features: (1) organizes around an open-ended driving question or challenge; (2) creates a need to know, practice, and apply essential content and skills; (3) requires inquiry to learn and create something new; (4) requires 21st-century skills such as critical thinking, problem solving, collaboration, and various forms of oral and written communication; (5) allows some degree of student voice and choice, which increases motivation and engagement; (6) incorporates feedback and critique from peers and teachers; and (7) results in a publicly presented product, project, or performance (www.bie.org/about/what_is_pbl). Nevertheless, the curriculum at NTHS is under constant revision because teaching partnerships have to be developed every time new teachers come on board or partnerships are reorganized for whatever reason.

One example of the creative mash-up of courses we saw at NTHS was the 9th-grade BioFitness class mentioned earlier, which is co-taught by a New Tech veteran biology teacher and a new PE teacher she helped select. This course combines the biology, health, and PE curriculum in ways that focus students on learning about what makes their bodies work and how to stay healthy. On the day we observed, students were very engaged in a lab about DNA, and displays of student work around the room made this look like a class that would be very relevant to students because they were literally learning about themselves. The biology teacher also teaches an elective environmental studies class, and we learned that every teacher either offers an elective or offers a reader's/writer's workshop class for students who are struggling and need additional instruction and tutoring more than they need an elective class like literature and film, international current events, or yearbook and publications. Interestingly, when we asked teachers what they were most proud of, several of them said that teaching a reader's/writer's workshop class is what they were most proud of because they make a difference for students in these classes, help them improve their literacy skills, and work on personal development with them at the same time.

We also observed another example of how the curriculum content is integrated and applied at NTHS in a class that combines geometry and digital media design. These classes are taught in the same large classroom, with desktop computers at one end and interactive whiteboards at both ends of the room. The two teachers in this room work hard to teach their curriculum in depth and to collaborate so that the students can digitally represent some of the geometry they are studying in a variety of multimedia design projects. Some of the results are visible on the walls and windows of the classroom in the form of cityscapes created by combining three-dimensional geometric shapes, tessellation patterns, and designs for stained-glass windows done in the style of Frank Lloyd Wright. These two teachers also told us they are learning and trying out studio-based learning and the Bauhaus method, and are now working with the support of a National Science Foundation grant to incorporate aspects of studio-based learning such as workflow and desk and peer critiques to further structure the cross-pollination of mathematics concepts and digital media. Given the compatibility of the studio model with NTHS's model of interdisciplinary, project-based, and technology-infused curriculum, the goal of these NTHS teaching partners to incorporate aspects of studio-based learning into their curriculum makes logical sense. See http://peoplelearn.homestead. com/Module_10.Studio.pdf for definitions, examples, and features of studio-based learning.

Algebra II and physics are also co-taught, as are all the humanities courses at each grade level. In the 11th-grade humanities class the students were currently working on projects about the roles of women and minorities in World War II, with the project being a pitch for a documentary series about one of these groups, thus combining the required American studies curriculum with American literature for whatever they are studying. A similar situation was happening in a 10th-grade humanities class we observed that combined world history and world literature while placing a heavy emphasis on reading, writing, and oral communication skills as the students engage in book club discussions, create projects together, and use their laptops for research, writing, and creating presentations to represent their learning. The 9th-grade humanities class we observed, which focuses on improving and polishing students' communication skills, was reading Steinbeck's *Of Mice and Men*. When we observed, the students were editing and practicing "reader's theater" scripts they had created to provide alternate endings for this book. We observed some groups still writing and some rehearsing before the teachers called the group together to review the criteria on the rubric for this project as it was projected on the interactive whiteboard. After this, several groups performed their reader's theater scripts and the teachers moderated a discussion of these alternative endings and feedback provided by their peers.

When discussing changes in teaching practices, as a result of being at NTHS and also at American Canyon High School, several teachers said that it took them years, maybe as many as 3 years, "to get the curriculum down" for each new project they developed. And, since new courses and new projects were always being developed because of new assignments and new teaching partners, they felt they were always learning, always trying to make the projects better, or always trying out new projects, all while still tweaking some of their favorite projects. Bottom line, teachers told us that project-based learning was time consuming but very rewarding because the students produced great work.

Besides the fact that developing good project-based learning units is time consuming, and that it requires more time when done collaboratively with a teaching partner, sometimes adequate materials and resources were constraining factors for teachers wanting to do certain projects. However, they usually found a way around the problems they encountered—as most teachers do. Also, every NTHS teacher had to learn to adjust to working with and teaching 50–60 students at a time, even when the space is adequate. In fact, they told us that they quickly learned that whole-class teaching must be kept to a minimum and developed strategies for times when they do need everyone's attention. For example, they developed "campfire" time when everyone needs to huddle up to listen to instructions, view a film, have a brainstorming session, or see something projected on the interactive whiteboard. Some teachers use handheld microphones available in every classroom when they need to make an announcement, and students sometimes use these when they make presentations to the whole group.

Despite making these kinds of adjustments, NTHS teachers quickly realized that teaching is not telling and that the process of learning is often more powerful for the students than some of their final products. And while they still see some students struggle with working in groups, they have learned that attention to shared group norms has to be made explicit for each project to work, so they include time for students to develop norms and measures of accountability to their groups for each new project. They told us that the payoff for teachers using project-based learning is increased student engagement, students learning to think and problem-solve, and amazing growth in students' oral and written communication skills because they have more authentic learning experiences.

Noteworthy Outcomes

The students at NTHS recognize both what they are getting from attending this kind of high school and what they are giving up. However, they told us in no uncertain terms that the advantages of attending this small high school, which is focused on preparing them for work and life in the 21st century, far outweigh any disadvantages. Also notable is the success of NTHS students on standardized tests and their college-going success rate. The fact that students continue to seek entrance to this school is noteworthy. Further, once they begin as 9th-graders, very few NTHS students change their mind, so a high percentage graduate 4 years later and 100% of the graduates go on to higher education of some kind.

Another noteworthy outcome of NTHS is that this model of education started in Napa has been replicated more than 90 times across the nation. Furthermore, this model has been recognized and supported financially by philanthropic foundations like the Bill and Melinda Gates Foundation, as well as by other partners of the New Tech Network that include Hewlett-Packard and the Carnegie Foundation. And thousands of visitors have made their way to NTHS in Napa to see how this model looks in action, which is both notable and a challenge to manage. However, in the spirit of the 21st-century skill of being entrepreneurial, the students and the leadership at NTHS are thinking about charging a fee for tours in the near future.

Challenges

From the perspective of teachers and administrators at Napa's New Tech High School, the biggest challenge is dealing with budget cuts for school districts in California that result in teachers and other important personnel either getting laid off or having their time reduced. Not more than a week after we visited, a disproportionate number of NTHS staff received pink slips because they were new to NVUSD, or because their jobs were not directly connected to classroom teaching. While some of these people will end up being able to stay at NTHS, the disruption and loss of morale affects everyone and potentially jeopardizes being able to continue some of the key features of this school. And while budget and personnel issues are a problem throughout the public education system in the United States, it feels like small schools and districts, including places like NTHS where teachers all co-plan and co-teach their classes, are disproportionately affected because there are fewer degrees of freedom.

At the new American Canyon High School the challenge of budget cuts is also salient, as is getting all teachers on board with project-based learning and using it as the foundation of their curriculum because many teachers were forced transfers from other schools due to enrollment imbalances. This also means it is challenging to find enough time for teachers to collaborate, being careful about giving teachers too many different course preps, and figuring out ways that the school culture and distributed leadership are going to work well for everyone at a large, new, comprehensive school with a growing but changing staff.

From the perspective of a former teacher at Napa New Tech who is currently the assistant director of school design at New Tech Network, the

challenges that still face all the New Tech schools around the country include the need to identify assessments of critical thinking that are robust, to
develop Benchmark projects that can also be used for assessment, to use the
Student Clearinghouse data being supported by the Bill and Melinda Gates
Foundation to track students, and assessing the cultural aspects of project-
based learning to see how using it transfers to humanitarian issues like toler-
ance of religion and different lifestyles. The people at New Tech Network are
also working hard to get a stable learning management system that does everything they want for students, parents, teachers, and administrators, which
also seems to be a challenge in other school systems around the country.

And finally, other financial concerns are always a challenge in addition
to personnel. Technology infrastructure costs money, as does ongoing teacher professional development related to project-based learning, and morale is
affected by budget constraints and fear of losing one's position.

Lessons Learned: Key Factors for Success

There are many things that can be learned from the original New Tech High
School in Napa, California, because the leaders, faculty, and staff have been
working to create and enact a 21st-century curriculum that includes ubiquitous computing for 15 years, maybe longer than any other secondary school
in the country. Further, we believe that many of these lessons are valuable
for other schools and districts, large or small, even if they still have a traditional curriculum and faculty who work alone in classrooms using mostly
traditional instructional strategies. Although your school or district may not
be planning to use project-based learning, there are ideas from NTHS that
can be emulated regarding school culture, innovative instruction, teaching
roles, technology integration, and what teaching 21st-century skills should
look like. Based on our interviews with administrators and teachers (N=15)
at both Napa New Tech and American Canyon (plus some students too,
N=6), and classroom observations (N=14), these are the lessons we think
are most valuable:

- Having a vision about what an education for the 21st century
  can and should look like, feel like, and be like is the first lesson
  learned from New Tech. In this case that vision is about putting
  students on the path toward becoming engaged citizens in the
  21st century.
- Developing a set of core values that will help everyone to
  enact the vision with fidelity must follow. As examples, the
  core values at New Tech are Trust, Respect, and Responsibility;
  and Relationships, Relevance, and Achievement are the core

values at American Canyon High School. To achieve fidelity, all decisions are based on those core values, and the leadership is constantly checking in with students, teachers, and staff to see if the school's climate and culture is in synch with its core values.

- The leadership at New Tech talked explicitly about the importance of distributing leadership among teachers, staff, and students. This included listening to students and staff because they will be honest about what is working and what is not, and also seeking consensus as the first choice for decision-making whenever possible.

- The leadership at New Tech learned early a lesson that everyone needs to know, which is that piecemeal change is a hindrance to real change. Therefore, when improving your school and developing new models, the advice from the leadership at New Tech would be to start with the end in mind by changing the graduation requirements to include more than just credits earned. For example, New Tech included requirements for digital portfolios, service learning, internships, college credits, and so forth.

- When the New Tech Network was established to scale up the New Tech Model for 21st-century high schools, the leadership knew they had to be committed to innovations like ubiquitous technology use, project-based learning, co-teaching, interdisciplinary curriculum, and community service. Such commitment is a lesson all leaders need to learn if real change is to occur.

- Lessons learned about financing curriculum innovation and partnering with businesses and higher education came out of necessity at New Tech. By engaging the local business community, the leadership was able to find ongoing support for its innovative curriculum and its technology infrastructure, as well as garner support in the form of places for student internships as well as scholarships for students. The value of partnering with the local business community to support the school's goals is a lesson learned from New Tech and several other cases in this book.

- Partnerships with nearby institutions of higher education also provided opportunities for students to take college classes for credit both on-site and at a nearby college. Such partnerships not only supported the vision and goals of this school but also enhanced the curriculum that could be provided by a small high school.

- The value of seeking grants, both large and small, to support innovative ideas is another lesson learned from many of the schools and districts we studied about sustainability for innovations. Sometimes just articulating a goal is the trigger to look for other financial support if the grant is not successful.
- Having the necessary technical staff to manage your technology infrastructure on-site is an important lesson learned from all the cases in this book. However, at New Tech this also meant being persistent in getting the right learning management and assessment tools in the hands of teachers, students, and parents. Ultimately, whether you purchase a learning management system (LMS), develop your own, or use a free LMS tool, finding one that meets all of your needs is a lesson learned from most of the schools we studied.
- However, getting out of the hardware business as soon as possible and allowing students to use their own personal computing devices at school is another lesson learned by the leadership at New Tech. Given that New Tech has been a 1:1 environment for 15 years, it is important we learn from their experience. In other words, if you put your available funds into infrastructure and cloud computing and allow students to bring their own personal computing devices to use at school, then you only have to rent or loan computers to students who cannot afford their own. This is an important lesson for schools of all sizes, but arguably one that should be heeded from the beginning when planning how to use technology as a lever for school reform and improvement.
- Regarding changing the curriculum and professional development, the lesson learned from New Tech is that you have to continue to provide ongoing PD for teachers so everyone is on board and up to speed with regard to the school's vision, values, goals, standards, and instructional strategies. However, this also means that you have to give teachers who are new to integrating technology, or in the case of New Tech, teachers new to PBL (or whatever curriculum innovation you decide to employ), enough time to get their content reorganized so that it can be taught in an appropriate and effective manner (e.g., in this case, as problems and projects).
- When your vision includes preparing students to use 21st-century skills, this will lead to changes in both curriculum and school culture. With expectations that all students would seek

higher education and also engage in community service, the lessons learned from New Tech tell us you can:

a. Trust students to be actively engaged in and responsible for their learning when they are treated with trust, respect, and responsibility.

b. Give students the responsibility for learning from opportunities that include internships as well as community service both within and outside of the school.

c. Trust that students will learn the content needed for success on standardized tests, even when the curriculum is based on ill-structured problems and projects that are at the heart of project-based learning.

- This also means you can trust that your teachers will find ways to "cover" the required local or state curriculum while integrating technology, or as is the case at New Tech, use project- and/or problem-based learning. Trusting teachers to be professional and students to learn with new tools and new teaching strategies is a palpable lesson learned from New Tech.

- The result of changing graduation requirements to include more than just credits earned, and giving students as many opportunities as possible to enact 21st-century skills yielded a culture where students understand that assessments are feedback that provide them with direction for improvement. This was accomplished at New Tech and American Canyon by providing regular feedback to students on more than just grades (e.g., on their progress toward 21st-century skills such as oral and written communication, collaboration, technology use, creativity and innovation, critical thinking and problem solving, leadership, etc.), and encouraging students to set goals for themselves based on feedback they are receiving.

CHAPTER 10

Putting It All Together
Lessons Learned About Leadership, Technology, and School Improvement

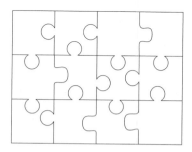

The purpose of this chapter is to summarize the lessons learned from all eight cases in this book, based on a cross-case analysis. Therefore, we combine what we gleaned from our study of exemplary, award-winning secondary schools (both middle and high schools) to better understand the many ways the leadership in these schools and districts has leveraged technology for school improvement. However, our goal in this chapter is not to present a typical cross-case analysis that would reduce the lessons learned to general patterns and themes but rather to share the many valuable lessons learned from the schools and districts we visited in a logical, organized fashion.

At the outset we knew from the research literature, which is laid out in Chapter 1, that distributed leadership was one of the keys to school reform/ school improvement, and that we needed to take a systems approach to data collection and data analysis because many factors are implicated in school improvement beyond just using more technology. Therefore, in addition to interviewing school and district leaders, our data collection needed to include classroom observations as well as interviews with teachers and other school and district-level staff, some parents, school board members, and other key informants. Taking all these perspectives into account provided us with a more nuanced view of each case study site than we would have had by limiting our data collection solely to school and district leaders. Further, by using both purposeful and snowball sampling techniques to identify and develop *intrinsic* case studies (Yin, 2008) we interviewed over 150 people and also observed in 150 classrooms in selected school districts in Virginia, North Carolina, Colorado, California, Washington, Maryland, Minnesota, and Michigan. We also examined hundreds of web pages and documents to learn more about our research sites.

One of the main findings from our research is that employing technology as a lever for school reform, and believing in or even acting on the principles of distributed leadership, is not enough. We found that it is just not that simple! In fact, we found that unless all actions in the bulleted list below are attended to intentionally, and (nearly) simultaneously, schools and/or districts will not be able to achieve their goals just by adding technology, or just by acting on the principles of distributed leadership. What we learned from doing these case studies is that school and district leaders have to purposefully and wholeheartedly address all these factors to be successful at improving and/or reforming their schools. Furthermore, because of the interaction among these factors, as well as others we may not have uncovered in our research, we caution against simplifying the items in our list. We describe them in the order presented in this list because of the linear nature of printed text, but this should not imply that the list represents a particular order to be followed, nor do we see these factors as a checklist for school improvement. Rather, in practice these factors can be seen as pieces of a puzzle that must be completed before any real improvement can be seen in the hoped for results of school improvement efforts, such as increased engagement, achievement, and other outcomes like increasing rates of graduation and college attendance, better attendance and decreasing numbers of dropouts, etcetera. Despite these caveats, the data from our case studies indicate that school and district leaders who have successfully used technology to leverage school improvement must:

- Have a clear vision/mission and systemically execute goals to carry out the vision/mission
- Act on the principles of distributed leadership, develop teams of leaders, build on individual strengths, and encourage the development of others
- Plan, plan, and plan some more in order to make changes and implement goals
- Identify realistic, sustainable sources of funding by thinking outside the box
- Create structures and processes for technology infrastructure and support

- Provide ongoing, high-quality, formal and informal professional development that is not one-size-fits-all
- Focus on improving school culture
- Revise the curriculum to promote more student-centered instruction and focus on 21st-century knowledge and skills
- Collaborate with parents, families, and community members, and also build partnerships with nearby businesses, industries, and colleges or universities

Interestingly, these findings from our case studies match the Interstate School Leaders Licensure Consortium (ISLLC) Standards for School Leaders developed in 2008 by the Council of Chief State School Officers in collaboration with the National Policy Board on Educational Administration (NPBEA) to guide the preparation of school leaders (www.ccsso.org/Documents/2008/ Educational_Leadership_Policy_Standards_2008.pdf). While we did not use these standards in our analysis of lessons learned from these cases, the leaders of the eight exemplary, award-winning schools and districts we studied epitomize these standards. In other words, the leaders of the schools/districts we studied showed us what the ISLLC Standards look like in practice.

What follows next is a more elaborate summary of each of the key factors and lessons learned during our research that we hope leaders who seek to make the best use of technology as a lever for school reform can take away from our research. We include details and examples of what we learned across all eight cases about these main factors, and we also include examples from some individual cases to emphasize some of the important lessons learned from all eight cases.

Having Clear Vision, Mission, and Goals

The leadership at all eight schools and districts we visited talked about the necessity of having a vision, and the importance of a clearly articulated mission statement regarding their purpose(s) for using technology for improving their school(s). Many of these leaders were forward-thinking and trusted that their ideas for technology integration would contribute to helping improve their school(s) by improving student outcomes. In addition, many leaders also expressed an understanding of the importance of having 100% buy-in to the district's vision and mission. To get buy-in they told us they worked tirelessly to get input from all their constituent groups in developing their mission statement and the specific goals that followed from it.

Of course, we realize that every school and district in this country has a strategic plan, but these leaders made sure that technology had a prominent place in their strategic planning. Further, both superintendents and principals told us they continuously test every new idea that comes up against their vision and work tirelessly to achieve what is articulated in their mission statement and strategic plan; therefore, these documents are not just an exercise they go through because this is what is expected of school and district leaders.

Core values were also obvious in several sites we visited, and these core values were actually visible in the schools and repeated by everyone—students, teachers, and even parents. Core values such as "Trust, Respect, and Responsibility" or "Every Kid Every Day" or "Respect, Responsibility, Integrity, Doing Your Best, Courage, and Curiosity" were actually the mantra in places we visited; in other places core values were evident in documents we reviewed, or were prominently displayed on walls and on shirts.

The visions, missions, and strategic plans varied by the context and situation of each school and district we studied. For some of the school and district leaders, their mission is to get technology directly into the hands of students because they understand that their students have changed and need something different. Of course they are concerned about student achievement, but they know that before they can raise achievement they have to get students engaged or re-engaged in learning. Therefore, many of these leaders are passionate about making instruction in their school(s) more student-centered and less teacher-directed, which leads them to working to improve school culture and both curriculum and instructional practices. For others, the goal is to use technology to help provide a 21st-century education for their students and to prepare their graduates for work and life in our highly technological world. They want both curriculum and instruction to be more relevant to the world their students will enter when they graduate. Others hoped that integrating technology into their curriculum would help raise achievement scores for their students, and still others see technology as providing students with opportunities they may not otherwise have. For school and district leaders, we assume that all of these are goals they would like to achieve as a result of improving their schools and districts, but both we and they know this cannot be accomplished with technology alone. For example, one school district stated this explicitly on their website by noting that their digital conversion is not a technology project, but a curriculum project.

The leaders we talked to also understand that systematic and systemic change takes time, and that piecemeal tinkering can be a hindrance to change. They expressed understanding that they needed to see the big picture as well as think and plan for several years down the road, which is why many talked about taking a systems approach to enacting their vision. Some district leaders we talked with felt it was important *not* to promote cookie-cutter schools; so they established a climate for innovation and allowed schools in their districts to customize their goals for achieving the district's mission regarding the use of various technologies for school improvement. Other district leaders felt the need to have one cohesive school system rather than a system of schools; as a result, their goals and policies were the same for all schools in the district.

In both large and small school districts the sheer expense of adding or increasing the use of technology for instruction, as well as the added costs for needed infrastructure and for using technology for assessment, data analysis, and for managing other systems required them to phase in the desired technology in order to eventually meet their goals and achieve their vision. For example, while several of the schools and districts we visited were fully 1:1 and provided laptops or netbooks for every student, none of these places did this without some kind of pilot project and a phase-in period. And along the way, leadership in the schools and districts realized that just providing technology to every student, or even to every teacher, would not automatically help them achieve their goals for school improvement. As a matter of fact, we know from the research literature that many districts are rethinking their 1:1 technology initiatives (Weston & Bain, 2008) because they have not achieved expected benefits. Fortunately, the leaders we interviewed understand that they need to attend to many more pieces of the puzzle in order to achieve their vision beyond just purchasing new computers or going 1:1.

Making Changes to Achieve Your Goals

In fact, in order to make the changes they were seeking, the school and district leaders in this study told us that they knew they had to create new initiatives, blow up existing programs that were not working, and sometimes just plunge in and get people to try new things. Some of the goals that all eight schools and districts had in common included moving to using more online content and Web 2.0 tools to deliver the curriculum, and changing textbook policies so that they could use these funds to purchase hardware and software that would be used as learning materials. They all realized that funding technology made more sense than purchasing new textbooks that are quickly outdated, or more encyclopedias, atlases, and maps that are not well used and also become out of date quickly.

Many of the places we visited were also revising their curriculum, changing some of their traditional instructional strategies, and tweaking their favorite projects to integrate more technology. We noted this in places that had more experience with technology integration and/or had leaders who realized that both curriculum and instructional practices needed to be revised if their school and district was going to be able to achieve their goals. Some examples of real curriculum changes included schools that were either using or experimenting with problem-based and project-based learning (see www.bie.org), or challenge-based learning, which is a similar concept promoted by Apple computer company (see http://ali.apple.com/cbl). Other examples include schools that were beefing up their traditional senior projects to include technology for both research and presentation, and/or encouraging and supporting their teachers to conduct action research projects in order to determine the actual outcomes of using various new technologies in their teaching. Across the board, most school and district leaders were trying to get technology into the hands of students, and several places were not planning to purchase any more interactive whiteboards (i.e., from SMART or Promethean) because they wanted the students to have and use the technology themselves. In all cases they knew they needed to collect and use data to track the changes they were working to achieve.

To make these changes, almost all school leaders expressed the expectation that everyone needed to just plunge in, be willing to move ahead on a trial-and-error basis, and to be okay making mistakes—as long as they at least tried. Some school and district leaders also told us they believed that those who did not get on board with new initiatives should look for work elsewhere, although most were willing to let teachers move at their own pace as long as they were moving forward and not resisting changes and new expectations. Most school leaders in this study specifically said that every lesson did *not* have to make use of technology. Rather, they wanted teachers using appropriate technologies when they made sense. However, we often heard students asking when they entered classrooms, "Are we going to use the laptops [or iPads or netbooks] today?" which seemed to push some of the teachers to do more because they saw their students' interest and engagement improve when they incorporated technology into their lessons.

Enacting Distributed Leadership Practices

We all know that in order to accomplish desired change, and to reform or improve schools, leadership is paramount. Based on our data and our review of the research literature about leadership, we found extensive evidence that the leaders of the schools and districts we studied engage in practices known as distributed leadership. That is, they were very aware that improving their schools and districts could not be accomplished by virtue of their position as principal or superintendent—not even with the help of their leadership teams. Rather, they understood the reciprocal and interdependent nature of schools and districts (Spillane, 2005), and knew that the involvement of their many constituents would be crucial in whether or not an innovation like integrating technology would be successful. They understood and valued that it was the interaction among students, parents and families, teachers, community members, and other professionals in leadership positions that would yield results or not. Among our case studies, not one school or district leader tried to improve their school or district on his or her own. Instead each leader relied on many others in their constituency, identified and recruited other professionals and community members, and then worked together with them as a team to accomplish change. Furthermore, technology was just one of the tools these leaders leveraged to help make changes and improve their schools. In each case the technology tools they chose were enacted in unique ways depending on the situation or context. What we observed among our case studies corresponds to how Spillane (2005) has described the system of distributed leadership:

> From a distributed perspective, leadership is a system of practice comprised of a collection of interacting components: leaders, followers, and situation. These interacting components must be understood together because the system is more than the sum of the component parts or practices. (p. 150)

As a result of interviewing district-level and building-level leaders, their faculty and staff, and other important constituents including some parents and school board members, we learned the following lessons about distributed leadership. First, in every school and district we visited leadership was discussed in terms of building teams, working as a team, and being sure the entire leadership team was on board with the vision, mission, and goals of the school and district. In seven of eight locations leaders talked explicitly about believing in and practicing distributed leadership, and letting people find their niche and lead from their strengths. Second, the importance of being strategic with networking and hiring, especially hiring the right people for the right job, was also evident. Third, leaders in this study were both publicly and privately recognizing strengths in others that they may not recognize themselves and encouraging them to take on leadership roles. This was also expressed as finding and trusting the right people, giving people what they need, and getting out of their way. Fourth, several leaders talked about the importance of cross-pollinating ideas between and among the schools in their district, region, and state, and also about the value of connecting with other leaders who think outside the box.

In more than half of the places we visited, teachers and other staff described their leaders as being willing to try new things, and engaging the community in planning for changes and/or new initiatives. Teachers and staff in at least half the schools talked about valuing their leaders because they were engaging in the following practices: supporting teachers, especially early adopters; being an integral member of the community beyond their role as principal or superintendent; providing instructional coaches and/or technology specialists to work with teachers; not thinking all veteran teachers are reluctant to change; being open and transparent about new initiatives and having no hidden agendas; advocating for teachers and their school(s) to get needed resources; planning, planning, and planning some more; and leading by example, with passion and focus. They also told us they appreciated having leaders they saw as supportive, visible, committed, and understanding of family obligations. Teachers and other staff also appreciated the fact that their leadership was engaging in practices that included experimenting with 1:1 computing in their school as well as supporting the use of more digital curriculum, and that they were actively seeking partnerships with business and industry, and/or collaborating with nearby universities, tech companies, or tech consortiums.

Some of the leaders described themselves as engaging in the following practices: believing that their teachers want to change and improve their teaching; being adept at managing multiple projects and changes at one time; being willing to blow up programs that are not working; and being consistent, on message, and doing what they say they will do—following through. We also heard from many of the leaders that they value knowing every student, being forward-thinking, making open communication a goal, and using multiple ways to communicate. They also believe in practices such as providing honest, constructive feedback to teachers, and in connecting and building relationships with all constituents—students, teachers, staff, and parents. Modeling what they want others to be doing with technology was another practice mentioned by several school and district leaders. In at least two places we visited we also heard leaders say that they practice listening to teachers and students because they are honest about what is working or not; find that reading, asking questions, listening, and watching others is a valuable way to learn; believe in enabling teachers with good ideas; and are not willing to settle for even 90% success because they want 100% success. Toward this end we heard multiple times from leaders, teachers, and other staff we interviewed that their leadership is working toward its goals every day in every way, questioning everything, working tirelessly to fulfill their vision, and quickly admitting mistakes with decency and fixing them.

While these descriptions of the leadership of the eight exemplary, award-winning schools and districts in our study are impossible for any one individual to carry out, that is exactly the point about their understanding and practicing the principles of distributed leadership. That is, they knew that no one person can be or do all these things, but hopefully all these aspects of leadership are possible within and across broad-based leadership teams that work together to improve schools and districts. In other words, it takes many leaders and followers engaged in the situation (Spillane, 2005) all involved in planning how improve education. Further, while acting on the principles of distributed leadership may be one of the largest pieces of the puzzle that is school improvement, it is nevertheless just one of the pieces of this puzzle.

Planning, Planning, and More Planning

Some schools were at the beginning of 1:1 laptop or netbook initiatives and working toward developing a digital curriculum when we visited (e.g., WMS in Virginia, Rose Hill in Washington, etc.), while other schools we observed had been 1:1 for several years (Mooresville in North Carolina and STEM Academy in Colorado), or for over 15 years (Napa New Tech in California). Nevertheless, what we observed was that all these schools had done two crucial things: First, they put the technology they were going to roll out to students into the hands of the teachers first, preferably the year before their planned rollout. Second, they involved parents and families in the plans for their 1:1 digital conversion and clearly communicated what this change would mean for students and families early on. This, of course, is an example of the level of planning in which the school and district leaders in this study engaged. As the school and/or district leaders told us, they had to plan, plan, and plan some more to be sure their technology initiatives would be successful. They had to let students and parents, and even the entire community, know what students were going to be doing with new technologies at school.

They also had to communicate whether or not students would be bringing in their own personal computing devices as they are doing at the high school in Godfrey-Lee, Michigan; had been doing at New Tech High School in Napa, California, for many years; and were also doing in the newest high school in this same district. They had to decide whether or not the school would be providing a laptop or netbook for every student, or renting or subsidizing these devices for students who could not afford them. Communication was crucial because some parents told us they were concerned about cyberbullying or having their students vulnerable to others stealing their laptops. In addition, not every household has access to the Internet, so schools and districts needed to plan for this and either (1) partner with a local cable company to serve as the Internet Service Provider for a very reasonable cost, as they were able to do in Mooresville, North Carolina, or (2) establish policies that precluded requiring Internet access for homework, and/or open the school's media center early and stay open late, or (3) make sure students and families could access the Internet in the town's public libraries, or have wireless access in the school's parking lot.

These are examples of just some of the many issues that had to be planned for, and all contingencies had to be considered well before the rollout of new technology in a school or district, especially for places where grade levels or entire schools were going 1:1. Fortunately, most school and district leaders are very good at planning and thinking through all possible contingencies, even if systems thinking does not come naturally to everyone as it did to many of the leaders in our study. Nevertheless, planning is a key piece of the puzzle, and the case studies in this book can be mined for many other things that school and district leaders considered when planning for technology to be one of the levers for school reform.

Figuring Out Funding Sources for Technology

Of course one of the first things to plan for is having funding in place for both initiating and sustaining technology initiatives, including whatever the plans are for purchasing and supporting hardware, software, and related infrastructure needs. Without a viable financial plan in place, one of the pieces of the puzzle called school improvement will be missing, so this is a crucial aspect of planning that leaders have to figure out. In fact, finding ways to devote enough resources for their technology initiatives was mentioned by nearly every school and district leader we interviewed because without sufficient funding their vision could not be achieved. In this study, all leaders talked about the importance of partnering with nearby businesses, industries, and/or universities or colleges, and of seeking grants both large and small. However, partnerships with business, industry, or higher education included not just potential financial backing in the form of donations or grants, but also expertise in the form of membership on planning committees and advisory boards, plus the potential for receiving additional human and technical resources. For example, in several places we visited such partnerships were the source of internships for students, collaborators on grant applications, sponsorship of special projects or competitions, and locations for faculty externships during the summer that allowed teachers to bring what they learned in the real work of business, industry, and research into their curriculum.

Perhaps one of the most intriguing things we learned about the school and district leaders in this study is how creative they are in seeking new funds and redirecting funds for technology. For example, they used new building funds to pay for the technology infrastructure and the hardware for new or renovated buildings, and they also used textbook funds to purchase software as well as other kinds of digital devices by changing their district's textbook policy into a broader, more flexible instructional materials policy. Additionally, they endorsed or engaged in numerous fund-raisers, redirected rental income for their school buildings into a technology fund, and partnered with local businesses to get a percentage of their sales for the school's technology fund. In other words, they all were able to think outside the box in order to find funds to direct toward technology purchases.

Some schools with 1:1 initiatives self-insured their laptops to defray maintenance costs, and also recycled their computers at a profit when it was time to upgrade them. Other districts put together and worked to pass bond issues even when they were skeptical about their success in a weak economic climate. They worked tirelessly to get the school board on their side with regard to bond issues and changing policies, and to get community members to see the value added for students in exchange for tax increases for schools. They also scoured their budgets to carve out money from other funds. Several districts made sure to include its chief financial officer in all their planning and deliberations because that person was better informed and able to help in finding other sources of funds; so this is something we highly recommend.

Technology Infrastructure and Support

Another key piece to the puzzle of achieving goals related to using technology as a tool for school reform has to do with the people leading school and district technology teams. These leaders may include a district-level chief technology officer and his or her team, or they may include people serving as technical liaisons, technical support staff, or tech facilitators housed either in the district office or in the schools. These professionals come with all kinds of titles and have all kinds of different backgrounds, but we learned that having tech support on-site in the buildings in various forms, especially help desk personnel who can fix digital devices that break, and tech facilitators who can do professional development and work directly with teachers, is ideal. If that is not possible, then having a quick response team at the district level was the next best thing. In those places that had full 1:1 initiatives, we were also told that getting parents on board early and educating them about how to take care of laptops that come home is also key; thus, involving parents and family members is another piece of the puzzle.

In many schools and districts we visited, having a robust learning management system (LMS) in place and getting *all* users trained on it really made a difference in terms of changing teachers' instructional practices so that they could more easily differentiate instruction and monitor student progress. This worked especially well when the LMS they selected had features that included online testing and a gradebook program linked to the testing features of the LMS. The people we interviewed also liked learning management systems that had a database for storing and sharing lesson plans, and one that could be used readily for communicating with students and parents. Having other systems in place for school and districtwide data management, monitoring student progress toward graduation, supporting multiple forms of communication, and even running HVAC systems and school cafeterias were also highly desired. Unfortunately, some schools and districts we visited had been through several different LMS programs, sometimes two or three different versions or new systems in as many years, which was frustrating for everyone. Except for Moodle, these programs are not free and while they are very useful, no one seemed to have found the perfect system that did everything they wanted it to do. Fortunately, learning management systems continue to evolve and respond to the needs of schools and districts, so this may become less of an issue in the future.

The types and brands of technology that were being used varied greatly among the schools and districts we visited. Some places elected to standardize the brand of laptops or netbooks and operating systems that every student would use to try to limit the amount of troubleshooting and tech support needed. Some only wanted to have Apple products while others only wanted Windows machines. One school bought dual-boot Apple computers so that their teachers could use the operating system with which they were most familiar. However, several other schools and districts decided to put their money into a robust network infrastructure that would support whatever personal computing devices the students owned and could bring to use at school—including cell phones, iPods, iPads, and multiple brands of laptops and netbooks. They did this because they knew they could not sustain the costs of purchasing, maintaining, and upgrading personal computing devices for every student. With the advent of cloud computing and the availability of open source networking tools, these schools and districts changed their policies and encouraged students to bring and use their own personal computing devices at school, which meant they only had to buy or rent out computers to students who had nothing of their own to bring to school.

Actually, those districts in our study with both the longest and shortest history of being 1:1 realized that having students use their own personal computing devices at school was the wave of the future and the only way to sustain their 1:1 goals. Obviously these decisions required a mind shift on the part of teachers and different kinds of tech support, plus network, server, and other infrastructure decisions to make a completely open system work. However, even in schools and districts that were still funding 1:1 initiatives, teams needed to be in place to support their infrastructure and maintain all the devices in their building or district. In all cases the demand for quick technical support, either within the school or from the district office, became a necessity so that there would be no downtime for students and teachers who were becoming very dependent upon various computing devices for teaching and learning.

Providing Ongoing Professional Development

If you are going to add or increase the amount of technology in a school or district to achieve goals related to school improvement this should include using more digital curriculum, increasing the use of Web 2.0 tools, and focusing on 21st-century skills. The result of doing these things is that school becomes more relevant for students (and young teachers) who are digital natives who do not want to power down when they come to school. However, you have to provide ongoing professional development (PD) for all faculty and staff. Without the PD piece of the puzzle in place, any change in teaching practices will be very slow, or potentially non-existent. Ongoing PD, not just one-shot overviews or introductions to new tools, has to be a priority because the tools are always changing. Further, we learned that both new and veteran teachers need and want to become adept with new technology tools so they can use them appropriately and fully in their teaching.

While some places we studied expected everyone to plunge in and figure things out, most schools and districts found many good ways to continue to provide PD without spending a lot of money. In fact, in-house PD was clearly the norm in most places we visited. They did this to keep costs down, but also to keep PD relevant to their needs. As a result, we observed a cooperative culture in these places that encouraged peer-to-peer collaboration and informal sharing in which risk-taking was encouraged and celebrated. Also, in these schools everyone knew which teachers or other staff members they could consult for help in learning about or troubleshooting a particular software tool or piece of hardware. In addition, faculty and department meetings were regularly used to communicate what teachers had tried and found successful when using new technologies.

Other ways we observed in-house PD occurring included meetings of teacher-initiated user groups; menus of workshops delivered by teachers but organized by a building-level tech facilitator; one-on-one or small-group sessions offered on-site by a tech facilitator, a teacher, or a librarian; and the availability of brief how-to videos and demonstration lessons created by teachers and/or tech facilitators. The best examples of in-house PD we observed were in schools where the school's leadership and tech teams regularly surveyed teachers about their needs for PD and then managed to deliver it at three levels (novice, intermediate, and advanced) to those who wanted to learn to use a particular device or piece of software. Teachers also liked the summer PD sessions they described to us, as well as workshops offered during early-release days, or on Tech Days set aside by the district and offered by teachers on-site or at other schools. A few districts either sponsored or collaborated with other districts to offer summer PD, which was very well received by teachers because they were paid for attending and had the time to focus on what they were learning. Two of the districts we studied actually make money by sponsoring and leading summer technology events that people from other districts attend, and that money becomes a revenue stream for maintaining their technology initiatives. Some wealthier districts have passed bond issues focused on technology for 21st-century schools, and can actually pay teachers generous stipends for attending PD and taking what they learn back to their schools using a trainer-of-trainer model. Other districts have funds to offset the cost of graduate-level courses and certificates or degrees in technology leadership because of their partnerships with local universities. And some districts fund grants to get new technology in the hands of students whose teachers are willing to do action research in their classroom, which is actually another form of in-house PD for these teachers.

Attending to School Culture

You have to have a vision, good leadership, and a workable plan for managing the finances and technology infrastructure to even start seeing technology as a lever for school improvement. However, these are only some of the pieces of the puzzle, and without putting together all the remaining pieces you will not be able to see or achieve the full picture. For example, we learned from our case studies that without attending to school culture, and making revisions to both the curriculum and the instructional practices being used, real change and sustained improvement will not happen. And although the people we interviewed typically talked about changes in school culture as a result of integrating more technology, we observed that school culture included additional things like the importance of knowing every student, building relationships with students, improving student-teacher mentoring relationships, creating a supportive environment for teachers, and building successful leadership teams.

We also learned that all the exemplary schools and districts in our study had cultural norms around how they interacted with technology that expected everyone to plunge in, try new things, use the method of trial and error, be okay with making mistakes, but also a culture where everyone at least tried to do new things with technology. In these cases, messages from both school and district-level leadership made staff members feel that it was all right not to know everything and not to be perfect. In fact, one school realized that with their laptop initiative every teacher was like a first-year teacher for a while, but that this was okay because everyone was in the same boat, learning from one another, and being praised for even small successes. Teachers also learned that their students were sometimes their best technical resources.

At the same time, all the schools and districts in this study created cultural norms that included celebrating successes publicly, acknowledging even small successes, celebrating successes on a regular basis, and acknowledging everyone's contributions–and none of this cost anything. In addition, the culture in the majority of schools and districts made it all right for teachers not to use technology in every lesson. However, those same schools/districts expected the best from their students, teachers, and other staff, while also holding them accountable.

In some schools data-driven instruction became a part of the culture because the teachers created common assessments across disciplines and grades, and students were able to access and use data to track their own progress through their LMS. As a result, a climate was created where students saw assessments as providing feedback and direction for improvement. In other schools in this study the culture was one of trusting that students will learn the required content and be successful on standardized tests without using direct instruction as often; encouraging communication, collaboration, and sharing among teachers and between teachers and students; and getting people involved in helping to make decisions and empowering others to take on leadership roles. Still other schools created a culture that valued using technology to support different kinds of learners, helping them to discover their talents and strengths, focusing on culturally responsive teaching, and creating a more student-centered culture that provided the students with resources, activities, or whatever it takes to help them be successful. Some schools also expected and trusted their students to be good digital citizens, while others made this an explicit part of their curriculum.

In all cases, the schools and districts we visited that had a long history with their 1:1 initiatives also had a more unique and palpable school culture than those that were just getting started. We speculate that this is probably because they had enough time to consciously focus on their school's culture as well as on transforming their curriculum and making their instructional practices more student-centered. This indicated to us that some changes in school culture may be a result of integrating technology, but we recommend that school and district leaders be proactive in developing the kind of culture they want simultaneously with attending to enacting their vision, strategic planning, arranging funding, and developing the infrastructure for technology initiatives designed to improve their school(s).

Changing Curriculum and Instruction

We observed that changes occur in how students experience school when technology is used regularly as a tool for teaching and learning, which influences school culture and vice versa. In other words, school culture and changes in curriculum and instruction are two pieces of the puzzle that are usually focused on simultaneously. In this study of exemplary schools, working to improve school culture appeared to go hand in hand with working to revise the curriculum and change instruction from traditional, mainly teacher-centered instructional practices to using more 21st-century, student-centered instructional practices, which included a lot more group and independent work than lectures and independent practice. As a result of using new technologies, one of the most talked about changes during our research that relates to school culture, curriculum, and instruction was increased communication among students and between teachers and students both in and out school. We heard stories about teachers encouraging students to contact them electronically using various features of their LMS with any questions about homework, and setting up times at night to do online reviews for an upcoming test. Some teachers told us they communicated with their students using instant message or even through Facebook. An unintended consequence, but one seen as positive by all the teachers who talked to us about it, was getting to know their students better because they had more opportunities and different ways to communicate with them.

Educators at the exemplary schools we visited were explicit about trying to make instruction more student-centered and revising both the curriculum and their favorite projects to include more technology. Teachers in the places we visited were clearly exposing students to many 21st-century tools and skills—especially for communication and collaboration, and also problem solving and critical thinking—and trying to find ways to make global awareness a part of the curriculum. Rather than purchasing expensive software licenses, most schools were using more digital curriculum by trying out the many free Web 2.0 tools available on the Internet, as well as free applications (apps) available for iPads and iPods. We also observed that several of the schools went beyond changing current curricular practices; they implemented new courses to take advantage of the availability of new technology. For example, we observed courses titled "Robots and Roller Coasters" and "Digital Media," and simulations taking place in a virtual learning lab that evolved from taking curriculum and technology to another level.

Also, all the exemplary schools in this study were explicit about using data to try to close achievement gaps and giving students immediate feedback following assessments because the technology made this much easier for teachers. Several schools were also doing online testing, which they did quarterly as well as at the end of the term or year. One school even does daily assessments in most classes. As a result, in at least half the schools we visited many students were using the LMS to track their own progress and teachers were using data to plan for reteaching. Most of the schools we visited were also rearranging their class schedules to create time for tutoring, and/or for enrichment, student internships, and completing senior projects that now required technology to be integrated in various ways.

In sum, adding technology to these schools triggered new learning opportunities for students and caused teachers to revise both their curriculum and their instructional practices in a variety of ways. Also, the 6- or 7-period day was favored less over block or modified-block scheduling in schools using technology with their students because the longer periods allowed them to go more in-depth with the content, do more research, and complete project- or problem-based learning assignments. Clearly, in the exemplary, award-winning schools and districts we visited changes in school culture, curriculum, and instruction when technology is used as a lever for school improvement means these pieces of the puzzle must be manipulated (nearly) simultaneously with all the other puzzle pieces that are a part of the picture that is school improvement.

Collaborations and Partnerships

As discussed earlier in this summary of the lessons we learned by interviewing and observing in eight exemplary, award-winning schools and districts around the United States, partnering with businesses, industries, and colleges or universities is another important part of successfully improving these schools and districts. For many this is an important lesson to be learned but it may be one piece of the puzzle that is too frequently missing for many schools and districts with regard to their technology initiatives. As described above, such partnerships may include financial resources for schools in the form of grants or donations, but also in the form of human resources and technical support. For example, a few schools we visited had mentors come in from nearby businesses, industries, or universities to participate in special projects and/or mentor students as a way to build relationships and provide real-world connections to the curriculum.

Partnering with parents and families is an important part of the puzzle as well. As mentioned previously, involving and communicating early on with parents and families when moving to integrate new technologies into their children's education is crucial. And it is even more crucial when students are asked to bring in their own personal computing device to school, or will be bringing home laptops or netbooks provided by the school. Communication with parents and families is also important when families are asked to pay a part of the cost of these devices either as insurance or rent that might range from $50 to $150 each year. Because parents didn't have the same kind of access to technology when they were going to school, this change in their children's education requires that they are consulted and included in the process. However, the advantages of new systems of communication, including the use of multiple learning management systems, which allow parents to be aware of how their students are doing on tests and what the homework is for the night, were very well received by parents we talked with. Parents liked being involved in and knowledgeable about what their students are doing at school, and they especially liked being able to be in communication with their children's teacher and know what is going on in their schools.

Implications for Districts and Policy Makers

We believe the cases in this book will be useful to school leaders at both the building and district level who want to learn about strategies and models that other leaders have used to leverage technology for school improvement. The lessons learned from the schools and districts we studied lead us to conclude that there are many pieces of the school improvement puzzle that leaders must attend to (nearly) simultaneously. Therefore, when district leaders are considering the use of technology as a lever for school improvement we recommend that they take a long-term view and a systems approach when planning how they will evaluate the success of their initiatives. That is, even though district leaders have a vision, goals, and a strategic plan in place, they must understand that just putting technology into schools will not really change or improve anything unless the following additional factors are also addressed: providing ongoing, high-quality professional development that is not just one-size-fits-all; focusing on improving the school culture; making changes in the curriculum to focus on 21st-century knowledge and skills; and promoting more student-centered instructional practices that engage students. Further, from our perspective, school reform, driven by technology or not, will not happen unless leaders understand and practice the principles of distributed leadership. Leading a technology initiative with the goals of creating a relevant curriculum that engages today's learners, improving student achievement, and preparing students for college and work in the 21st century cannot be done alone and cannot be mandated; it is too complex and too dependent on attending to multiple factors for any one leader, no matter how competent or charismatic, to accomplish alone.

In addition, when technology is one of the tools for school improvement, the district has to create a robust and effective infrastructure and processes for technical support so that teachers and students do not lose time and opportunities for teaching and learning. Schools cannot and should not be left to do this on their own. Finding appropriate funding sources to start up, maintain, and sustain technology initiatives is also a piece of the puzzle that districts have to deal with at both the policy level and with regard to their budgets. Finally, for best results collaborating with parents, families, and community members can probably be handled at the school level, but we believe that building partnerships with businesses, industries, and colleges or universities should be undertaken at both the school and the district level.

Policy makers at the state and national level must also take a long-term view and a systems approach when considering technology as a lever for school improvement. This means creating policies and establishing criteria for grants that address all pieces of the puzzle, if they want to see real improvement in schools. Toward this end, in addition to the findings of the research we have presented in this book, we recommend the RED Report (Greaves, Hayes, Wilson, Gielniak, & Peterson, 2010) to policy makers who want to understand additional factors related to cost effectiveness and student achievement when full 1:1 initiatives are undertaken. We also recommend policies that lead to creating cooperative associations like TIES in Minnesota (www. ties.k12.mn.us/home.html) to provide comprehensive, cost-effective technology support to schools and districts for instructional, professional development, communication, technical, human resource, and transportation needs. While several states provide a similar resource to schools and districts, most do not; and since such collaborations save money, it seems policy makers in other states would want to emulate this kind of comprehensive support for technology use in schools. Similarly, we recommend looking at the comprehensive model for school reform used in the IMPACT Model Schools grants in North Carolina, which are funded by the Enhancing Education Through Technology (EETT) and American Recovery and Reinvestment Act (ARRA) competitive grant awards (www.ncwiseowl.org/impact). This collaborative model for school reform has a 10-year track record and provides guidelines and assessment instruments that may be useful for others using technology as a tool for school improvement.

Summary and Conclusion

We focused our research on how technology was leveraged for school improvement, and on the ways in which school and district leadership undertook the process of using technology as a tool for school improvement, but we learned that it is just not that simple. We learned that employing technology as a lever for school reform, and believing in or even acting on the principles of distributed leadership, is not enough. Nevertheless, this study does reinforce what we know about the important role that leaders have to play in school reform, because without leadership nothing will change. Further, as a result of our research we found that numerous factors beyond technology are relevant to school transformation, including visions, mission, and goals; organization and structure; planning, decision-making, and governance; school culture, including student policies, programs, and activities; assessment and evaluation systems and uses of data; personnel and other resources; mentoring, coaching, and professional development; curriculum and instructional practices; partnerships with business, industry, and colleges and universities; and communication and relationships within the school community. However, because of the interaction among these factors, we also found that in practice they are like pieces of a puzzle that must be completed (nearly simultaneously) before real transformation is possible.

The case studies in this book offer detailed descriptions of successful transformation in large and small schools and districts, in wealthy and poor communities, and in places with more or less experience using technology for improving teaching, learning, and achievement. Despite the diversity of these cases, or maybe because of their diversity, perhaps their greatest value is the accumulation of possibilities in the form of numerous lessons learned that other school and district leaders can heed, borrow, adapt, or try. The cases reveal strategies that worked in particular contexts, but we believe these strategies are worth adapting and trying in other situations as well. We hope you read these case studies and take advantage of what other school and district leaders have learned while working toward similar goals.

References

Abramovich, S. (2006). Early algebra with graphics software as a type II application of technology. *Computers in the Schools, 22*(3–4), 21–33.

Alexander, B. (2008). Web 2.0 and emergent multiliteracies. *Theory into Practice, 47*(2), 150–160.

Anderson, R., & Dexter, S. (2005). School technology leadership: An empirical investigation of prevalence and effect. *Educational Administrator Quarterly, 41*(1), 49–82.

Berends, M., Bodilly, S. J., & Kirby, S. N. (2002). *Facing the challenge of whole school reform: New American schools after a decade.* Santa Monica, CA: Rand.

Brown, C. (2007). Learning through multimedia construction: A complex strategy. *Journal of Educational Multimedia and Hypermedia, 16*(2), 93–124.

Camburn, E., Rowan, B., & Taylor, J. (2003). Distributed leadership in schools: The case of elementary schools adopting comprehensive school reform models. *Educational Evaluation and Policy Analysis, 25*(4), 347–373.

Creswell, J. W. (1998). *Qualitative inquiry and research design: Choosing among five designs.* Thousand Oaks, CA: Sage.

Crum, K. S., & Sherman, W. H. (2008). Facilitating high achievement: High school principals' reflections on their successful leadership practices. *Journal of Educational Administration, 46*(5), 562–580.

Crum, K. S., Sherman, W. H., & Myran, S. (2009). Best practices of successful elementary school leaders. *Journal of Educational Administration, 48*(1), 48–63.

Darling-Hammond, L., Meyerson, D., LaPointe, M., & Orr, M. T. (2010). *Preparing principals for a changing world: Lessons from effective school leadership programs.* San Francisco: Jossey-Bass.

Dawson, C., & Rakes, G. (2003). The influence of principals' technology training on the integration of technology into schools. *Journal of Research on Technology in Education, 36*(1), 29–49.

Dimmock, C. (1999). The management dilemmas in school restructuring: A case analysis. *School Leadership & Management, 19*(1), 97–113.

Drago-Severson, E. (2004). *Helping teachers learn: Principal leadership for adult growth and development.* Thousand Oaks, CA: Corwin Press.

Ertmer, P. A., & Ottenbreit-Leftwich, A. (2010). Teacher technology change: How knowledge, confidence, beliefs, and culture intersect. *Journal of Research on Technology in Education, 42*(3), 255–284.

Firestone, W. A., & Riehl, C. (Eds.). (2005). *A new agenda for research in educational leadership: Critical issues in educational leadership.* New York: Teachers College Press.

Frey, N., Fisher, D., & Gonzalez, A. (2010). *Literacy 2.0: Reading and writing in 21st century classrooms.* Bloomington, IN: Solution Tree Press.

Gemberling, K., Peterkin, R., Rohr, P., & Sneed, M. (2000). *Transition team report: For the superintendent of the Baltimore County Public Schools.* Baltimore, MD: BCPS.

Greaves, T., Hayes, J., Wilson, L., Gielniak, M., & Peterson, R. (2010). *The technology factor: Nine keys to student achievement and cost-effectiveness.* Mason, MI: Project Red.

Gronn, P. (2002). Distributed leadership as a unit of analysis. *The Leadership Quarterly, 13,* 423–451.

Guskey, T. R. (1995). Professional development in education: In search of the optimal mix. In T. R. Guskey & M. Huberman (Eds.), *Professional development in education: New paradigms and practices* (pp. 114–131). New York: Teachers College Press.

Hallinger, P., & Heck, R. H. (1998). Exploring the principal's contribution to school effectiveness: 1980–1995. *School Effectiveness and School Improvement, 9,* 157–191.

Harris, A. (2006). Opening up the "black box" of leadership practice: Taking a distributed leadership perspective. *Leadership and Management, 34*(2), 37–45.

Katz, R. L., & Kahn, D. (1978). *The social psychology of organizing* (2nd ed.). New York: John Wiley & Sons.

Kopcha, T. J. (2010). A systems-based approach to technology integration using mentoring and communities of practice. *Educational Technology Research & Development, 58,* 175–190.

Lei, J., & Zhao, Y. (2007). Technology uses and student achievement: A longitudinal study. *Computers and Education, 49,* 284–296.

Leithwood, K., Jantzi, D., & McElheron-Hopkins, C. (2006). The development and testing of a school improvement model. *School Effectiveness and School Improvement, 17*(4), 441–464.

Lemov, D. (2010). *Teach like a champion: 49 techniques that put students on the path to college.* San Francisco: Jossey-Bass.

Lincoln, Y. S., & Guba, E. G. (1985). *Naturalistic inquiry.* Thousand Oaks, CA: Sage.

Mayrowetz, D. (2008). Making sense of distributed leadership: Exploring the multiple usages of the concept in the field. *Educational Administration Quarterly, 44*(3), 424–435. doi: 10.1177/0013161X07309480.

McLeod, S., & Richardson, J. W. (2011). The dearth of technology leadership coverage. *Journal of School Leadership, 21*(2), 216–240.

Merriam, S. B. (1998). *Qualitative research and case study application in education: Revised and expanded from case study research in education.* San Francisco: Jossey-Bass.

Moos, L., & Johansson, O. (2009). The international successful school principals' project: Success sustained? *Journal of Educational Administration, 47*(6), 765–780.

Mulford, B., Edmunds, B., Kendall, L., Kendall, D., & Bishop, P. (2008). Successful school principalship, evaluation and accountability. *Leading and Managing, 14*(2), 19–44.

Murphy, J., Smylieb, M., Mayrowetz, D., & Louis, K. S. (2009). The role of the principal in fostering the development of distributed leadership. *School Leadership and Management, 29*(2), 181–214.

Park, V., & Datnow, A. (2009). Co-constructing distributed leadership: District and school connections in data-driven decision-making. *School Leadership and Management, 29*(5), 477–494.

Patton, M. Q. (1990). *Qualitative evaluation methods* (2nd ed). Thousand Oaks, CA: Sage.

Sandholtz, J. H., Ringstaff, C., & Dwyer, D. D. (1997). *Teaching with technology: Creating student-centered classrooms.* New York: Teachers College Press.

Schrum, L., & Levin, B. (2009). *Leading a 21st century school: Harnessing technology for engagement and achievement.* Thousand Oaks, CA: Corwin Press.

Schrum, L., Galizio, L. M., & Ledesma, P. (2011). Educational leadership and technology integration: An investigation into preparation, experiences, and roles. *Journal of School Leadership, 21*(2), 241–261.

Spillane, J. P. (2005). Distributed leadership. *The Educational Forum, 69,* 143–150.

Spillane, J. P., Camburn, E. M., & Pareja, A. S. (2007). Taking a distributed perspective to the school principal's workday. *Leadership and Policy in Schools, 6*(1), 103–125.

Spillane, J. P., Diamond, J. B., & Jita, L. (2003). Leading instruction: The distribution of leadership for instruction. *Journal of Curriculum Studies, 35*(5), 533–543.

Spillane, J. P., Halverson, R., & Diamond, J. B. (2001). Investigating school leadership practice: A distributed perspective. *Educational Researcher, 30*(3), 23–28.

Stake, R. E. (1995). *The art of case study research.* Thousand Oaks, CA: Sage Publications.

Stuart, L. H., Mills, A. M., & Remus, U. (2009). School leaders, ICT competence and championing innovations. *Computers & Education, 53,* 733–741.

Timperley, H. S. (2005). Distributed leadership: Developing theory from practice. *Journal of Curriculum Studies, 37*(4), 395–420.

Wenger, E. (1998). *Communities of practice: Learning, meaning, and identity.* Cambridge, UK: Cambridge University Press.

Weston, M. E., & Bain, A. (2008). Engaging with change: A model for adopting and evaluating school-based innovation. *Journal of Educational Administration, 47*(2), 156–175.

Wiggins, G., & McTighe, J. (2005). *Understanding by design* (expanded 2nd ed.). Alexandria, VA: Association for Supervision and Curriculum Development.

Williams, P. (2008). Leading schools in the digital age: A clash of cultures. *School Leadership and Management, 28*(3), 213–228.

Yin, R. K. (2008). *Case study research: Design and methods* (4th ed). Thousand Oaks, CA: Sage Publications.

Index

AUTHOR INDEX

SUBJECT INDEX

About the Authors

Barbara B. Levin is a professor in the Department of Teacher Education and Higher Education and Director of the Teachers Academy at the University of North Carolina at Greensboro. She was an elementary school teacher for 17 years before earning her PhD at the University of California, Berkeley. Previously Dr. Levin was assistant department chair and director of graduate studies for 8 years. She also served as an associate editor for *Teacher Education Quarterly* for 8 years. Dr. Levin was awarded the first Mentoring-Advising-Supervising (MAS) Award in the School of Education at UNCG in 2008. Dr. Levin's research focuses on understanding how teachers' beliefs and pedagogical understandings develop across their careers, case-based and problem-based learning, and leading, teaching, and learning with technology. Dr. Levin has published six books and numerous articles in well-respected journals.

Lynne Schrum is a professor and coordinator of Elementary Education in the College of Education and Human Development at George Mason University. Previously she was chair of the Department of Teaching and Learning at the University of Utah. Her research and teaching focus on appropriate uses of technology, preparing teachers for the 21st century, and effective and successful online teaching and learning. She is a past elementary school and special education teacher. She has written and edited nine books and numerous articles. Dr. Schrum recently finished 10 years as editor of the *Journal of Research on Technology in Education (JRTE)* (2002–2012) and is a past president of the International Society for Technology in Education (ISTE). She has had the honor to work with teachers and leaders in many states and countries as they strive to establish 21st-century schools, develop STEM initiatives, and design effective learning environments.